DURAN DURAN

All The Top 40 Hits

Craig Halstead

First Edition

for Aaron

BY THE SAME AUTHOR ...

Christmas Number Ones

This book details the Christmas No.1 singles in the UK from 1940 to date, and also reveals the Christmas No.2 single and Christmas No.1 album. The book also features the Christmas No.1s in five other countries, namely Australia, Germany, Ireland, the Netherlands and the United States, and is up-dated annually in January.

The '*All The Top 40 Hits*' Series

This series documents, in chronological order, all the Top 40 Hit Singles and Albums by the featured artist:

ABBA
Annie Lennox (incl. Eurythmics)
Bee Gees
Blondie
Boney M.
Boy George & Culture Club
Carpenters
Chi-Lites & Stylistics
Donna Summer
George Michael (incl. Wham!)
Janet Jackson
Kate Bush
Kim Wilde
Lionel Richie (incl. Commodores)
Marvin Gaye
Michael Jackson
The Jacksons (Jackson 5/Jacksons/Jermaine/La Toya/Rebbie/3T)
Olivia Newton-John
Sam Cooke & Otis Redding
Dame Shirley Bassey
Slade
Spice Girls
Tina Turner
Whitney Houston

The '*For The Record*' Series

The books in this series are more comprehensive than the 'All The Top 40 Hits' volumes, and typically include: The Songs (released & unreleased), The Albums, The Home Videos, The TV Shows/Films, The Concerts, Chartography & USA/UK Chart Runs, USA Discography & UK Discography.

Donna Summer
Janet Jackson
Michael Jackson
Whitney Houston

Fiction

The James Harris Trilogy

The Secret Library
Shadow Of Death
Twist Of Fate

Cataclysm

Book 1: The First 73 Days
Book 2: A New Year

Stand Alone Novel

Tyranny

Novellas

Alone
Passion
Taboo

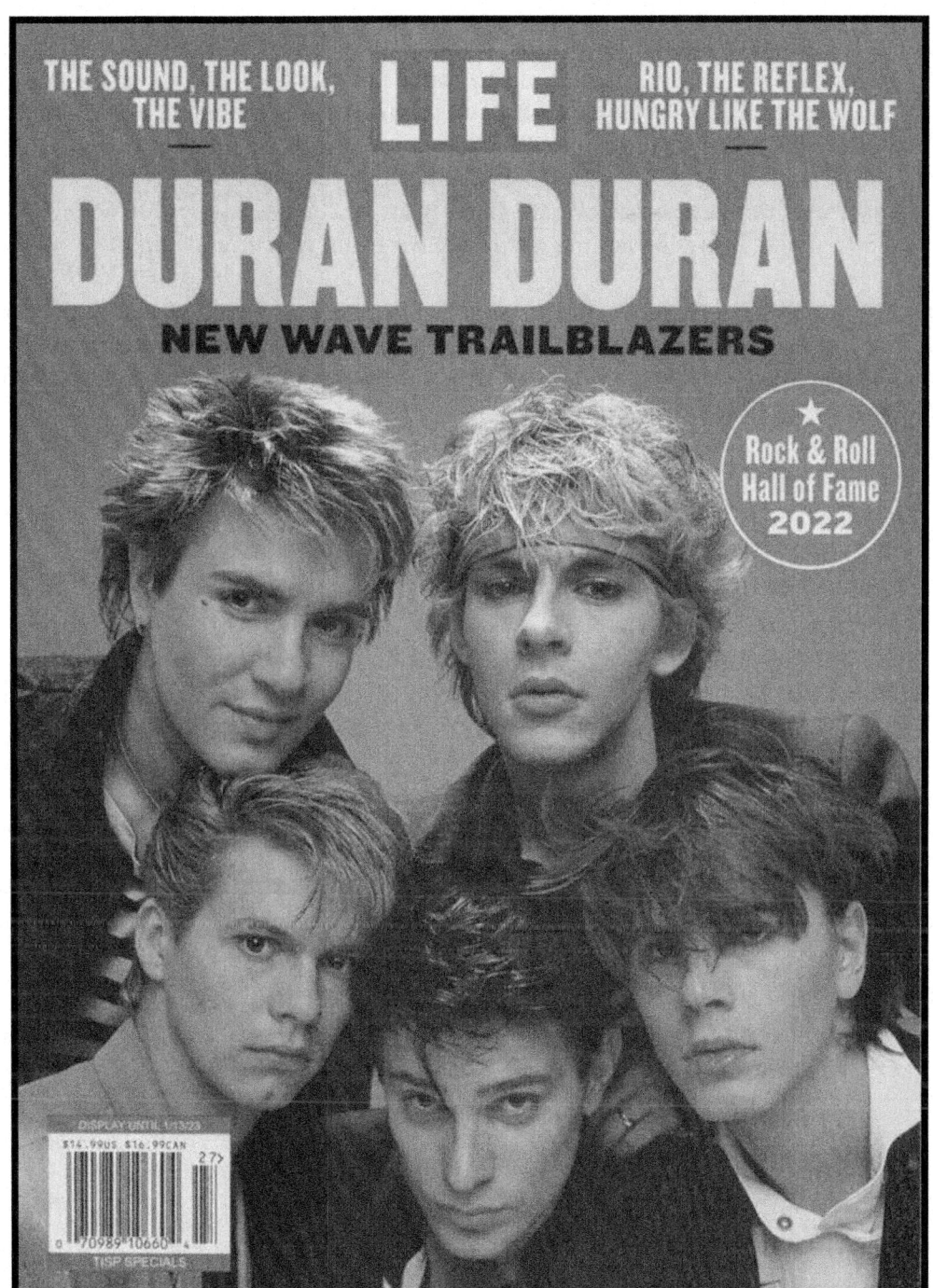

ACKNOWLEDGEMENTS

I would like to thank Chris Cadman, my former writing partner, for helping to make my writing dreams come true. It's incredible to think how far we have come, since we got together to compile 'The Complete Michael Jackson Discography 1972-1990', for Adrian Grant's *Off the Wall* fan magazine in 1990. Good luck with your future projects!

Chris Kimberley, it's hard to believe we have been corresponding and exchanging chart action for 30+ years! A big thank you, I will always value your friendship.

I would like to thank the online music community, who so readily share and exchange information at: Chartbusters (chartbusters.forumfree.it), ukmix (ukmix.org/forums), Haven (fatherandy2.proboards.com) & Buzzjack (buzzjack.com/forums). In particular, I would like to thank:

- 'BrainDamageII' & 'Wayne' for posting current Canadian charts on ukmix;
- 'flatdeejay' & 'ChartFreaky' for posting German chart action, and 'Indi' for answering my queries regarding Germany, on ukmix;
- 'Davidalic' for posting Spanish chart action on ukmix;
- 'Shakyfan, 'CZB', 'beatlened' & 'trebor' for posting Irish charts on ukmix;
- 'janjensen for posting Danish singles charts from 1979 onwards on ukmix;
- 'Hanboo' for posting and up-dating on request full UK & USA chart runs on ukmix. R.I.P., Hanboo, your posts on ukmix are sadly missed;

If you can fill any of the gaps in the chart information in this book, or have chart runs from a country not already featured in the book, I would love to hear from you. You can contact me via email at: **craig.halstead2@ntlworld.com** ~ thank you!

CONTENTS

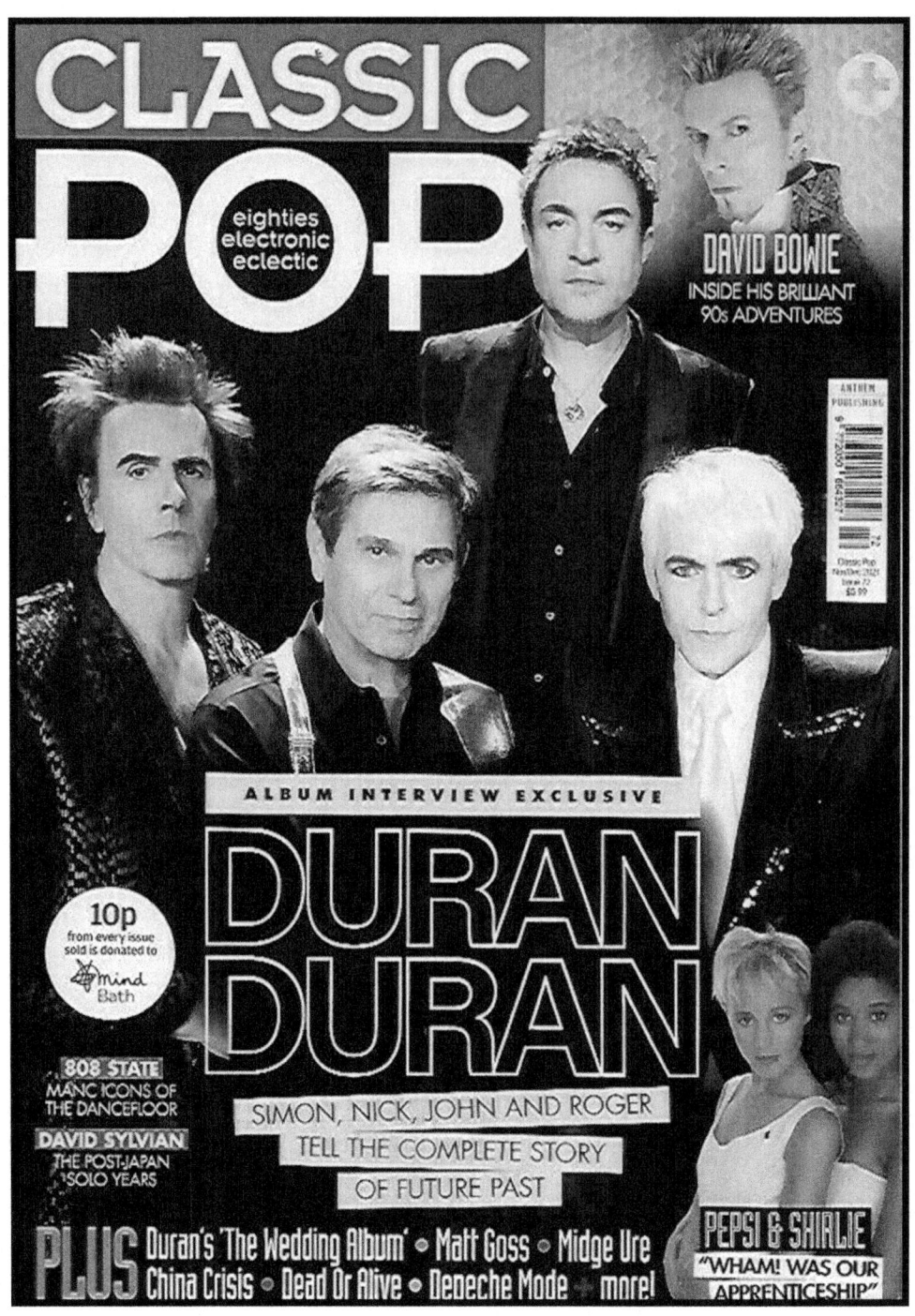

CLASSIC POP

eighties
electronic
eclectic

DAVID BOWIE
INSIDE HIS BRILLIANT
90s ADVENTURES

ANTHEM
PUBLISHING

Classic Pop
Nov/Dec 2021
Issue 72
£5.99

ALBUM INTERVIEW EXCLUSIVE

DURAN
DURAN

SIMON, NICK, JOHN AND ROGER
TELL THE COMPLETE STORY
OF FUTURE PAST

10p
from every issue
sold is donated to
mind
Bath

808 STATE
MANC ICONS OF
THE DANCEFLOOR

DAVID SYLVIAN
THE POST-JAPAN
SOLO YEARS

PEPSI & SHIRLIE
"WHAM! WAS OUR
APPRENTICESHIP"

PLUS Duran's 'The Wedding Album' • Matt Goss • Midge Ure
China Crisis • Dead Or Alive • Depeche Mode ... more!

INTRODUCTION

An English new wave band, Duran Duran was formed in 1978 in Birmingham, West Midlands, by John Taylor, Nick Rhodes and Stephen Duffy. The band was named after Dr. Durand Durand, a character played by Milo O'Shea in the 1968 sci-fi film, *Barbarella*.

The following year, Roger Taylor joined the band, which experienced a number of changes before May 1980, when Duran Duran's classic line-up was established.

Introducing Duran Duran

- Simon John Charles Le Bon ~ lead singer. Simon was born near Bushey, Hertfordshire, on 27th October 1958, and he studied drama at the University of Birmingham. He has been a member of Duran Duran since 1980, and was also a member of Arcadia.

- Roger Andrew Taylor ~ drummer. Roger was born in Birmingham, West Midlands, on 26th April 1960, and was a member of Duran Duran between 1979-85, 1994-95 and 2001 to date. He was also a member of Arcadia.

- Nigel John Taylor ~ guitar/bass. John was born in Solihull, West Midlands, on 20th June 1960, and he has been a member of Duran Duran between 1978-97 and 2001 to date. He was also a member of The Power Station.

- Andrew Arthur Taylor ~ guitar. Andy was born in Tynemouth, Northumberland, on 16th February 1961. He made what he called 'that fateful train journey down to Birmingham' in April 1980, and was a member of Duran Duran between 1980-86 and 2001-2006. He was also a member of The Power Station.

- Nicholas James Bates *aka* Nick Rhodes ~ keyboards. Nick was born in Birmingham, West Midlands, on 8th June 1962, and he has been a member of Duran Duran since 1978. He was also a member of Arcadia.

Despite sharing the same surname, Roger Taylor, John Taylor and Andy Taylor are not related.

Duran Duran recorded two demos in 1980, and the band played gigs in numerous clubs in both Birmingham and London. Later the same year, as her opening act, they toured with Hazel O'Connor. The positive attention the band attracted led to a bidding war between two record companies, EMI and Phonogram, for their signatures. Being fans of The Beatles, Duran Duran decided to sign with EMI, which they did in December 1980.

Early the following year, Duran Duran headed to London, to record their self-titled debut album with producer Colin Thurston. The band's debut single, *Planet Earth*, gave them their first hit, when it rose to no.12 in the UK. The follow-up, *Careless Memories*, was less successful, but it did make the Top 40, peaking at no.37.

Duran Duran's third single, *Girls On Film*, became the band's first Top 10 hit in the UK ~ it achieved no.5. Sales were boosted by a controversial music video directed by Godley & Creme, which featured topless women mud wrestling and pillow fighting. Predictably, the promo was banned by the BBC in the UK, and was heavily edited when it was aired on the brand new music channel MTV in the United States.

The hits kept on coming, with two singles ~ *Is There Something I Should Know?* and *The Reflex* ~ and the band's third album, *SEVEN AND THE RAGGED TIGER*, all going to no.1 in the UK.

Then, taking their fans by surprise, Duran Duran split into two side project, The Power Station and Arcadia. Andy Taylor and John Taylor teamed up with Robert Palmer and Tony Thompson, to form the rock supergroup The Power Station, while Nick Rhodes, Roger Taylor and Simon Le Bon formed Arcadia. Although not officially a member, Roger Taylor also played percussion with The Power Station. The Power Station and Arcadia released one album each, *THE POWER STATION* and *SO RED THE ROSE*, respectively, before disbanding (The Power Station did later reform).

Nick Rhodes later described the two side projects as 'commercial suicide … but we've always been good at that'.

Duran Duran contributed to Band Aid's mega-selling charity single *Do They Know It's Christmas?* in 1984, and following the two side projects the five members of Duran Duran did get back together, to record the theme song for the 1985 James Bond film, *A View To A Kill*, which became the first Bond theme to hit no.1 in the United States.

On 13th July 1985, Duran Duran participated in the hugely successful Live Aid concerts, playing before 90,000 people at Pennsylvania's John F. Kennedy Stadium. Although no knew it at the time, this was the last time the five members of Duran Duran would play together until July 2003.

In 1986, Roger Taylor quit the band, and retired to the English countryside.

'I was burned out,' he later explained. 'I think I was just exhausted. It was a very intense five years. We didn't stop. It was constant touring, constant writing, recording. We broke internationally, as well ~ instantly, pretty well. It's a non-stop schedule, really. I lost myself somewhere.'

The same year, Duran Duran lost Andy Taylor as well ~ he signed a solo contract with MCA in Los Angeles. The three remaining band members took legal action against Andy, to try to force him back into the studio with them, but after numerous delays they agreed to let him go.

John Taylor wrote and recorded *I Do What I Do …*, which was the theme song for the film *9½ Weeks*, in 1986, and it gave him his only Top 40 success as a solo artist. The same year, Andy Taylor released two movie-related singles, *Take It Easy* (from *American Anthem*) and *When The Rain Comes Down* (from *Miami Vice II*). The former was a Top 40 hit, but the latter could only manage no.73 in the United States.

Andy Taylor released his debut solo album, titled *THUNDER*, in 1987, which was a Top 40 hit in Sweden. He followed this three years later with a covers album, *DANGEROUS*, which failed to chart anywhere.

The three remaining members of Duran Duran recruited co-producer Nile Rodgers, formerly a member of Chic, to play guitar on new material, and hired Steve Ferrone to play drums. Eventually, the band hired Warren Cuccurullo as a session guitarist, and he contributed to Duran Duran's fourth studio album, *NOTORIOUS*, which was released in October 1986.

Towards the end of the 1980s, and into the 1990s, Duran Duran's popularity began to fade, and the band found success harder to come by. During this period, the band's most successful project was their second eponymous album, also known as *THE WEDDING ALBUM*, which was issued in 1993 and gave rise to two sizeable hit singles, *Ordinary World* and *Come Undone*.

Roger Taylor briefly rejoined Duran Duran in 1995, for the band's covers album, *THANK YOU*. He played drums on two tracks, *Perfect Day* and *Watching The Detectives*, plus *Jeepster*, which failed to make the final track listing.

In 1995, John Taylor released a solo album, *FEELINGS ARE GOOD AND OTHER LIES*.

Then, in early 1997 after touring with Neurotic Outsiders, John Taylor announced he was leaving Duran Duran, once again reducing the band to a trio: Nick Rhodes, Simon Le Bon and Warren Cuccurullo.

Three years later, while they were on tour in the United States, Nick Rhodes and Simon Le Bon were invited to lunch at this home by John Taylor. There was talk of Duran Duran's classic five-man line-up reforming, and while Nick and Simon resumed their tour, John contacted first Roger Taylor, and then Andy Taylor, and both said yes to getting back together again.

But, at the time, Warren Cuccurullo was a member of Duran Duran, and he had no idea what was being planned. It wasn't until the band's tour ended and he headed home that he received a letter by special delivery ~ sacking him from the band.

Naturally, Warren was shocked to learn he was no longer a member of Duran Duran, and angry no one had the guts to tell him to his face. But the decision had already been made, so Warren resumed working with his 1980s band Missing Persons, and this was quickly followed by official confirmation the three Taylors, Andy, John and Roger, were rejoining Duran Duran. However, it wasn't until July 2003 that the reformed band played any concerts together, with a new album *ASTRONAUT* finally released in September 2004.

Meanwhile, in 2002, following a chance meeting at a fashion show, Nick Rhodes teamed up with fellow Duran Duran founder member Stephen Duffy, to form The Devils. Together, they re-recorded some old pre-Duran Duran songs, which they released on an album titled *DARK CIRCLES*.

Andy Taylor quit the band for a second time in October 2006, due to what the other members of Duran Duran described as an 'unworkable gulf' on their official website. In his autobiography, *Wild Boys*, Andy cited tensions between himself and the band's management, plus the fact he was suffering from clinical depression following the death of his father, as reasons he decided to leave the band. Andy was replaced by Dom Brown, a guitarist who had previously toured with Duran Duran.

In 2013, as TVMania, Nick Rhodes and Warren Cuccurullo recorded an album together titled *BORED WITH PROZAC AND THE INTERNET?* but it wasn't a hit.

In a ceremony held on 5th November 2022, Duran Duran was inducted into the Rock and Roll Hall of Fame. The ceremony was attended by four members of the classic Duran Duran line-up, the one exception being Andy Taylor, who revealed he was 'massively disappointed' he was unable to attend, as he had been diagnosed with cancer in 2018 and was battling stage four prostate cancer.

All The Top 40 Hits

For the purposes of this book, to qualify as a Top 40 hit, a single or album must have entered the Top 40 singles/albums chart in at least one of the following countries: Australia, Austria, Belgium, Canada, Denmark, Finland, France, Germany, Ireland, Italy, Japan, the Netherlands, New Zealand, Norway, South Africa, Spain, Sweden, Switzerland, the United Kingdom, the United States of America and Zimbabwe (formerly Rhodesia).

The Top 40 singles and albums are detailed chronologically, according to the date they first entered the chart in one or more of the featured countries. Each Top 40 single and album is illustrated and the catalogue numbers and release dates are detailed, for the UK, followed by the chart action in each featured country, including any chart re-entries. Where full chart runs are unavailable, peak position and weeks on the chart are given.

The main listing is followed by 'The Almost Top 40 Singles', which gives an honorable mention to singles that peaked between no.41 and no.50 in one or more countries (no albums did so). There is also a points-based list of the Top 30 Singles and Top 20 Albums, plus a fascinating 'Trivia' section at the end of each section which looks at the most successful singles and albums in each of the featured countries.

The Charts

The charts from an increasing number of countries are now freely available online, and for many countries it is possible to research weekly chart runs. Although this book focuses on Top 50 hits, longer charts runs are included where available, up to the Top 100 for countries where a Top 100 or longer is published.

Nowadays, charts are compiled and published on a weekly basis – in the past, however, some countries published charts on a bi-weekly or monthly basis, and most charts listed far fewer titles than they do today. There follows a summary of the current charts from each country featured in this book, together with relevant online resources and chart books.

Australia
Current charts: Top 100 Singles & Top 100 Albums.
Online resources: current weekly Top 50 Singles & Albums, but no archive, at **ariacharts.com.au**; archive of complete weekly charts dating back to 2001 at **pandora.nla.gov.au/tep/23790**; searchable archive of Top 50 Singles & Albums dating back to 1988 at **australian-charts.com**.
Books: 'Australian Chart Book 1970-1992' & 'Australian Chart Book 1993-2009' by David Kent.

Austria
Current charts: Top 75 Singles & Top 75 Albums.
Online resources: current weekly charts and a searchable archive dating back to 1965 for singles and 1973 for albums at **austriancharts.at**.

Belgium
Current charts: Top 50 Singles & Top 200 Albums for two different regions, Flanders (the Dutch speaking north of the country) and Wallonia (the French speaking south).
Online resources: current weekly charts and a searchable archive dating back to 1956 for singles and 1995 for albums at **ultratop.be**.
Book: '*Het Belgisch Hitboek – 40 Jaar Hits In Vlaanderen* by Robert Collin.
Note: the information in this book for Belgium relates to the Flanders region.

Canada
Current charts: Hot 100 Singles & Top 100 Albums.
Online resources: weekly charts and a searchable archive of weekly charts from the Nielsen SoundScan era at **billboard.com/biz** (subscription only); incomplete archive of weekly RPM charts dating back to 1964 for singles and 1967 for albums. The archive is in transition at the moment, but googling 'search RPM charts' should locate it. Scans of RPM Weekly magazine can be viewed at **https://3345.ca/rpm-magazine/** and **https://worldradiohistory.com/RPM.htm** (RPM folded in 2000).
Book: 'The Canadian Singles Chart Book 1975-1996' by Nanda Lwin.

Denmark

Current Charts: Top 40 Singles & Albums.

Online resources: weekly charts at **hitlisten.nu**, and an archive dating back to 2001 at **danishcharts.com**. No archive currently exists for charts before 2001. 'CZB' has posted weekly Top 20s from September 1994 to December 1999 on **ukmix.org**, and 'janjensen' has posted singles charts from January 1977 onwards on the same forum.

Finland

Current charts: Top 20 Singles & Top 50 Albums.

Online resources: current weekly charts and a searchable archive dating back to 1995 at **finnishcharts.com**.

France

Current charts: Top 200 Singles & Top 200 Albums.

Online resources: current weekly and archive charts dating back to 2001 can be found at **snepmusique.com**; a searchable archive dating back to 1984 for singles and 1997 for albums is at **lescharts.com**; searchable archive for earlier/other charts at **infodisc.fr**.

Book: '*Hit Parades 1950-1998*' by Daniel Lesueur.

Note: Compilation albums were excluded from the main chart until 2008, when a Top 200 Comprehensive chart was launched.

Germany

Current charts: Top 100 Singles & Top 100 Albums.

Online resources: current weekly and archive charts dating back to 1977 can be found at **offiziellecharts.de/charts**.

Books: '*Deutsche Chart Singles 1956-1980*', '*Deutsche Chart Singles 1981-90*' & '*Deutsche Chart Singles 1991-1995*' published by Taurus Press.

Ireland

Current charts: Top 100 Singles & Top 100 Albums.

Online resources: current weekly charts are published at IRMA (**irma.ie**); there is a searchable archive for Top 30 singles (entry date, peak position and week on chart only) at **irishcharts.ie**; an annual Irish Chart Thread has been published annually from 2007 to date, plus singles charts from 1967 to 1999 and album charts for 1993, 1995-6 and 1999, have been published at ukmix (**ukmix.org**); weekly album charts from March 2003 to date can be found at **acharts.us/ireland_albums_top_75**.

Note: the information presented in this book for albums is incomplete, and only covers the years 1993, 1995-6, 1999 and March 2003 to date.

Italy

Current charts: Top 100 Singles & Top 100 Albums.

Online resources: weekly charts and a weekly chart archive dating back to 2005 at **fimi.it**; a searchable archive of Top 20 charts dating back to 2000 at **italiancharts.com**; pre-2000 information has been posted at ukmix (**ukmix.org**).

Books: *Musica e Dischi Borsa Singoli 1960-2019 & Musica e Dischi Borsa Album 1964-2019* by Guido Racca.
Note: as the FIMI-Neilsen charts didn't start until 1995, the information detailed in this book is from the Musica & Dischi chart prior to this date.

Japan
Current charts: Top 200 Singles & Top 300 Albums.
Online resources: current weekly charts (in Japanese) at **oricon.co.jp/rank**; selected information is available on the Japanese Chart/The Newest Charts and Japanese Chart/The Archives threads at **ukmix.org**.

Netherlands
Current charts: Top 100 Singles & Top 100 Albums.
Online resources: current weekly charts and a searchable archive dating back to 1956 for singles and 1969 for albums at **dutchcharts.nl**.

New Zealand
Current charts: Top 40 Singles & Top 40 Albums.
Online resources: current weekly charts and a searchable archive dating back to 1975 at **nztop40.co.nz**.
Book: 'The Complete New Zealand Music Charts 1966-2006' by Dean Scapolo.

Norway
Current charts: Top 20 Singles & Top 40 Albums.
Online resources: current weekly charts and a searchable archive dating back to 1958 for singles and 1967 for albums at **norwegiancharts.com**.

South Africa
Current charts: no official charts.
Online resources: none known.
Book: 'South Africa Chart Book' by Christopher Kimberley.
Notes: the singles chart was discontinued in early 1989, as singles were no longer being manufactured in significant numbers. The albums chart only commenced in December 1981, and was discontinued in 1995, following re-structuring of the South African Broadcasting Corporation.

Spain
Current charts: Top 50 Singles & Top 100 Albums.
Online resources: current weekly charts and a searchable archive dating back to 2005 at **spanishcharts.com**.
Book: *'Sólo éxitos 1959-2002 Año a Año'* by Fernando Salaverri.

Sweden
Current charts: Top 60 Singles & Top 100 Albums.

Online resources: current weekly charts and a searchable archive dating back to 1975 at **swedishcharts.com**.

Note: before 1975, a weekly Top 20 *Kvällstoppen* charts was published, which was a sales-based, mixed singles/albums chart.

Switzerland

Current charts: Top 75 Singles & Top 100 Albums.

Online resources: current weekly charts and a searchable archive dating back to 1968 for singles and 1983 for albums at **hitparade.ch**.

UK

Current Charts: Top 100 Singles & Top 200 Albums.

Online resources: current weekly and archive charts dating back to 1960 at **officialcharts.com**; weekly charts are posted on a number of music forums, including ukmix (**ukmix.org**), Haven (**fatherandy2.proboards.com**) and Buzzjack (**buzzjack.com**).

Note: weekly Top 200 album charts are only available via subscription from UK ChartsPlus (**ukchartsplus.co.uk**).

USA

Current charts: Hot 100 Singles & Billboard 200 Albums.

Online resources: current and archive weekly charts are available at **billboard.com**; weekly charts are also posted on a number of music forums, including ukmix (**ukmix.org**), Haven (**fatherandy2.proboards.com**) and Buzzjack (**buzzjack.com**).

Zimbabwe

Current charts: no official charts, and no known online resources.

Books: 'Zimbabwe Singles Chart Book' & 'Zimbabwe Albums Chart Book' by Christopher Kimberley.

Note: Zimbabwe was, of course, known as Rhodesia before 1980, but the country is referred to by its present name throughout this book.

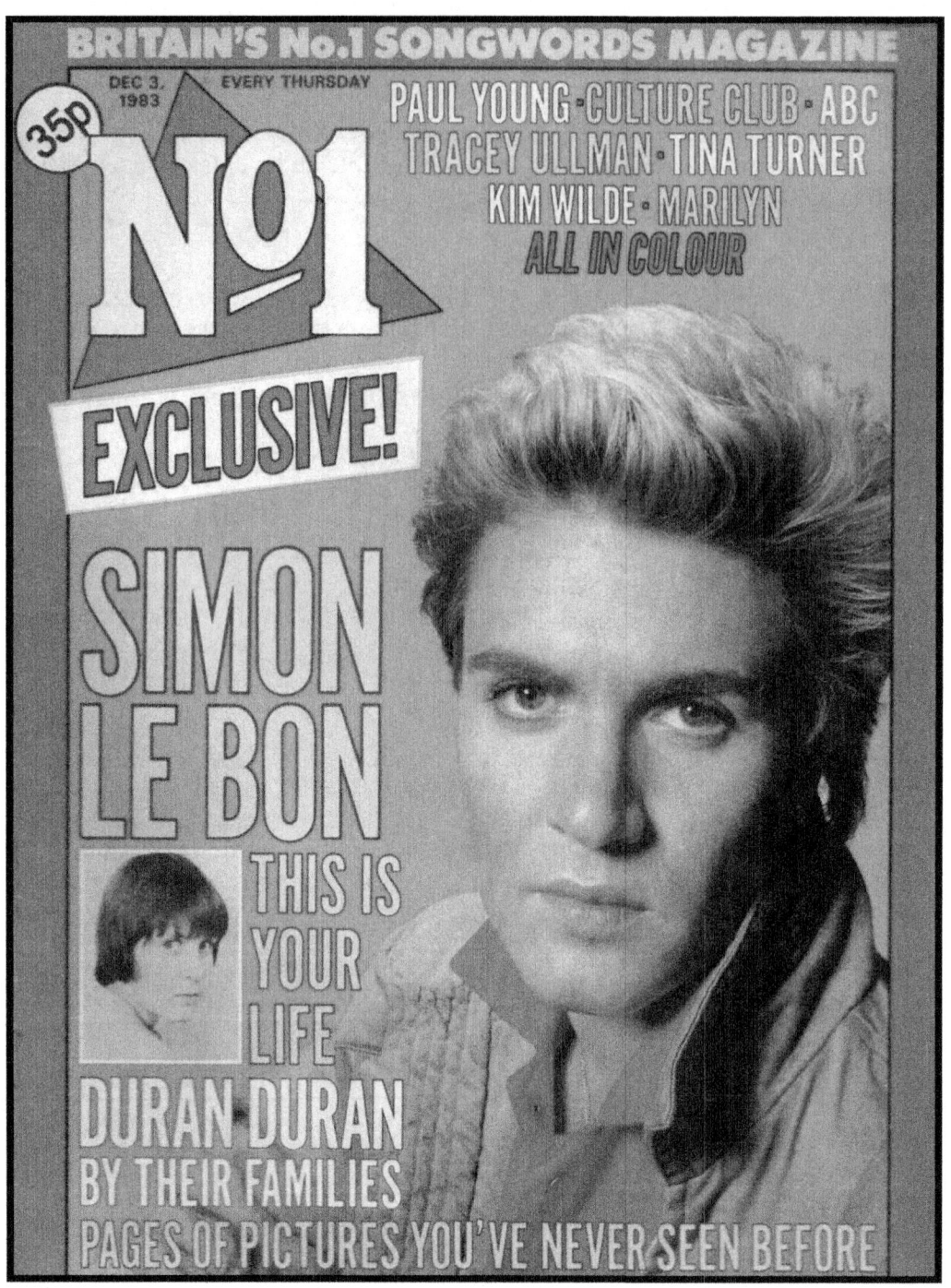

All The Top 40 Singles

1 ~ Planet Earth

UK: EMI 5137 (1981).
  B-side: *Late Bar.*

21.02.81: 67-52-47-26-20-**12**-16-22-23-40-47

Australia
4.05.81: peaked at no.**8**, charted for 26 weeks
26.04.82: peaked at no.19, charted for 8 weeks (b/w *Girls On Film* / Night Versions)

France
9.10.81: peaked at no.**70**, charted for 5 weeks

Ireland
29.03.81: 25-**14**-18-28

Duran Duran, with Nick Rhodes credited as James Bates, wrote their debut single *Planet Earth* themselves, and the band recorded the song at London's Red Bus Studios in December 1980.

'*Planet Earth* was influenced by German techno as much as it was by punk and New York dance,' said John Taylor. 'Lyrically, it was new. *Planet Earth* was a celebration of youth, of the possibility of youth, about feeling good to be alive.'

Planet Earth served as the lead single from Duran Duran's self-titled debut album, which was released in June 1981. The accompanying music video, directed by Russell Mulcahy, featured the four elements: air, earth, fire and water. The promo was later recreated by The Dandy Warhol's, for their 2003 single *You Were The Last High*, which Duran Duran's Nick Rhodes produced.

Planet Earth rose to no.8 in Australia, no.12 in the UK and no.14 in Ireland, and it was a minor no.70 hit in France.

Duran Duran created a 'night version' of *Planet Earth* ~ essentially, an extended version for release as a 12" single. However, as the technology was still in its infancy at the time, the night version featured a new arrangement based on the way the band performed the song live.

The night version of *Planet Earth*, released with the night version of *Girls On Film*, charted at no.19 in Australia a year after the original single was a Top 10 hit.

'I remember two things about recording *Planet Earth*,' John Taylor later reflected. 'Staying in a horrible hotel in Fulham, where I got very sick, and John Lennon dying.'

2 ~ Careless Memories

UK: EMI 5168 (1981).
  B-side: *Khanada*.

9.05.81: 55-38-**37**-**37**-38-48-65

Australia
3.05.82: peaked at no.**60**, charted for 8 weeks

Like *Planet Earth*, *Careless Memories* was written by Duran Duran, and was recorded at London's Red Bus Studios in December 1980.

Duran Duran promoted *Careless Memories* with a music video directed by Perry Haines, which was filmed in Soho.

'I believe that is the worst video we've ever made,' reflected Nick Rhodes. 'It did nothing for the song. It was all done in a very 'Habitat' manner.'

No extended 'night version' of *Careless Memories* was created so, as a bonus, a cover of David Bowie's 1975 hit, *Fame*, was included on the 12" single.

Despite the inclusion of *Fame*, *Careless Memories* struggled to match the success of *Planet Earth*, and stalled at no.37 in the UK, where it spent two weeks before falling down the chart. The single was also a minor no.60 hit in Australia, but it failed to chart anywhere else.

'We all wanted to release *Girls On Film* as the follow-up', said John Taylor, 'and were keen to get it out quickly, but EMI claimed to know better, saying *Careless Memories* was the right follow-up to *Planet Earth*. It had more integrity as a song, apparently, and would show the audience our deeper, more serious side. Maybe it did all that, but it didn't sell, and in some corners of the industry we were swiftly written off as one-hit wonders.'

A live version of *Careless Memories*, recorded at London's Hammersmith Odeon in December 1981, was issued as the B-side of Duran Duran's 1982 single, *Hungry Like The Wolf*.

3 ~ Girls On Film

UK: EMI 5206 (1981).
  B-side: *Faster Than Light*.

25.07.81: 29-23-15-6-**5**-7-12-19-27-41-65

Australia
30.11.81: peaked at no.**11**, charted for 22 weeks
26.04.82: peaked at no.19, charted for 8 weeks (b/w *Planet Earth* / Night Versions)

Belgium
24.10.81: 32-**30**-40

Ireland
16.08.81: 22-22-20-**16**-22

New Zealand
17.01.82: 40-23-23-5-7-6-5-**4**-6-8-8-9-11-18-14-14-15-16-27-24-26-30-x-49-x-15-12-7-
  11-11-15-26-32-43-48

Sweden
12.01.82: **15**-18 (bi-weekly)

Girls On Film was originally written and demoed in 1979, before Simon Le Bon joined
Duran Duran ~ the lead vocalist on the demo was Andy Wickett, and he was also largely

responsible for writing the song, which he sold to Duran Duran in July 1981 for a paltry £600.

The band's new line-up re-wrote the song, and Duran Duran recorded the new version of *Girls On Film* at London's Red Bus Studios in December 1980, for their self-titled debut album.

With *Careless Memories* having struggled, EMI agreed to release *Girls On Film* as the band's third single, and it proved to be the final and most successful release from *DURAN DURAN*.

Duran Duran filmed a raunchy and hugely controversial music video ~ it featured semi-naked women mud-wrestling and pillow-fighting ~ to promote *Girls On Film*. The promo was directed by Godley & Crème, and was shot at London's Shepperton Studios in July 1981 ~ just weeks before the music station MTV was launched in the United States.

The music video was banned by the BBC in the UK, and an edited 'day version' featured on MTV in the United States. Simon Le Bon later stated he felt the controversy surrounding the promo overshadowed the song's message, which focused on the exploitation of models in the fashion industry.

'My memories of it (the video) are not great.' admitted John Taylor. 'I remember being a bit embarrassed about it. You have a bunch of guys around and put a nearly naked girl in the room with them and it turns them all into idiots.'

Girls On Film gave Duran Duran their first Top 10 success in the UK, where the single achieved no.5. Elsewhere, the single charted at no.4 in New Zealand, no.11 in Australia, no.15 in Sweden, no.16 in Ireland and no.30 in Belgium.

A year later, the night versions of *Girls On Film* and *Planet Earth* gave Duran Duran a no.19 hit in Australia.

In March 1983, the music videos for *Girls On Film* and *Hungry Like The Wolf* were released as *Video 45* in the United States.

The VHS release featured the edited 'day version' of *Girls On Film*, while the Betamax and CED Videodisc formats included the uncensored 'night version'. Duran Duran picked up their first Grammy Award for *Video 45*, for Best Music Video, Short Form.

4 ~ My Own Way

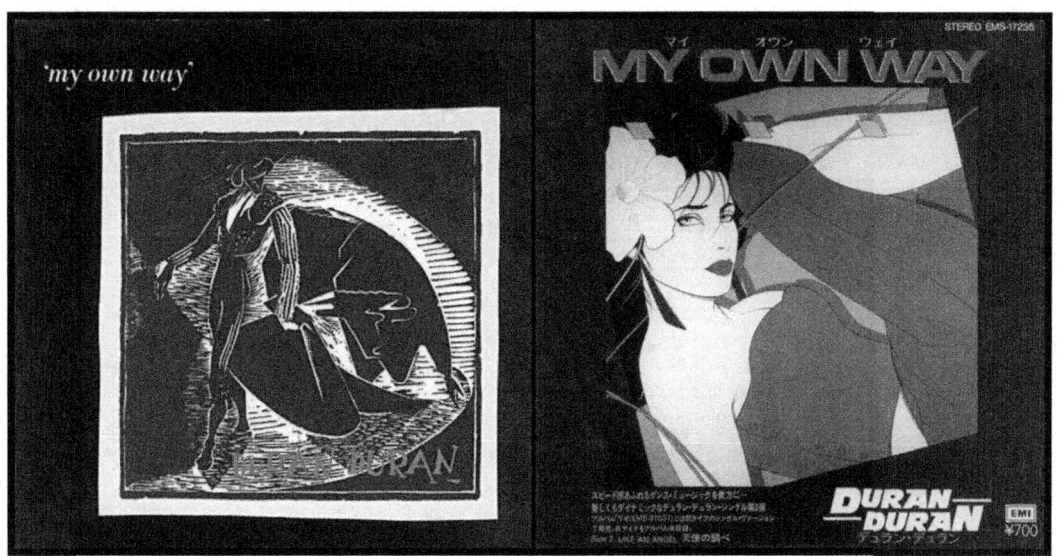

UK: EMI 5254 (1981).
  B-side: *Like An Angel*.

28.11.81: 37-26-22-**14**-15-15-16-16-27-44-59

Australia
8.03.82: peaked at no.**10**, charted for 16 weeks

Finland
04.82: peaked at no.**14**, charted for 8 weeks

Ireland
20.12.81: 21-**20-20-20**-22-23

New Zealand
30.05.82: 32-26-**12**-28-31-30-34-42

My Own Way was written by Duran Duran, and the band recorded the song at London's
Townhouse Studios in October 1981.

'It was the only time we actually sat down and said, "Okay, we've got to write a hit
single",' said Nick Rhodes. 'Biggest mistake of our career. Ever. We'll never do it again.'

My Own Way was issued as a non-album single, to cash-in on the success of *Girls On
Film*. It was promoted with a music video directed by Russell Mulcahy, which featured
flamenco dancers and a matador played by Adrian Paul.

The single was moderately successful, and achieved no.10 in Australia, no.12 in New Zealand, no.14 in Finland and the UK, and no.20 in Ireland.

Duran Duran re-recorded *My Own Way* for their second studio album, *RIO*, which was released in May 1982. This version was more of a ballad, with slightly re-written lyrics and the disco strings omitted.

The members of Duran Duran didn't have a very high opinion of *My Own Way*, as evidenced by its omission from the band's compilation albums, *DECADE* (1989) and *GREATEST* (1998).

5 ~ Hungry Like The Wolf

UK: EMI 5295 (1982).
  B-side: *Careless Memories (Live Version).*

15.05.82: 35-20-12-8-6-6-**5**-8-16-27-43-68

Australia
7.06.82: peaked at no.**5**, charted for 18 weeks

Canada
22.01.83: 48-?-34-26-16-9-6-3-**1**-2-2-3-4-5-7-11-19-23-30

Finland
06.82: peaked at no.**5**, charted for 8 weeks

Ireland
30.05.82: 17-13-14-10-8-**4**-13-25

Netherlands
3.07.82: **50**

New Zealand
1.08.82: 24-21-16-14-5-**4**-13-12-16-26-30-29-28-43

South Africa
4.09.82: peaked at no.**4**, charted for 14 weeks

USA
25.12.82: 77-77-65-53-34-27-22-19-9-6-5-5-4-**3-3-3**-6-11-16-33-42-66-94

Billboard Hot 100				WEEK OF MARCH 26, 1983		
THIS WEEK			AWARD ⓘ	LAST WEEK	PEAK POS.	WKS ON CHART
1		**Billie Jean** Michael Jackson	+	**1**	**1**	**10**
2		**Do You Really Want To Hurt Me** Culture Club	+	3	2	17
3		**Hungry Like The Wolf** Duran Duran	+	4	3	14

Hungry Like The Wolf was a song Duran Duran originally wrote and recorded in a single day, at the basement studios of EMI's London headquarters, in early 1982.

'That track came from fiddling with the new technology that was starting to come in,' said Andy Taylor.

Nick Rhodes was on his way to the studio when he came up with the idea for the backing track, which merged a Roland TR-808 drum machine with a sequencers and a Roland Jupiter-8 keyboard. When Simon Le Bon began working on the song's lyrics, he was inspired by the tale of *Little Red Riding Hood*.

Keeping the demo's original electronic backing track, Duran Duran re-recorded *Hungry Like The Wolf* for their second album, *RIO*, at London's AIR Studios, with producer Colin Thurston.

'He (Colin Thurston) was a great organiser and arranger,' said Andy Taylor. 'We gave him far more ideas and music than the track actually needed, and he was important in the process of whittling them down to the essential elements.'

Not counting *My Own Way*, which was originally issued as a non-album single, *Hungry Like The Wolf* was released as the lead single from *RIO*. The band promoted its release with an exotic music video directed by Russell Mulcahy, which was filmed on location in the jungles of Sri Lanka. Andy Taylor described the promo's storyline as 'Indiana Jones is horny and wants to get laid'.

Hungry Like The Wolf broke Duran Duran in North America ~ it went to no.1 in Canada and spent three weeks at no.3 in the United States.

'The success was totally unbelievable for us,' said John Taylor, 'because we sort of watched it from across the channel.'

In the UK, *Hungry Like The Wolf* gave the band their second Top 5 hit, and it charted at no.4 in Ireland, New Zealand and South Africa, no.5 in Australia and Finland, and no.50 in the Netherlands.

Duran Duran won a second Grammy Award for *Hungry Like The Wolf*, once again in the Best Music Video, Short Form, category.

6 ~ Save A Prayer

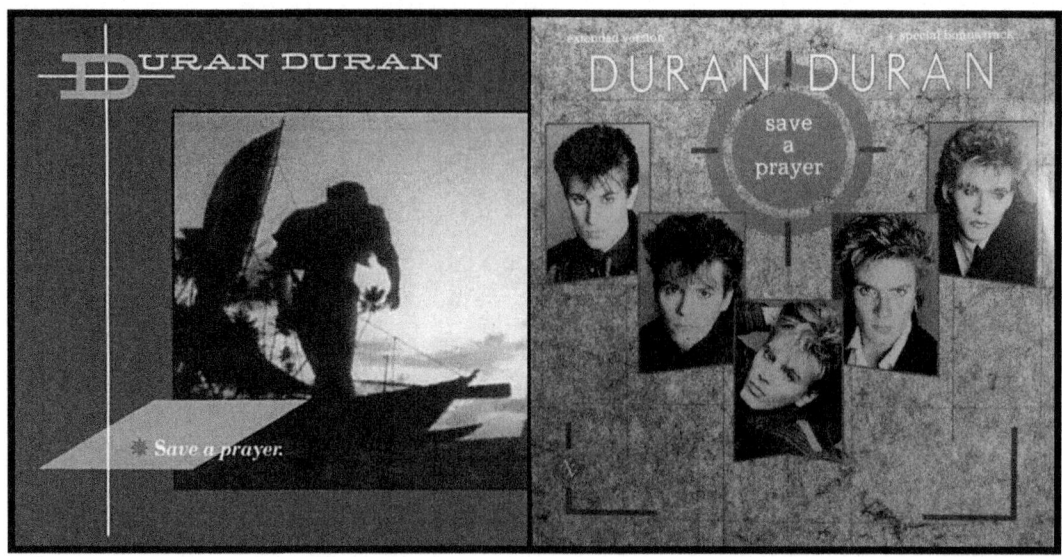

UK: EMI 5327 (1982).
  B-side: *Hold Back The Rain (Remix)*.

21.08.82: 27-5-3-**2**-3-7-18-34-62

Pos	LW		Title, Artist		Peak Pos	WoC
1	1		**EYE OF THE TIGER** SURVIVOR	SCOTTI BROTHERS	1	7
2	3 ↑		**SAVE A PRAYER** DURAN DURAN	EMI	2	4
3	2 ↓		**COME ON EILEEN** DEXY'S MIDNIGHT RUNNERS WITH THE EMERALD EXPRESS MERCURY		1	11

Australia
8.08.83: peaked at no.**56**, charted for 10 weeks

Belgium
30.10.82: 40
9.03.85: 32-26-**19-19**-30 (Special Edited Version)

Canada
9.02.85: 74-53-37-30-26-24-22-19-**17**-25-34-49-49-58-66-72-76-85-98

Germany

18.02.85: 61-33-**27**-29-31-43-44-46-54-67-65 (Special Edited Version)

Ireland

5.09.82: 8-4-**2**-5-11-30

Japan

1.03.85: peaked at no.**81**, charted for 3 weeks (Special Edited Version)

Netherlands

2.03.85: **17**-19-**17**-23-35-39-49 (Special Edited Version)

New Zealand

5.12.82: 50-36-**35**

USA

2.02.85: 53-42-35-29-23-21-**16-16**-22-33-49-67-79-97

Duran Duran wrote *Save A Prayer*, and the band recorded the song in early 1982 at London's AIR Studios, for their *RIO* album.

The song's lyrics were penned by Simon Le Bon while the band was on tour, and he described his inspiration as a 'realistic, not romantic' take on a one-night stand following a chance encounter.

As with *Hungry Like The Wolf*, Duran Duran promoted *Save A Prayer* with a music video filmed in Sri Lanka, which Russell Mulcahy directed. Venues included the ruins of a Buddhist temple at Polonnaruwa, where tensions were high as the country was on the verge of civil war, and Sigiriya, an ancient rock fortress. Members of the band were seen riding elephants, with one of the elephants spraying water at John Taylor from its trunk. During filming, miming playing his guitar while perched on a branch over a lagoon, Andy Taylor fell into the water, some of which he swallowed, leading to him developing a disease caused by a tropical virus, which resulted in him being hospitalised when the band moved on to Australia.

Save A Prayer gave Duran Duran their highest charting single to date in the UK, where it rose to no.2, kept off the top spot by Survivor's *Eye Of The Tiger*. The single also achieved no.2 in Ireland, and charted at no.35 in New Zealand, no.40 in Belgium and no.56 in Australia.

Save A Prayer wasn't released as a single in North America until 1985, when a live version from the band's *ARENA* album was issued. This version was recorded in April 1984, and during the concert Simon Le Bon dedicated the song to Marvin Gaye, who had been shot dead by his own father the day before the concert was recorded. This 'US Single Version' of *Save A Prayer* charted at no.16 in the United States and no.17 in Canada.

Also in 1985, a 'Special Edited Version' of *Save A Prayer* ~ which was 11 seconds longer than the US Single Version ~ was released outside North America, and achieved no.17 in the Netherlands, no.19 in Belgium, no.27 in Germany and no.81 in Japan.

7 ~ Rio

UK: EMI 5346 (1982).
  B-side: *The Chauffeur (Blue Silver)*.

13.11.82: 32-13-11-10-**9**-14-21-21-23-33-71

Australia
6.09.82: peaked at no.**60**, charted for 8 weeks

Canada
2.04.83: 49-33-25-20-15-10-5-**3-3**-6-7-26

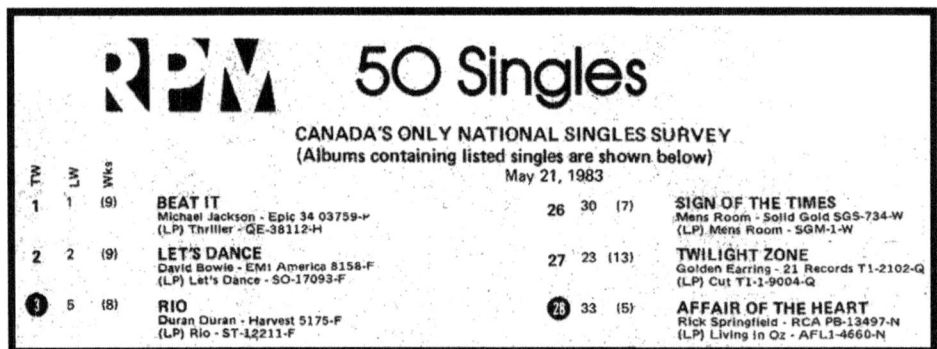

Finland
10.82: peaked at no.**19**, charted for 4 weeks

Ireland
21.11.82: 23-**9**-19-25-24-30-30

New Zealand
18.11.84: **36**-41

USA
2.04.83: 58-40-35-31-17-16-**14-14**-21-38-63-72-98

Duran Duran wrote *Rio*, and the band recorded the song at London's AIR Studios in early 1982, for their album with the same title.

John Taylor came up with the idea for a song about Rio de Janeiro, a city he described as 'the truly foreign, the exotic, a cornucopia of earthly delights, a party that would never stop.'

However, when Simon Le Bon wrote the lyrics for *Rio*, he chose to do so about a girl called Rio, rather than about the Brazilian city.

Duran Duran promoted *Rio* with a music video directed by Russell Mulcahy, which was filmed on and around the Caribbean island of Antigua. The promo featured the band on the yacht *Eilean*, and co-starred a beautiful body-painted woman played by Reema Ruspoli.

'In retrospect,' said Nick Rhodes, 'it's easy to look at the *Rio* video and say, "My God, it's like a Martini advert" … for us, it was like, "Wow, we can get the record company to pay for us to go to the Caribbean islands and make a video?" Of course we were going to go, we were kids!'

Rio was the final single released from the album with the same title, and it charted at no.9 in Ireland and the UK, no.19 in Finland, no.36 in New Zealand and no.60 in Australia.

The single was largely ignored, and failed to chart, when it was first issued in North America. This led to the single being reissued in March 1983, and this time *Rio* was much more successful, and achieved no.3 in Canada and no.14 in the United States.

Nicole Scherzinger, the former lead singer of Pussycat Dolls, recorded a cover of *Rio* in 2008, to promote Caress Brazilian body wash.

'When we were first approached about Nicole doing a version of *Rio* for this campaign,' said Simon Le Bon, 'we thought it was the perfect fit. She's exotic and beautiful and embodies everything that inspired the original version. Because it's one of our signature songs very few people have covered it over the years, so it has been great for us to hear a new interpretation.'

Nicole Scherzinger's cover of *Rio* was released as a single, but it wasn't a hit.

Too Shy

UK: EMI 5359 (1982).
  B-side: *Too Shy (Instrumental).*

22.01.83: 33-10-5-2-**1-1**-3-6-14-29-42-54-72

Pos	LW		Title, Artist		Peak Pos	WoC
1	2 ↑		**TOO SHY** KAJAGOOGOO	EMI	1	5
2	1 ↓		**DOWN UNDER** MEN AT WORK	EPIC	1	7
3	4 ↑		**SIGN OF THE TIMES** THE BELLE STARS	STIFF	3	6

Australia
21.03.83: peaked at no.**6**, charted for 14 weeks

Austria
15.04.83: 8-**4**-6-7-9-18-20 (bi-weekly)

Canada
14.05.83: 44-34-26-22-21-17-14-11-9-**8**-14-27-34

Belgium
19.03.83: 36-10-6-**1**-3-5-12-25

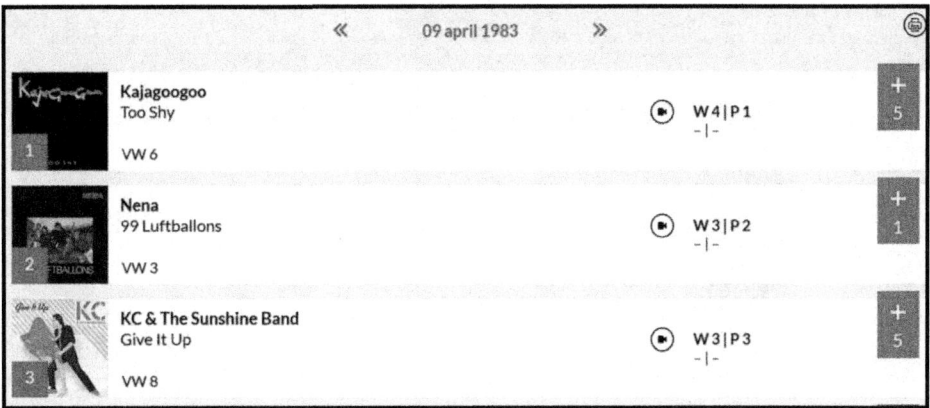

Finland
02.83: peaked at no.**1** (4), charted for 16 weeks

Germany
14.03.83: 36-27-12-**1-1-1-1-1**-3-6-11-13-17-30-36-54-47-59-64-69

Ireland
6.02.83: 17-8-5-**1**-3-8-19

Italy
7.05.83: peaked at no.**6**, charted for 11 weeks

Netherlands
5.03.83: 49-10-7-**5**-6-8-15-14-24-45

South Africa
26.03.83: peaked at no.**11**, charted for 15 weeks

New Zealand
6.03.83: 34-23-12-8-5-5-5-**2**-3-**2**-7-9-11-25-37-36

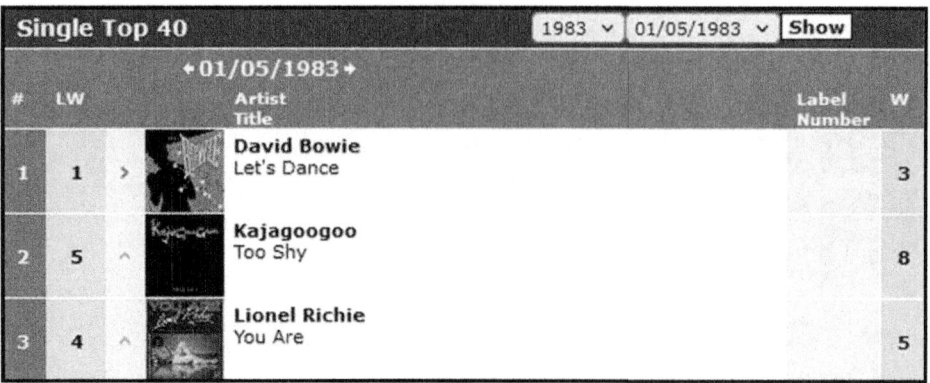

Sweden
22.03.83: 7-6-6-5-**4**-6-10-17

Switzerland
20.03.83: 14-7-3-3-3-**2**-3-4-7-13

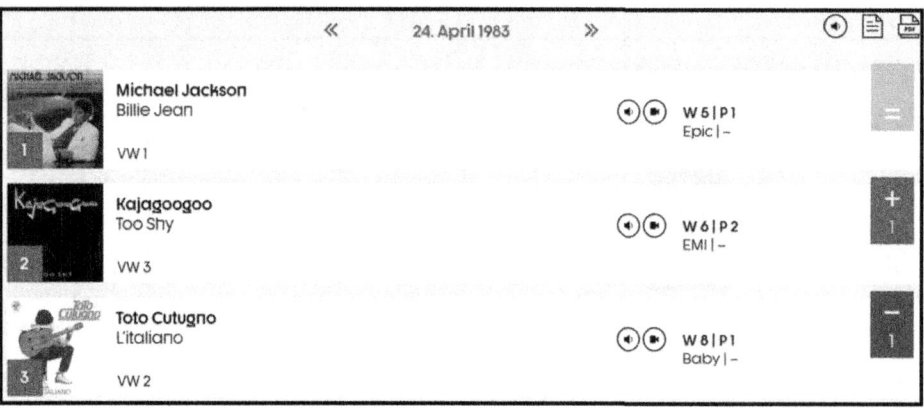

USA
23.04.83: 81-70-50-41-30-26-20-17-15-10-7-**5**-7-13-21-34-53-59-98

Too Shy was written and recorded by the British new wave band Kajagoogoo, namely Christopher 'Limahl' Hamill, Jez Strode, Nick Beggs, Steve Askew and Stuart Neale. The recording was produced by Duran Duran's Nick Rhodes and the band's producer, Colin Thurston, for Kajagoogoo's debut album, *WHITE FEATHERS*.

Too Shy got Kajagoogoo's career off to a flying start. The single hit no.1 in Belgium, Finland, Germany, Ireland and the UK, and achieved no.2 in New Zealand and Switzerland, no.4 in Austria and Sweden, no.5 in the Netherlands and the United States, no.6 in Australia and Italy, no.8 in Canada and no.11 in South Africa.

8 ~ Is There Something I Should Know?

UK: EMI 5371 (1983).
  B-side: *Faith In This Colour*.

26.03.83: **1-1**-2-3-11-27-34-44-66

Pos	LW	Title, Artist			Peak Pos	WoC
1	New		IS THERE SOMETHING I SHOULD KNOW? DURAN DURAN	EMI	1	1
2	1 ↓		TOTAL ECLIPSE OF THE HEART BONNIE TYLER	CBS	1	6
3	2 ↓		SWEET DREAMS (ARE MADE OF THIS) EURYTHMICS	RCA	2	7

Australia
2.05.83: peaked at no.**4**, charted for 15 weeks

Belgium
16.04.83: 39-17-**16**-18-18

Finland
04.83: peaked at no.**3**, charted for 8 weeks

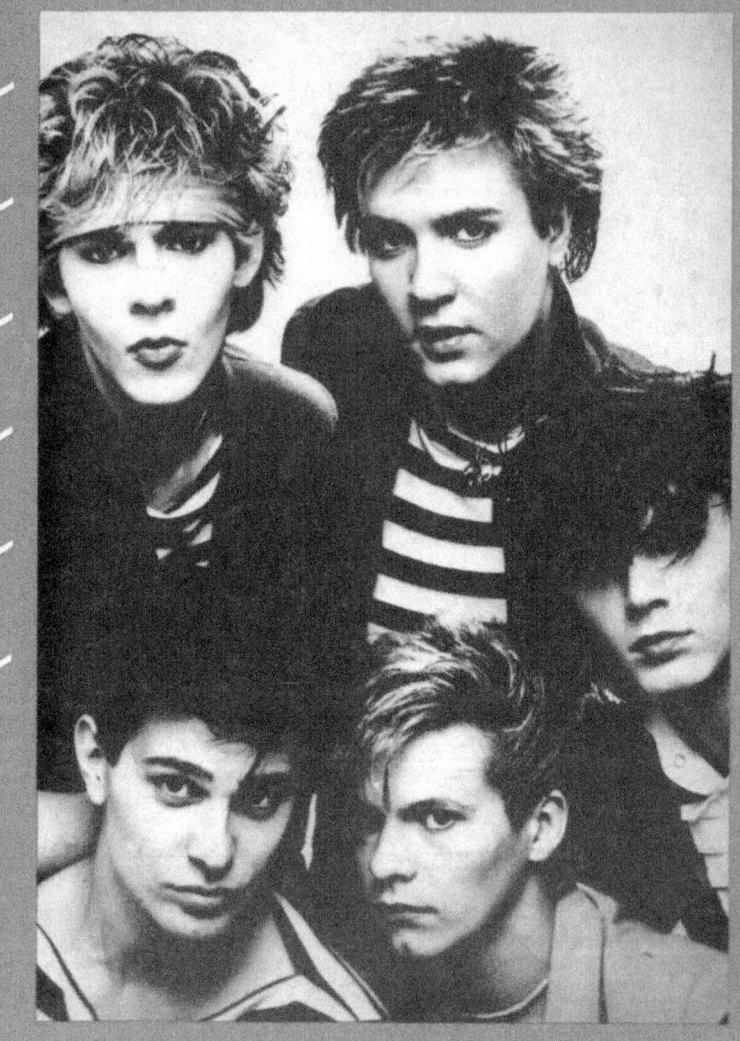

Canada
18.06.83: 49-37-28-21-13-10-7-**3-3**-5-13-19-28

RPM 50 Singles

CANADA'S ONLY NATIONAL SINGLES SURVEY
(Albums containing listed singles are shown below)
August 6, 1983

TW	LW	Wks				
1	5	(18)	**WHITE WEDDING** Billy Idol - Chrysalis CHS-2648-F (LP) Billy Idol - CHR-1377-F	26	30 (5)	**MANIAC** Michael Sembello - Casablanca - NBS-2367-Q (LP) Soundtrack/Flashdance - NDLP-7278-Q
2	2	(11)	**EVERY BREATH YOU TAKE** Police A&M - AM-2542-W (LP) Synchronicity - SP-3735-W	27	23 (13)	**CHANGE** Tears For Fears - Vertigo - SOV-2322-Q (LP) The Hurting - VOG-1-3323-Q
3	7	(8)	**IS THERE SOMETHING I SHOULD KNOW** Duran Duran - Capitol B-5233-F (LP) Duran Duran - ST-12158-F	**28**	36 (3)	**I'LL TUMBLE 4 YA** Culture Club - Virgin VS-1169-Q (LP) Kissing To Be Clever - VL-2248-Q

Germany
2.05.83: 29-31-**28-28**-29-35-42-54-57-69-x-74

Ireland
27.03.83: 22-**2-2**-6

Italy
4.06.83: peaked at no.**20**, charted for 3 weeks

Japan
1.06.83: peaked at no.**43**, charted for 14 weeks

Netherlands
16.04.83: 39-**24**-29-35-39-49

New Zealand
24.04.83: 28-7-7-6-**5**-6-7-10-15-14-16-15-17-32-42-x-x-39

Norway
21.05.83: **10**

Sweden
3.05.83: **16** 19-17 (bi weekly)

Switzerland
8.05.83: 15-11-**7**-8-14

USA
4.06.83: 57-44-32-25-17-13-9-8-5-**4**-5-7-15-29-45-66-97

Is There Something I Should Know? was written by Duran Duran, and the band recorded the song at Soho's Good Earth Studios in December 1982 ~ however, the single was remixed several times before the band was happy with it.

Is There Something I Should Know? was issued as a non-album single, and Duran Duran promoted its release with a colour and monochrome music video directed by Russell Mulcahy.

'The only part of a (Duran Duran) video I would change,' Roger Taylor later commented, 'is the end of *Is There Something I Should Know?* where I am singing to the camera. I look very uncomfortable doing this and cringe every time I see it to this day.'

On early pressings of the single, the B-side *Faith In This Colour* featured sound effects taken from *Star Wars*, which were used without permission. As a result, to avoid a lawsuit, the track was hastily remixed and the *Star Wars* sample was removed, and this is the version found on most pressings of the single.

In the UK, *Is There Something I Should Know?* not only gave Duran Duran their first no.1 single, it made its chart debut at no.1 ~ a rare feat at the time.

Elsewhere, the single achieved no.2 in Ireland, no.3 in Finland and Canada, no.4 in Australia and the United States, no.5 in New Zealand, no.7 in Switzerland, no.10 in Norway, no.16 in Belgium and Sweden, no.20 in Italy, no.24 in the Netherlands, no.28 in Germany and no.43 in Japan.

When Duran Duran's self-titled debut album was reissued in the United States in 1983, *Is There Something I Should Know?* was added to the track listing.

In 2001, allSTARS* recorded a cover of *Is There Something I Should Know?*, which was released as a double A-side single with *Things That Go Bump In The Night*. The single charted at no.12 in the UK.

Ooh To Be Ah

UK: EMI 5383 (1983).
  B-side: *Animal Instincts*.

2.04.83: 20-**7**-**7**-8-16-27-40-70

Australia
6.06.83: peaked at no.**68**, charted for 9 weeks

Germany
9.05.83: 57-32-25-**20**-22-28-41-38-37-49-53-64-64

Ireland
10.04.83: 11-**7**-14-26

New Zealand
3.07.83: **50**

Ooh To Be Ah was written by Limahl, and was recorded by Kajagoogoo for their *WHITE FEATHERS* album ~ the recording was produced by Nick Rhodes and Colin Thurston.
    Ooh To Be Ah was the second single released from Kajagoogoo's debut album, but it couldn't match the success of *Too Shy*. Nevertheless, the single charted at no.7 in Ireland and the UK, no.20 in Germany, no.50 in New Zealand and no.68 in Australia.

Hang On Now

UK: EMI 5394 (1983).
   B-side: *Hang On Now (Instrumental).*

4.06.83: 39-15-**13**-18-27-39-71

Finland
08.83: peaked at no.**15**, charted for 4 weeks

Germany
25.07.83: 50-**41**-45-42-49-59-67

USA
27.08.83: 85-80-**78**-99

Hang On Now was written and recorded by Kajagoogoo for their *WHITE FEATHERS* album ~ the recording was produced by Nick Rhodes and Colin Thurston.
   Hang On Now was the third and final single released from Kajagoogoo's debut album, and it achieved no.13 in the UK, no.15 in Finland and no.41 in Germany. The single was also a minor no.78 hit in the United States, but it failed to chart in most countries.

9 ~ Union Of The Snake

UK: EMI 5429 (1983).
  B-side: *Secret Oktober.*

29.10.83: 4-**3**-6-13-28-45-73-x-75-75-66-73

Pos	LW	Title, Artist		Peak Pos	WoC
1	7 ↑	**UPTOWN GIRL** BILLY JOEL	CBS	1	5
2	2	**ALL NIGHT LONG (ALL NIGHT)** LIONEL RICHIE	MOTOWN	2	6
3	4 ↑	**UNION OF THE SNAKE** DURAN DURAN	EMI	3	2

Australia
31.10.83: peaked at no.**4**, charted for 16 weeks

Belgium
3.12.83: 29-**19-19**-20

Denmark
18.11.83: 14-12-**7**

Canada
5.11.83: 45-42-30-22-16-13-10-7-7-4-**2**-6-7-10-11-23-35

Finland
10.83: peaked at no.**1** (7), charted for 16 weeks

Germany
14.11.83: 44-41-**37**-58-44-47-60-65-58-69-69-75-63-63-66-72

Ireland
30.10.83: 9-**5**-8-24

Italy
19.11.83: peaked at no.**16**, charted for 8 weeks

Japan
21.10.83: peaked at no.**48**, charted for 18 weeks

New Zealand
30.10.83: 19-4-**3**-6-4-5-7-5-5-5-5-5-17-33-33-46

Netherlands
5.11.83: 49-20-25-**17**-19-24-28-40

Norway
3.12.83: 9-10-**8**-x-x-**8**

Spain
5.03.84: peaked at no.**16**, charted for 5 weeks

Sweden
15.11.83: **16**-19 (bi-weekly)

USA
5.11.83: 59-42-24-14-11-7-5-**3-3-3**-4-11-13-25-49-64-96

Zimbabwe
11.02.84: peaked at no.**2**, charted for 10 weeks

Union Of The Snake, which was originally titled 'The Union At Stake', was written by Duran Duran, and the band recorded the song for their third studio album, *SEVEN AND THE RAGGED TIGER*, which was released in November 1983. The song was recorded at George Martin's AIR Studios on the Caribbean island of Montserrat.

Union Of The Snake was released as the lead single from *SEVEN AND THE RAGGED TIGER*, and was promoted with an expensive music video filmed in the sand dunes outside Cronulla, a suburb of Sydney, Australia. The storyline was conceived by Russell Mulcahy, however, as he was busy preparing to direct the band's Arena concert film, Simon Milne was recruited to direct the promo, which saw members of the band ~ with the main focus on lead singer Simon Le Bon ~ crossing the Australian dessert, pursued by a strange half-man, half-snake creation.

'The video for *Union Of The Snake* didn't work too well,' admitted John Taylor. 'It was too high concept, over-staged and over-dressed, and it lacked direction.'

Union of The Snake hit no.1 for seven weeks in Finland, and charted at no.2 in Canada and Zimbabwe, no.3 in New Zealand, the UK and the United States, no.4 in Australia, no.5 in Ireland, no.7 in Denmark, no.8 in Norway, no.16 in Italy, Spain and Sweden, no.17 in the Netherlands, no.19 in Belgium, no.37 in Germany and no.48 in Japan.

'*Union Of The Snake* went in at number two (sic),' said John Taylor, referring to the UK chart where the single actually debuted at no.4, 'and that was immensely disappointing, which gives some indication of the pressure we were under and the expectations we had for ourselves.'

10 ~ New Moon On Monday

UK: EMI DURAN 1 (1984).
  B-side: *Tiger Tiger*.

4.02.84: 12-**9-9**-20-22-45-70
5.05.84: 91

Australia
6.07.84: peaked at no.**48**, charted for 13 weeks

Canada
28.01.84: 43-39-34-26-19-17-**14-14**-21-22-27-30

Finland
03.84: peaked at no.**8**, charted for 4 weeks

Ireland
5.02.84: 13-**5**-10-28

Japan
1.03.84: peaked at no.**80**, charted for 3 weeks

Netherlands
18.02.84: 41-33-**28**-37-50

New Zealand
11.03.84: **32**-39-34-39-39-41-49

USA
14.01.84: 58-48-37-29-25-22-16-13-12-**10**-16-18-43-68-77-94

New Moon On Monday was written by Duran Duran, and the band recorded the song at Montserrat's AIR Studios for their *SEVEN AND THE RAGGED TIGER* album.

The track was released as the second single from the album, and Duran Duran promoted it with an ambitious music video filmed in the small French village of Noyers on 7th December 1983. Once again, Russell Mulcahy was too busy to direct, so Brian Grant was called in to do the honours.

In the video, the band played members of an underground resistance movement *La Luna* (French for 'The Moon'), and the lead female was played by a former Miss France winner, Patricia Barzyk.

'We set out to make a little movie,' said Brian Grant, but he admitted, 'I'm not sure we succeeded.'

The promo was 17 minutes long, and began with a lengthy non-musical opening. The song, when it finally started, was an extended remix. Initially, a shorter version with a spoken introduction in French was submitted to MTV, but the TV station requested an even shorter version ~ minus the introduction.

New Moon On Monday wasn't as successful as *Union Of The Snake*, but it did achieve no.5 in Ireland, no.8 in Finland, no.9 in the UK, no.10 in the United States, no.14 in Canada, no.28 in the Netherlands, no.32 in New Zealand and no.48 in Australia.

With hindsight, Duran Duran admitted the music video for *New Moon On Monday* wasn't the band's finest moment.

'The video was really awful,' said Nick Rhodes. 'When the director dresses up as a blind man, you know you've got a catastrophe on your hands.'

'Everybody hates it,' Andy Taylor agreed, 'particularly the dreadful scene at the end where we all dance together. Even today, I cringe and leave the room if anyone plays it.'

11 ~ The Reflex

UK: EMI DURAN 2 (1984),
  B-side: *Make Me Smile (Come Up And See Me) (Live)*.

28.04.84: 5-**1-1-1-1**-3-4-19-27-35-40-53-61-66

Pos	LW	Title, Artist		Peak Pos	WoC
1	5 ↑	**THE REFLEX** DURAN DURAN	EMI	1	2
2	2	**AGAINST ALL ODDS (TAKE A LOOK AT ME NOW)** PHIL COLLINS	VIRGIN	2	5
3	3	**I WANT TO BREAK FREE** QUEEN	EMI	3	4

Australia
14.05.84: peaked at no.**4**, charted for 18 weeks

Austria
15.07.84: 12-**11**-14-19 (bi-weekly)

Finland
05.84: peaked at no.**3**, charted for 12 weeks

Belgium
26.05.84: 23-16-5-2-**1-1-1-1**-2-2-8-10-18-21-26

Canada
28.04.84: 46-33-18-13-6-5-4-**3-3**-4-6-9-12-18-20-23-24-25-46-54-61-64

France
3.11.84: **15**-18-**15**-20-16-18-33-35-45-39-x-39

Germany
28.05.84: 28-20-12-11-**8**-9-9-10-17-17-20-31-31-33-54-71-67

Ireland
29.04.84: 8-3-**1-1**-2-**1**-4-16

Italy
9.06.84: peaked at no.**6**, charted for 15 weeks

Japan
1.06.84: peaked at no.**46**, charted for 12 weeks

Netherlands
19.05.84: 44-21-3-**1-1-1-1-1**-2-3-5-9-16-30-45-43

New Zealand
3.06.84: 25-**6**-15-7-8-10-9-13-15-26-19-29-29-40-45

Spain
6.11.84: peaked at no.**14**, charted for 17 weeks

Switzerland
3.06.84: 23-16-13-**10**-12-11-17-18-21-29-30-30

USA
21.04.84: 46-36-26-19-12-7-5-4-2-**1-1**-5-5-14-21-35-53-69-87-90-99

Duran Duran wrote and recorded *The Reflex* for their *SEVEN AND THE RAGGED TIGER*, and had wanted to release it as the album's lead single, but their record company insisted on releasing *Union Of The Snake* instead.

The Reflex was finally issued as the album's third ~ and what proved to be final ~ single, and the band's belief in the songs was justified, as it out-performed both *Union Of The Snake* and *New Moon On Monday*.

The single version of *The Reflex* was remixed by Chic's Nile Rodgers.

'I got the track and listened to it,' he said, 'and I picked up on this obvious little hook thing, "tra-la-la-la, tra-la-la-la" … and then I came up with the "Fle-fle-fle". I sent it to the guys. They loved it, they thought it was fantastic.'

Duran Duran's record company didn't agree.

'Nile, we've submitted it to the record company,' Nick Rhodes reported back, 'and they hate it, they said you've made us sound too black.'

But, on this occasion, Duran Duran stood their ground, and insisted their record company release the remix as is, which is what happened.

Duran Duran promoted *The Reflex* with a mostly live music video, which was filmed during the band's concert staged at the Maple Leaf Gardens in Toronto, Ontario, on 5th March 1984. The promo was directed by Russell Mulcahy, and ~ not wanting the music video to appear 'ordinary' ~ it did feature footage of a video screen above the stage showing clips of models wearing collars and chains and nothing else, illuminated by black light.

The B-side of *The Reflex* was a live cover of Steve Harley & Cockney Rebel's *Make Me Smile (Come Up And See Me)*, which hit no.1 in the UK in 1975. This was recorded at Duran Duran's concert at London's Hammersmith Odeon on 16th November 1982, when Steve Harley joined the band on stage to perform the song.

The Reflex gave Duran Duran their biggest hit in the UK, where it topped the chart for four straight weeks. It was the band's second chart topping single, after *Is There Something I Should Know?*, but it proved to be their last as well.

Elsewhere, *The Reflex* hit no.1 in Belgium, Ireland, the Netherlands and the United States, where it was the band's first single to top the Hot 100. The single also achieved no.3 in Canada and Finland, no.4 in Austria, no.6 in Italy and New Zealand, no.8 in Germany, no.10 in Switzerland, no.11 in Austria, no.14 in Spain, no.15 in France and no.46 in Japan.

12 ~ The Wild Boys

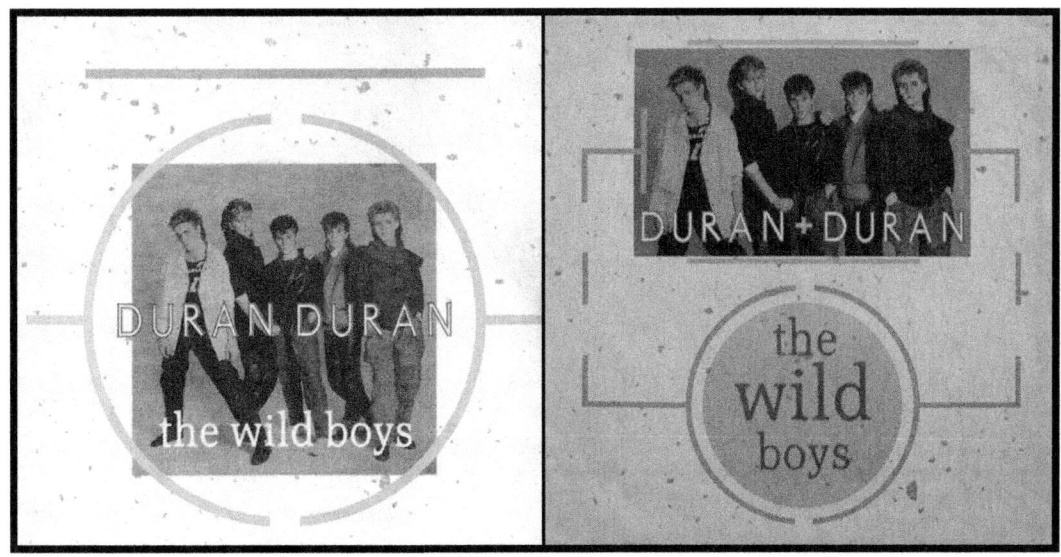

UK: Parlophone DURAN 3 (1984).
  B-side: *(I'm Looking For) Cracks In The Pavement (Live)*.

3.11.84: 5-3-**2**-3-9-19-29-32-31-26-23-39-50-70

Pos	LW	Title, Artist		Peak Pos	WoC
1	1	**I FEEL FOR YOU** CHAKA KHAN	WARNER BROTHERS	1	5
2	3 ↑	**THE WILD BOYS** DURAN DURAN	EMI	2	3
3	13 ↑	**I SHOULD HAVE KNOWN BETTER** JIM DIAMOND	A&M	3	4

Australia
19.11.84: peaked at no.**3**, charted for 17 weeks

Finland
11.84: peaked at no.**5**, charted for 8 weeks

France
2.03.85: 20-17-**13**-17-19-**13**-14-18-25-24-30-38-45-30-40-42

Austria
15.12.84: 10-3-**2**-5-7-13-28 (bi-weekly)

Belgium
10.11.84: 21-11-7-4-4-4-**2**-4-7-8-8-11-16-25

Canada
27.10.84: 85-64-44-30-18-5-4-**2**-3-3-3-5-6-8-15-21-30-45-49

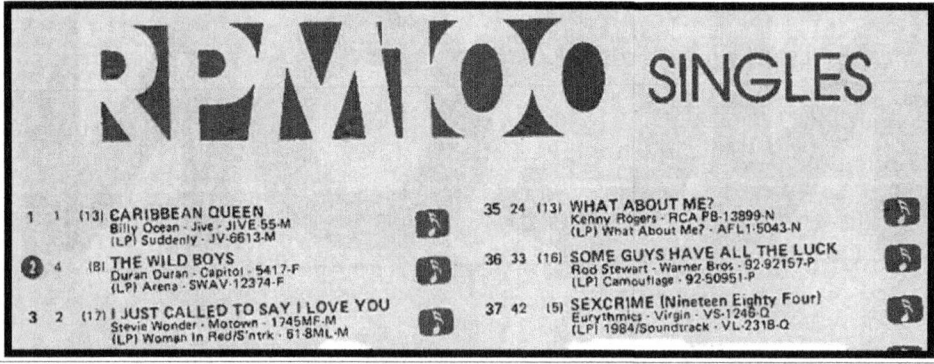

INCLUDES FULL-COLOR POSTER

PIANO • VOCAL • GUITAR

the wild boys

Words and Music by DURAN DURAN

Recorded by DURAN DURAN on Capitol Records

Denmark
23.11.84: 14-9-**4**-6-7-7-6-5-5-6-**4**-6-6-5-7-12

Germany
12.11.84: 60-24-5-2-**1-1-1**-2-3-3-10-12-23-32-48-59-68

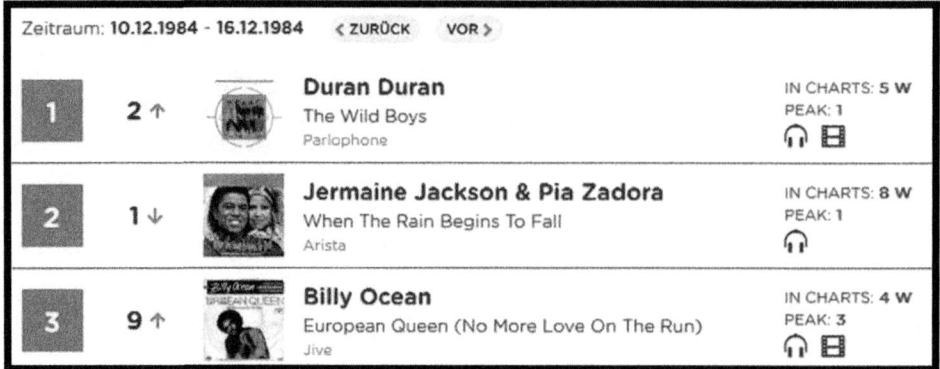

Ireland
4.11.84: 10-**2-2**-5-23

Italy
3.11.84: peaked at no.**3**, charted for 30 weeks

Japan
16.11.84: peaked at no.**47**, charted for 11 weeks
23.11 84: peaked at no.86, charted for 4 weeks (12")

Netherlands
10.11.84: 9-5-4-**3**-4-4-6-9-13-10-11-17-23-42

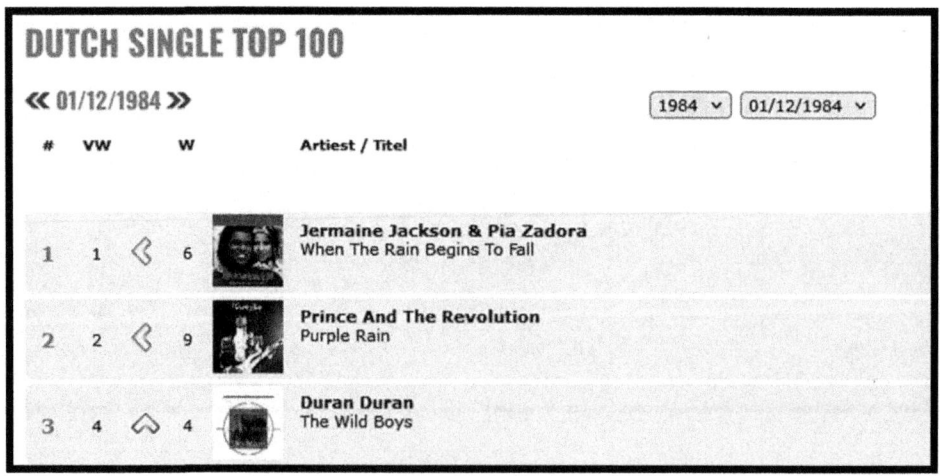

New Zealand
4.11.84: 28-9-8-**5**-7-9-13-13-13-13-13-18-34-49-35

Norway
22.12.84: **6**

South Africa
12.01.85: peaked at no.**1** (1), charted for 14 weeks

Switzerland
25.11.84: 15-9-5-**2-2-2-2-2**-4-7-10-15-27

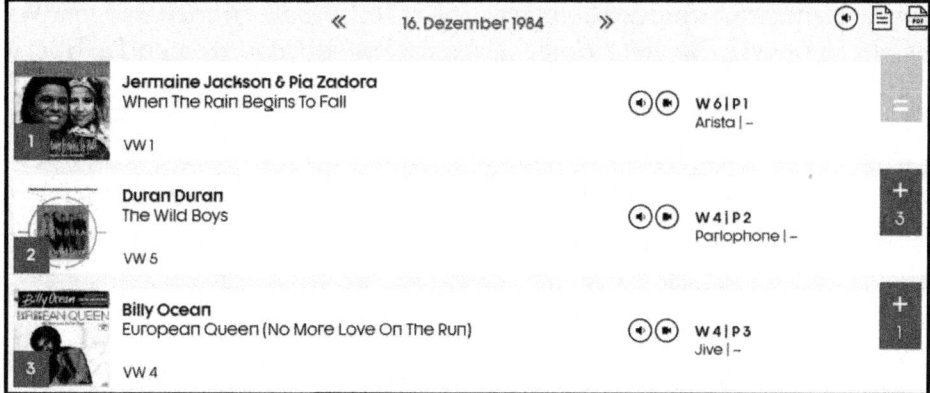

USA
3.11.84: 38-28-19-12-7-4-**2-2-2-2**-3-7-15-29-59-75-86-94

THIS WEEK			AWARD ⓘ	LAST WEEK	PEAK POS.	WKS ON CHART
1		Out Of Touch Daryl Hall John Oates	+	1	1	12
2		The Wild Boys Duran Duran	+	4	2	7
3		Like A Virgin Madonna	+	11	3	5

Billboard Hot 100 — WEEK OF DECEMBER 15, 1984

Spain
15.04.85: peaked at no.**3**, charted for 22 weeks

Sweden
23.11.84: **19** (bi-weekly)

The Wild Boys was written by Duran Duran, and the band recorded the song in July 1984 at London's Maison Rouge Studios ~ it was the only studio recording featured on the band's live album, *ARENA*, which was released in November 1984.

'We wanted to be more abrasive,' said Andy Taylor. '*Wild Boys* is the first song we have recorded that has captured the energy and power we have live.'

It was Duran Duran's music video director Russell Mulcahy who came up with the idea for the song, as he was interested in making a full length film based on William S. Burroughs' 1971 novel, *The Wild Boys: A Book Of The Dead*. Simon Le Bon wrote the lyrics for *The Wild Boys* based on Russell Mulcahy's brief synopsis of the book.

Russell Mulcahy directed the music video for *The Wild Boys*, which he saw as a teaser for a full length film that never materialised. The promo was filmed at Pinewood Studios, located just outside London, and cost an eye-watering £1 million to shoot. The elaborate stage featured a metal pyramid and a windmill over a deep pool. Simon Le Bon was strapped to one of the windmill's blades and, as it turned, his head was plunged into the water below the windmill. The other members of the band, dressed in ragged clothes, were similarly shown imprisoned and in dangerous situations.

In the UK, in a clever marketing ploy, *The Wild Boys* was issued with six different sleeve designs, one featuring the whole band and one depicting each individual member of the band.

Despite this, *The Wild Boys* peaked at no.2, kept off the top spot by Chaka Khan's *I Feel For You*.

It was a similar story in the United States, where *The Wild Boys* spent four straight weeks at no.2, behind first *Out Of Touch* by Daryl Hall & John Oates, and then Madonna's *Like A Virgin*.

The Wild Boys did hit no.1 in Germany and South Africa, and the single achieved no.2 in Austria, Belgium, Canada, Ireland and Switzerland, no.3 in Australia, Italy, the Netherlands and Spain, no.4 in Denmark, no.5 in Finland and new Zealand, no.6 in Norway, no.13 in France, no.19 in Sweden and no.47 in Japan.

At the 1985 Brit Awards, the music video for *The Wild Boys* was named British Video of the Year.

Phixx, a British-Irish group, recorded a cover of *The Wild Boys* in 2004, which was a no.12 hit in the UK.

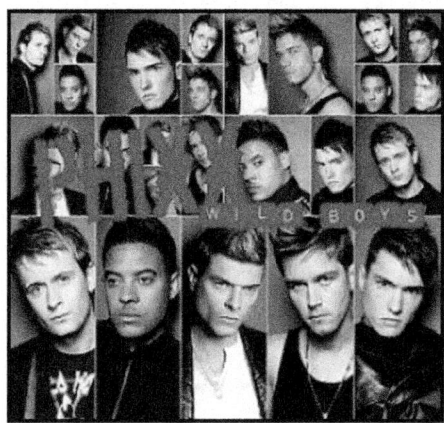

Do They Know It's Christmas?

UK: Mercury/Phonogram FEED 1 (1984).
  B-side: *Feed The World*.

15.12.84: **1-1-1-1-1**-2-9-17-30-38-57-71

Pos	LW		Title, Artist		Peak Pos	WoC
1	New		DO THEY KNOW IT'S CHRISTMAS? BAND AID	MERCURY	1	1
2	New		LAST CHRISTMAS/EVERYTHING SHE WANTS WHAM!	EPIC	2	1
3	1 ↓		THE POWER OF LOVE FRANKIE GOES TO HOLLYWOOD	ZTT	1	3

7.12.85: 24-6-3-3-4-13-47-x-91
20.12.86: 99-88-86
15.12.07: 38-27-24-57
13.12.08: 64-54-58-72
12.12.09: 65-53-61-50
11.12.10: 62-54-58-58
10.12.11: 62-34-42-41
8.12.12: 82-37-42-51
14.12.13: 62-57-63
29.11.14: 61-88-59-61-60-56

17.12.15: 71-59-38-86
15.12.16: 41-43-35-29
7.12.17: 85-16-12-12-7
6.12.18: 88-26-15-13-6
5.12.19: 77-23-15-17-7
26.11.20: 86-38-15-8-7-9-7
2.12.21: 66-23-14-13-14-12
25.11.22: 63-34-18-16-17-11

Australia
24.12.84: peaked at no.**1** (4), charted for 23 weeks
3.01.21: 19-34
20.12.21: 59-25-14
19.12.22: 61-29-10

Austria
15.01.85: **1**-8-13-17 (bi-weekly)

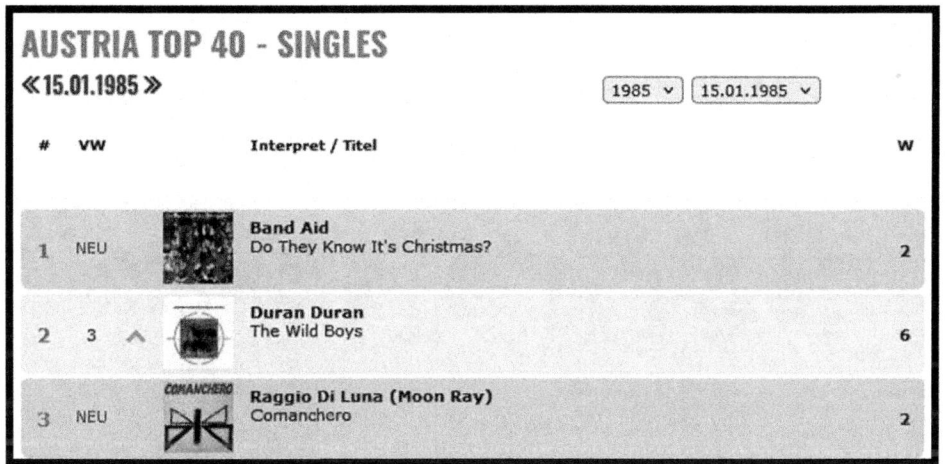

10.12.10: 43-55-45-59
9.12.11: 49-57-63
14.12.12: 57-61-74
13.12.13: 56-49-55
12.12.14: 62-61-54
25.12.15: 57-73
6.01.17: 58
15.12.17: 71-54-38
14.12.18: 45-37-22
13.12.19: 43-37-14
4.12.20: 55-13-11-13-10

3.12.21: 52-14-12-17-13
29.11.22: 32-14-14-16-18-17

Belgium
22.12.84: 7-**1-1-1-1**-3-5-21-28

31.12.22: 35

Canada
5.01.85: **1-1**-2-2-7-9-14-21-42-48-56-58-68-83

18.12.21: 44-42-29-33
31.12.22: 26-25

Denmark
29.11.19: 26-12-13-11-8
27.11.20: 25-10-9-8-**7**
4.12.21: 39-17-15-15-16-13
30.11.22: 28-12-12-12-12-11

Finland
12.84: peaked at no.**4**, charted for 4 weeks (monthly)
29.12.18: 11

France
9.02.85: 42-**34**-48

Germany
24.12.84: 6-**1-1**-2-3-7-10-15-35-56-69

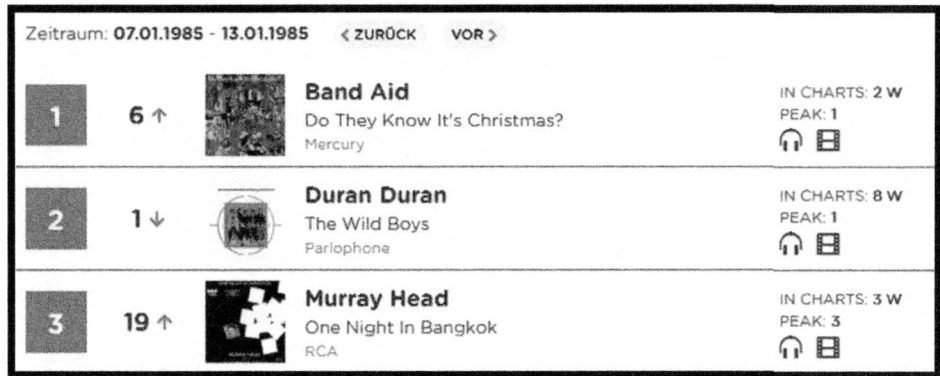

9.12.11: 74-79-72-51-73
14.12.12: 72-62-64-63
13.12.13: 83-60-59-57
28.11.14: 95-67-64-61-60-43
11.12.15: 97-100-37
9.12.16: 87-x-82-42
8.12.17: 82-67-62-29
7.12.18: 57-51-38-21
6.12.19: 81-68-51-17
4.12.20: 28-11-18-12-10
3.12.21: 40-29-29-23-19
25.11.22: 65-24-20-17-15-16

Ireland
16.12.84: **1-1-1-1-1-1**-2-4-4-5-13
22.12.85: 2-2-2
6.12.07: 37-28-33-37
11.12.08: 33-34-42
28.11.14: 61-88-85-63-63-58
18.12.15: 74-63-39-51
16.12.16: 62-55-40-35
8.12.17: 6-24-15-15-7

7.12.18: 86-41-25-17-9
13.12.19: 47-35-30-15
4.12.20: 60-34-20-24-12-21
26.11.21: 71-36-20-16-13-12
25.11.22: 64-32-19-17-15-10

Italy
5.01.85: peaked at no.**1** (2), charted for 15 weeks
9.12.21: 70-x-76-40
8.12.22: 86-78-75-30

Netherlands
22.12.84: **1-1-1-1**-2-2-8-18-40

4.01.86: 49-49
20.12.08: 37-27-45
19.12.09: 52-53-60
11.12.10: 90-58-62-68
17.12.11: 91-85-69
29.12.12: 76
21.12.13: 72-49
20.12.14: 42-29-78
12.12.15: 99-49-39-28
12.12.16: 81-64-29
16.12.17: 25-28-9
15.12.18: 30-23-11
14.12.19: 47-42-11
5.12.20: 76-33-19-14-9

11.12.21: 49-35-29-12
10.12.22: 39-24-20-13

New Zealand
20.01.85: **1-1-1-1**-6-10-16-27-28-42-45-39-47-13-13-10-17-21-28-35

2.01.17: 38
1.01.18: 15
12.12.18: 37-22-4
30.12.19: 6
28.12.20: 14
20.12.21: 38-21-12
12.12.22: 32-27-11-9

Norway
29.12.84: 3-3-3-3-**1-1-1**-2-2-4-6-5-8

30.12.89: 4-4-4-6-8-9
31.12.22: 38

South Africa
2.02.85: peaked at no.**13**, charted for 5 weeks

Spain
25.03.85: peaked at no.**22**, charted for 6 weeks

Sweden
21.12.84: 9-**1**-2-2-2-3-9-16-19 (bi-weekly)

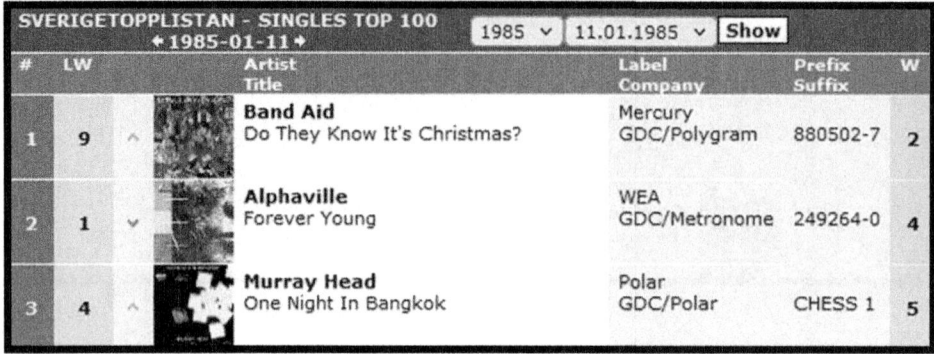

13.12.07: 60-52-23
18.12.08: 39-35-53
11.12.09: 57-41-37-47
24.12.10: 57-49
16.12.11: 53-42-23
7.12.12: 52-36-31-15
13.12.13: 41-38-21
5.12.14: 58-44-34-16-42
4.12.15: 43-31-21-16
2.12.16: 36-31-26-18-10
1.12.17: 59-20-18-11-7
30.11.18: 33-11-10-99
29.11.19: 92-37-39-29-15
27.11.20: 79-19-18-20-13-97
3.12.21: 40-33-30-28-25
25.11.22: 03-35-26-16-15-15

Switzerland
23.12.84: 7-**1-1**-3-2-4-6-11-18
30.12.07: 71-96
21.12.08: 70-44
3.01.10: 60
1.01.17: 98

Band Aid
Do They Know It's Christmas?

VW 7

W 2 | P 1
Mercury | –

+ 6

Duran Duran
The Wild Boys

VW 2

W 6 | P 2
Parlophone | –

Jermaine Jackson & Pia Zadora
When The Rain Begins To Fall

VW 1

W 8 | P 1
Arista | –

– 2

24.12.17: 75-54
16.12.18: 87-58-26
15.12.19: 97-62-19
6.12.20: 58-36-30-28-25
5.12.21: 84-52-45-37-26
11.12.22: 55-42-40-27

USA
22.12.84: 65-65-20-15-**13**-17-49-64-81

Zimbabwe
9.02.85: peaked at no.**3**, charted for 15 weeks

Bob Geldof (Boomtown Rats) and Midge Ure (Ultravox) wrote *Do They Know It's Christmas?* in response to harrowing TV reports about the famine in Ethiopia at the time.

'I was lucky in a way,' said Geldof, 'because I had already written this song, which I provisionally called 'It's My World', and I knew it would be suitable if I just changed the words a bit and called it *Do They Know It's Christmas?* Midge, reliable as ever, sent down this tune which is the sort of Christmassy bit at the end, and we married the two together.'

To record *Do They Know It's Christmas?* Bob Geldof brought together a supergroup of mostly British and Irish acts, and the song was recorded at London's Sarm Studios on 25th November 1984.

Simon Le Bon was one of the lead vocalists on *Do They Know It's Christmas?*, along with Paul Young (who opened the song), Boy George (Culture Club), George Michael (Wham!), Paul Weller (Jam), Tony Hadley (Spandau Ballet), Sting (The Police) and Bono (U2).

Other members of the above bands, including Duran Duran, formed part of the all-star chorus, as did Bananarama, Jody Watley, Kool & The Gang, Marilyn and Status Quo. Phil Collins played drums on the recording, while Andy Taylor played guitar and John Taylor played bass.

'The whole thing serves a dual purpose,' said John Taylor. 'It can raise a lot of money and I'm really proud because it's a celebration of British pop music.'

Do They Know It's Christmas? quickly became the fastest selling single in the history of the UK charts. It made its chart debut at no.1, ahead of Wham!'s *Last Christmas*, and held the top spot for five weeks. The single went on to outsell *Mull Of Kintyre* by Wings, thus becoming the UK's No.1 best-selling single of all-time. It was an accolade the song held until 1997, when it was outsold by Elton John's tribute to Diana, Princess of Wales, *Candle In The Wind 1997*.

Do They Know It's Christmas? hit no.1 in numerous countries around the world, including Australia, Austria, Belgium, Canada, Germany, Ireland, Italy, the Netherlands, New Zealand, Norway, Sweden and Switzerland. Elsewhere, the single achieved no.3 in Zimbabwe, no.4 in Finland, no.13 in South Africa and the United States, no.22 in Spain and no.34 in France.

Bob Geldof hoped the single would raise £70,000 ~ it actually raised, in just the first twelve months, in the region of £8 million, to aid famine relief in Ethiopia.

The digital age saw *Do They Know It's Christmas?* re-entering charts in several countries on an annual basis, albeit not terribly highly. This changed with the advent of streaming, and the inclusion of streaming 'sales' and *Do They Know It's Christmas?* on most festive streaming playlists, means the single regularly makes an annual appearance in the Top 20 in several countries every December.

New versions of *Do They Know It's Christmas?* were recorded in 1989, 2004 and 2014, but none featured any members of Duran Duran, while in 2022 LadBaby claimed the Christmas no.1 with a charity reworking of the song titled *Food Aid*.

13 ~ Some Like It Hot

UK: Parlophone R6091 (1985).
  B-side: *The Heat Is On*.

16.03.85: 37-17-**14**-15-21-28-43-58

Australia
8.04.85: peaked at no.**4**, charted for 20 weeks

Austria
1.06.85: 17-24-**10**-21 (bi-weekly)

Belgium
23.03.85: 36-18-14-10-**6**-13-32-35

Canada
9.05.85: 86-58-38-26-21-16-13-10-10-**9-9**-10-21-28-34-46-54-57-65-67-82-94

Denmark
12.04.85: 17-9-**6**-9

Germany
8.04.85: 34-29-21-17-20-**16**-22-33-40-45-45-62-63

Ireland
16.03.85: 23-26-18-**15**-28

Italy
18.05.85: peaked at no.**13**, charted for 7 weeks

Netherlands
23.03.85: 46-19-17-13-14-**9**-22-34

New Zealand
7.04.85: 31-16-**8**-9-11-20-16-23-25-39-41

South Africa
22.06.85: peaked at no.**10**, charted for 10 weeks

Spain
17.06.85: peaked at no.**14**, charted for 11 weeks

Switzerland
28.04.85: 16-17-**13**-20-22-24-25

USA
16.03.85: 57-43-30-24-17-12-8-7-**6-6**-9-16-27-37-60-76-98-100

After recording their third album, *SEVEN AND THE RAGGED TIGER*, Duran Duran planned to take a much needed break, which led to members of the band splitting into two side projects.

The first of these, The Power Station, involved Andy Taylor and John Taylor, who were keen to get away from the distinctive Duran Duran sound, and work on a hard funk/rock project.

'Andy and I had finished our third album, 'said John Taylor. 'We decided we weren't being heard, so we wanted to do a side project as soon as we got the touring done. We didn't know what it was going to be.'

Andy and John teamed up with singer Robert Palmer and Chic's drummer Tony Thompson, with Chic's Bernard Edwards producing, to form a supergroup. Originally, they planned to call themselves 'Big Brother', but changed this to The Power Station ~ the supergroup was named after the New York recording studio where their self-titled album was recorded.

Some Like It Hot was written by Andy Taylor, John Taylor and Robert Palmer.

'What we really wanted to do was put this drummer out there in a way that we felt he deserved,' said John Taylor, 'so that song particularly was sort of designed to really showcase Tony (Thompson). I flew to Nassau in the Bahamas, which was where Robert Palmer lived at the time, and played him the demo that Andy and I had written and said, "We've got this idea that we're calling *Some Like It Hot*" and he just looked at me and said, "And some sweat when the heat is on". I was, like, "Yes! That'll do!".'

The Power Station performed two songs, *Some Like It Hot* and a cover of Marc Bolan's *Get It On*, on the *Saturday Night Live* TV show on 16th February 1985 ~ this was the one and only time the four members of The Power Station performed live together.

Some Like It Hot was released as The Power Station's debut single, and it charted at no.4 in Australia, no.6 in Belgium, Denmark and The United States, no.8 in New Zealand, no.9 in Canada and the Netherlands, no.10 in Austria and South Africa, no.13 in Italy and Switzerland, no.14 in Spain and the UK, no.15 in Ireland and no.16 in Germany.

Some Like It Hot was issued as a 12" picture disc single in the UK.

14 ~ Get It On

UK: Parlophone R6096 (1985).
  B-side: *Go To Zero*.

11.05.85: 50-33-24-**22**-30-40-56

Australia
24.06.85: peaked at no.**8**, charted for 12 weeks

Canada
22.06.85: 69-52-44-39-31-28-26-24-19-**15-15-15**-25-32-40-52-67-77-86

Germany
17.06.85: 53-44-**37**-39-44-62-66

Ireland
19.05.85: 26-**12**

New Zealand
7.07.85: 42-37-37-20-**16-16**-24-25-24-42-34-44

USA
8.06.85: 58-43-35-30-25-18-14-10-**9-9**-14-28-45-69-88

Get It On was written by Marc Bolan, and he recorded the song with T. Rex for the 1971 album, *ELECTRIC WARRIOR*.

To avoid confusion with a similarly titled song by the group Chase, *Get It On* was re-titled *Bang A Gong (Get It On)* in North America. As a single, *Get It On* hit no.1 in Ireland and the UK, and charted at no.3 in Germany and Switzerland, no.6 in Norway, no.10 in the United States, no.12 in Canada, no.14 in Australia and no.15 in the Netherlands.

The Power Station recorded a cover of *Get It On* ~ titled *Get It On (Bang A Gong)* in North America ~ for their self-titled album. Originally, the plan was for a few friends to provide backing vocals for model and would-be single Bebe Buell, when she recorded a cover of *Get It On*. However, as the project evolved and a supergroup was formed, The Power Station recorded the song instead.

Get It On was released as The Power Station's second single, and it charted at no.8 in Australia, no.9 in the United States, no.12 in Ireland, no.15 in Canada, no.16 in New Zealand, no.22 in the UK and no.37 in Germany.

15 ~ A View To A Kill

UK: Parlophone DURAN 007 (1985).
  B-side: *A View To A Kill (That Fatal Kiss).*

18.05.85: 7-**2-2-2**-6-11-15-23-29-33-34-52-64-56-63-73

Pos	LW	Title, Artist		Peak Pos	WoC
1	1	**19** PAUL HARDCASTLE	CHRYSALIS	1	4
2	7 ↑	**A VIEW TO A KILL** DURAN DURAN	EMI	2	2
3	8 ↑	**LOVE DON'T LIVE HERE ANYMORE** JIMMY NAIL	VIRGIN	3	5

Australia
10.06.85: peaked at no.**6**, charted for 14 weeks

Austria
1.07.85: 9-**6**-13-14-12-15-22 (bi-weekly)

Denmark
7.06.85: 8-3-3-**1-1**-3-3-3-2-5-8-7-7-5-4-4-7-8

Belgium
1.06.85: 21-6-5-3-4-5-**2**-4-5-6-10-17-27

Canada
18.05.85: 69-55-34-20-11-4-**1**-2-3-3-6-15-21-25-34-39-49-65-75-88-90-99

Finland
05.85: peaked at no.**6**, charted for 8 weeks

France
13.07.85: 29-39-42-29-34-32-32-28-28-25-24-18-**11**-17-19-20-21-25-37-39

Germany
27.05.85: 65-45-12-**9**-10-11-12-13-15-15-18-20-20-20-21-18-23-35-44-58-75

Ireland
19.05.85: 13-3-**2-2**-5-12-14-28-25

Italy
11.05.85: peaked at no.**1** (6), charted for 23 weeks

Japan
1.06.85: peaked at no.**28**, charted for 14 weeks

Netherlands
25.05.85: 40-7-6-6-**3**-4-4-7-6-6-9-11-13-15-24-45

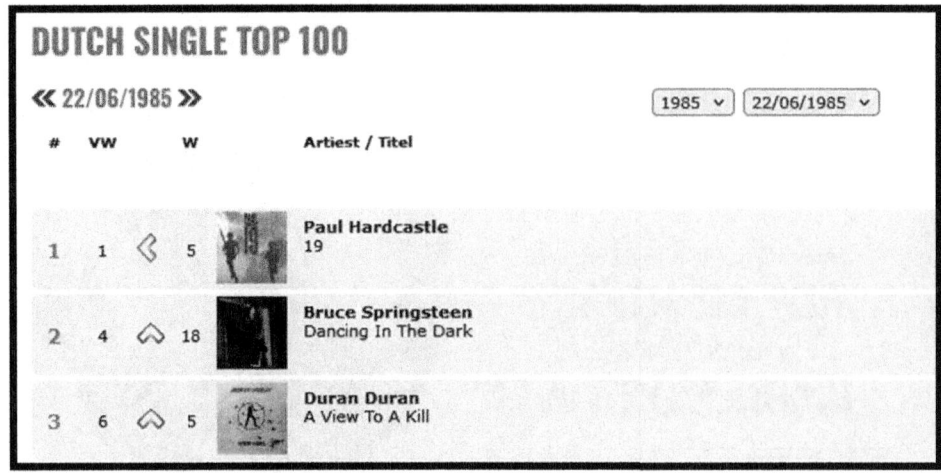

New Zealand
26.05.85: 31-17-**13-13-13**-28-25-31-29-33-32-42

Norway
8.06.85: 10-4-3-**2**-4-3-3-6-5-7-10-8-9

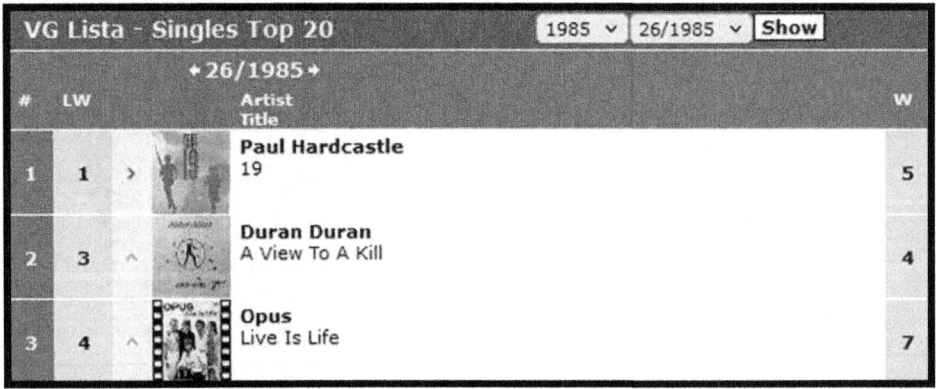

South Africa
29.06.85: peaked at no.**4**, charted for 11 weeks

Spain
12.08.85: peaked at no.**4**, charted for 25 weeks

Switzerland
9.06.85: 17-13-8-8-8-**7**-10-13-13-13-13-13-14-18-19-27-27

Sweden
31.05.85: 18-6-3-4-**1**-5-7-15 (bi-weekly)

#	LW		Artist Title	Label Company	Prefix Suffix	W
			SVERIGETOPPLISTAN - SINGLES TOP 100 ♦ 1985-08-09 ♦ 1985 ▾ 09.08.1985 ▾ Show			
1	4	∧	**Duran Duran** A View To A Kill	EMI EMI	2006307	5
2	1	∨	**Paul Hardcastle** 19	Chrysalis GDC/Sonet	107386	5
3	12	∧	**Eurythmics** There Must Be An Angel (Playing With My Heart)	RCA Electra	PB 40247	2

USA
18.05.85: 43-36-27-15-12-5-3-2-**1**-**1**-4-11-19-31-53-71-98

Billboard Hot 100 — WEEK OF JULY 13, 1985

THIS WEEK			AWARD	LAST WEEK	PEAK POS.	WKS ON CHART
1	↑	**A View To A Kill** Duran Duran	+	2	1	9
2	↓	**Sussudio** Phil Collins	+	1	1	10
3	→	**Raspberry Beret** Prince And The Revolution	+	3	3	9

Zimbabwe
10.08.85: peaked at no.**6**, charted for 9 weeks

A View To A Kill was written by Duran Duran with John Barry, and the band recorded the song at London's Maison Rouge and CTS Studios, with Bernard Edwards and Jason Corsaro producing. It was the theme song for the James Bond film with the same title, in which Roger Moore made his seventh and final appearance as 007.

Duran Duran were chosen to record the next James Bond theme after John Taylor, who was a big Bond fan, approached producer Cubby Broccoli at a party thrown by Michael Caine.

'We got to chatting,' he recalled. 'I said, "When are you going to have a decent theme song again?" He said, "Well, do you want to write the next one?" I said, "Absolutely!".'

The band was subsequently introduced to composer John Barry, and things progressed from there.

'He (John Barry) didn't really come up with any of the basic music ideas,' said Simon Le Bon. 'He heard what we came up with and he put them into an order. And that's why it happened so quickly, because he was able to separate the good ideas from the bad ones, and he arranged them. He has a great way of working brilliant chord arrangements. He was working with us as virtually a sixth member of the group, but not really getting on our backs at all.'

'It wasn't an easy song to write,' said John Taylor. 'Nick and John Barry didn't click. They found it hard just being in the same room. They were both stubborn and had very specific visions of how things should be done.'

A View To A Kill was promoted with a music video directed by Godley & Crème, which was filmed at Paris's Eiffel Tower. The promo featured scenes from the *A View To A Kill* film, and saw Roger Moore, *aka* James Bond, chasing Max Zorin's henchwoman, May Day. At the end of the video, Simon Le Bon blew up the Eiffel Tower, by accidentally activating the detonator hidden inside his Walkman.

As well as being released as a single, *A View To A Kill* featured on the soundtrack album that accompanied the film.

A View To A Kill became the first James Bond theme to hit no.1 in the United States, a feat no other Bond theme has equalled to date, but in the UK the single spent three weeks at no.2, behind Paul Hardcastle's *19*.

Around the world, *A View To A Kill* topped the chart in Canada, Denmark, Italy and Sweden, and achieved no.2 in Belgium, Ireland and Norway, no.3 in the Netherlands, no.4 in South Africa and Spain, no.6 in Australia, Austria, Finland and Zimbabwe, no.7 in Switzerland, no.9 in Germany, no.11 in France, no.13 in New Zealand and no.28 in Japan.

A View To A Kill was nominated for a Golden Globe, for Best Original Song, but Duran Duran lost out to Lionel Richie's *Say You, Say Me*, from the film *White Nights*.

16 ~ Communication

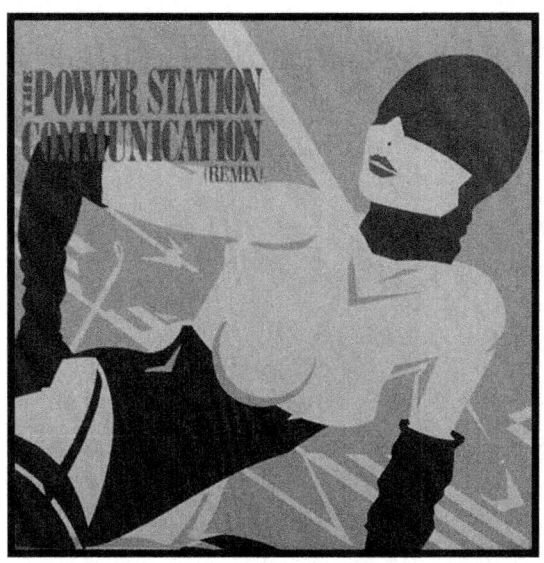

UK: Parlophone R6114 (1985).
  B-side: *Murderess*.

9.11.85: **75**

Australia
16.12.85: peaked at no.**95**, charted for 4 weeks

Canada
7.09.85: 86-79-65-56-50-**46-46**-49-60-70-76-98

USA
7.09.85: 65-52-47-42-37-**34-34**-42-69-99

Communication was written by Andy Taylor, John Taylor, Robert Palmer and Derek Bramble, and was recorded by The Power Station for their self-titled album.

Communication was issued as the third and final single recorded by The Power Station's original line-up, but it was only a minor hit. The single was a Top 40 success in the United States, where it rose to no.34. The single also charted at no.46 in Canada, but it struggled to no.75 in the UK and no.95 in Australia, and failed to chart in many countries.

17 ~ Election Day

UK: Parlophone Odeon Series NSR1 (1985).
  B-side: *She's Moody And Grey, She's Mean And She's Restless.*

26.10.85: **7**-10-16-32-52-66

Australia
18.11.85: peaked at no.**13**, charted for 13 weeks

Belgium
9.11.85: 35-30-18-**14-14**-20-20

Canada
2.11.85: 73-51-38-29-23-12-**8-8**-9-9-9-17-29-39-44-60-65-75

Denmark
15.11.85: 6-**5-5**-6-15

Finland
10.85: peaked at no.**3**, charted for 8 weeks

Germany
4.11.85: 72-26-24-**21**-24-31-39-47-51-58-59-71

Ireland
3.11.85: **5-5**-9-29

Italy
19.10.85: peaked at no.**1** (6), charted for 18 weeks

Netherlands
9.11.85: 31-14-**12**-17-19-23-27-41

New Zealand
27.10.85: 40-6-6-**4**-7-10-16-11-11-11-11-11-34-x-36

Norway
9.11.85: 10-**7**-8-10

Spain
24.02.86: peaked at no.**8**, charted for 13 weeks

Switzerland
17.11.85: 21-**18**-19-**18**-21-25

USA
26.10.85: 46-35-29-18-13-8-7-**6-6**-10-13-15-35-53-67-89

With the band's Andy Taylor and John Taylor having teamed up with Robert Palmer and Tony Thompson to form The Power Station, the three remaining members of Duran Duran ~ Nick Rhodes, Roger Taylor and Simon Le Bon ~ formed a trio, Arcadia. The name, reportedly, was inspired by a Nicolas Poussin painting, *Et In Arcadia Ego*, which was also known as 'The Arcadian Shepherd'.

The trio's debut single, *Election Day*, was written by Nick Rhodes and Simon Le Bon, and was recorded at Paris's *Studio de la Grande Armée*, for Arcadia's one and only album, *SO RED THE ROSE*, which was released in November 1985. *Election Day* featured guest vocals by Grace Jones.

'It's about having to make a decision,' said Nick Rhodes, 'and taking a chance about something special happening, so that it could be your election day.'

The three members of Arcadia dyed their hair black, as seen in promotional photographs and the music video for *Election Day*, which was directed by Roger Christian and filmed in Paris.

Election Day hit no.1 for six weeks in Italy, and charted at no.3 in Finland, no.4 in New Zealand, no.5 in Denmark and Ireland, no.6 in the United States, no.7 in Norway and the UK, no.8 in Canada and Spain, no.12 in the Netherlands, no.13 in Australia, no.14 in Belgium, no.18 in Switzerland and no.21 in Germany.

18 ~ The Promise

UK: Parlophone Odeon Series NSR2 (1985).
  B-side: *Rose Arcana*.

25.01.86: 61-40-**37**-47

Australia
24.02.86: peaked at no.**94**, charted for 2 weeks

Germany
3.03.86: 73-x-**72-72**

Ireland
2.02.86: 27-**24**

The Promise was written by the three members of Arcadia, and was recorded at Paris's *Studio de la Grande Armée*, for the trio's *SO RED THE ROSE* album. Pink Floyd's David Gilmour played guitar on the recording, which also featured uncredited backing vocals by Sting.

  Outside North America, *The Promise* was released as the follow-up to *Election Day*, but it couldn't match the success of Arcadia's debut single. Nevertheless, *The Promise* did achieve no.24 in Ireland and no.37 in the UK. The single was also a minor hit in Germany and Australia, where it peaked at no.72 and no.94, respectively.

19 ~ Goodbye Is Forever

UK: Not released.

USA: Capitol Records B-5542 (1986).
  B-side: *Missing*.

1.02.86: 64-55-46-43-36-**33**-34-56-69-94

Australia
5.05.86: peaked at no.**77**, charted for 3 weeks

Canada
8.02.86: 77-63-54-**39-39**-47-55-64-77-82

Goodbye Is Forever was written by the three members of Arcadia, and was recorded at Paris's *Studio de la Grande Armée*, for the trio's *SO RED THE ROSE* album.
  Goodbye Is Forever was released as the second single from the album in North America, and Arcadia promoted it with a music video directed by Marcello Anciano, which featured Nick Rhodes and Simon Le Bon as two figures stranded in time ~ Roger Taylor didn't appear in the promo.
  Goodbye Is Forever achieved no.33 in the United States and no.39 in Canada and, as the third single from *SO RED THE ROSE*, it was also a minor no.77 hit in Australia.

20 ~ I Do What I Do ... (Theme From 9½ Weeks)

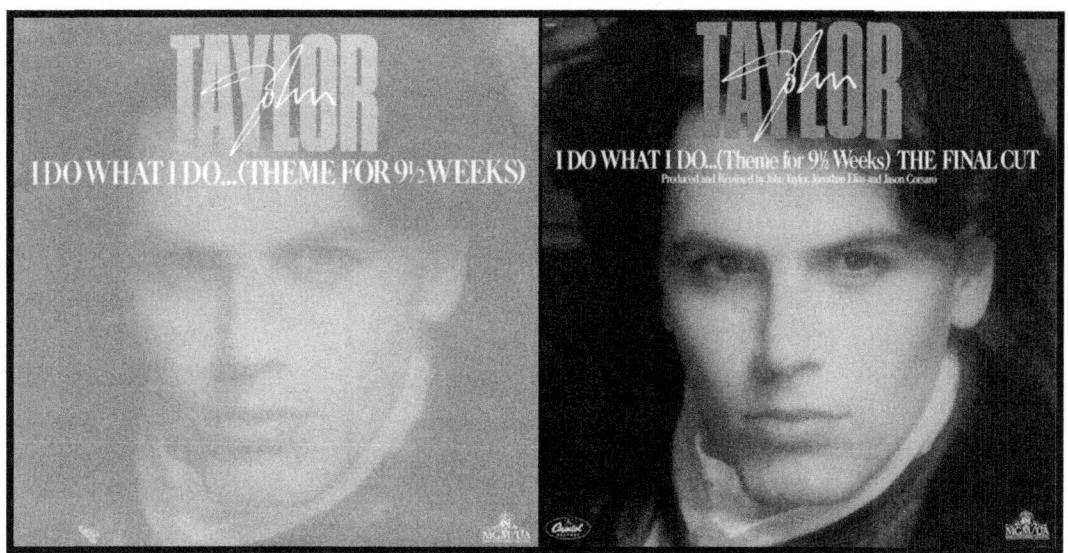

UK: Parlophone R 6125 (1986).
  B-side: *Jazz.*

15.03.86: 62-**42**-59-74

Australia
14.04.86: peaked at no.**35**, charted for 9 weeks

Canada
15.03.86: 87-70-64-54-50-47-44-40-**37**-39-45-49-57-62-71

Germany
19.05.86: 73-66-**58**-72-61

Italy
12.04.86: peaked at no.**6**, charted for 12 weeks

USA
8.03.86: 73-60-53-42-37-30-25-**23**-26-39-59-100

John Taylor wrote *I Do What I Do* ... with Jonathan Elias and Michael Des Barres, and he recorded the song as a solo single for the 1986 American film, *9½ Weeks*, which starred Kim Basinger and Mickey Rourke.

'I did a lot of promotion for the song,' he said, 'and learned a lot about myself. I wasn't a solo act. I could not carry the weight of the entire operation on my shoulders. I just didn't want it badly enough.'

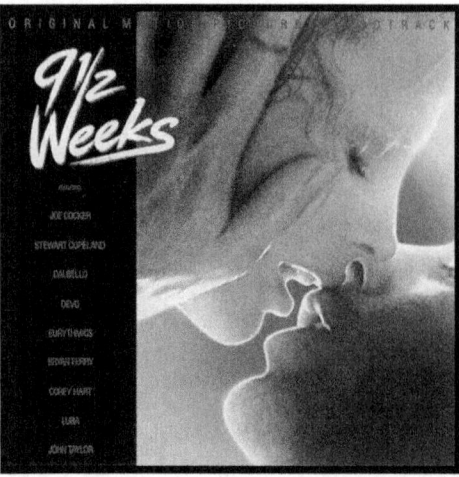

As well as featuring on the *9½ WEEKS* soundtrack album, *I Do What I Do …* was released as a single, and gave John Taylor his only Top 40 success as a solo artist. The single achieved no.6 in Italy, no.23 in the United States, no.35 in Australia, no.37 in Canada, no.42 in the UK and no.58 in Germany.

Addicted To Love

UK: Island Records IS 270 (1986).
  B-side: Remember To Remember.

3.05.86: 87-63-34-16-10-8-**5**-6-10-16-21-29-40-39-57-68
18.01.03: 42-81 (Shake B4 Use vs. Robert Palmer)

Australia
7.04.86: peaked at no.**1** (2), charted for 24 weeks

New Zealand
25.05.86: 33-17-16-6-**2-2-2-2**-5-12-27-28-29-48

Belgium
31.05.86: **34**-37-37

Canada
22.02.86: 84-72-54-42-32-28-21-16-12-8-6-**4**-**4**-5-6-9-12-16-20-26-27-41-53-58-65-77

Netherlands
31.05.86: 43-41-**34**-39-42-46

South Africa
22.06.86: peaked at no.**4**, charted for 12 weeks

USA
8.02.86: 83-68-57-46-38-32-18-13-9-6-3-2-**1**-2-10-17-24-31-45-49-61-99

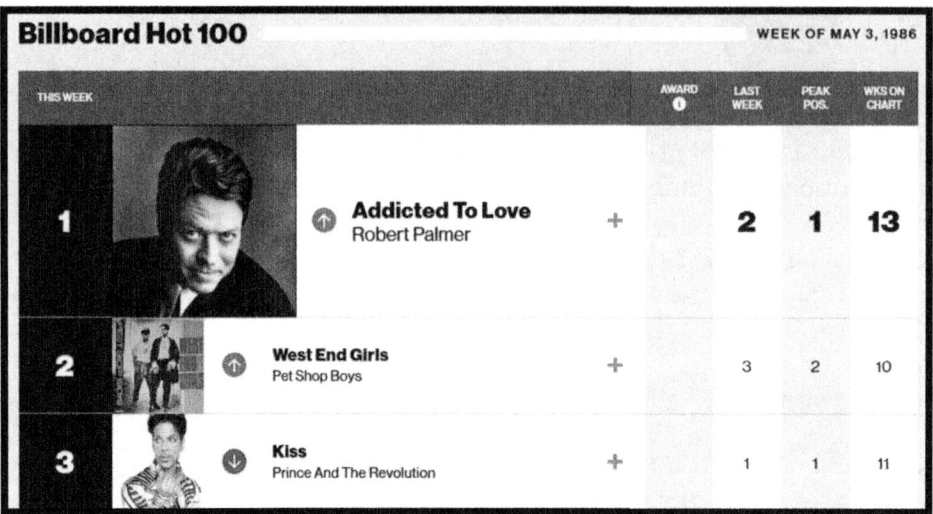

Robert Palmer wrote *Addicted To Love*, and he recorded the song at Compass Point Studios in Nassau, Bahamas, for his 1985 album, *RIPTIDE*.

The recording had a strong The Power Station connection, as it featured Andy Taylor playing guitar and Tony Thompson on drums, with Bernard Edwards responsible for production. Originally, Robert Palmer had planned to record the song as a duet with Chaka Khan, but her record company wouldn't allow her to work with an artist signed to a rival record label.

'Before working with this lot (The Power Station),' said Robert Palmer, 'I must admit I was turning into a bit of a crooner. This has set me back on the rails and I want to continue in a similar, strong direction.'

Addicted To Love was issued as the second single from *RIPTIDE* in most countries, following *Discipline Of Love*, and Robert Palmer promoted its released with an iconic music video directed by Terence Donovan. The promo featured a backing band of five high fashion models, each one of them with dark hair, and made-up and dressed exactly the same.

Addicted To Love was issued as a 7" shaped picture disc in the UK.

Addicted To Love hit no.1 in Australia and the United States, and achieved no.2 in New Zealand, no.4 in Canada and South Africa, no.5 in the UK, and no.34 in Belgium and the Netherlands.

Tina Turner released a live cover of *Addicted To Love* as a single in 1988, which charted at no.23 in Belgium, no.28 in the Netherlands and no.71 in the UK.

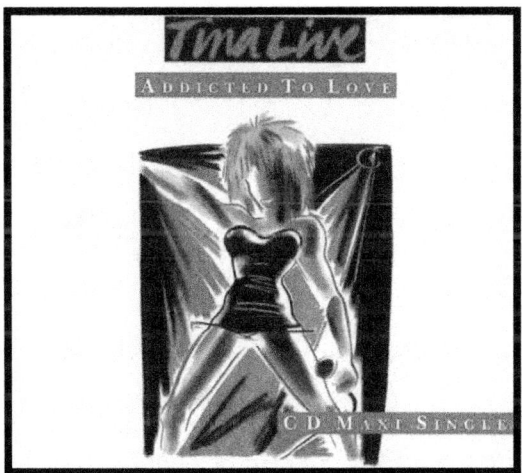

21 ~ Take It Easy

UK: Atlantic A9414 (1986).
  B-side: *Angel Eyes*.

16.08.86: **95**

Australia
21.07.86: peaked at no.**30**, charted for 15 weeks

Belgium
26.07.86: **35**

Canada
21.06.86: 99-88-86-76-53-45-40-34-24-20-**19**-24-30-38-39-43-48-59-75

USA
31.05.86: 85-74-64-52-43-38-35-29-26-**24**-25-38-47-57-75-76-89

Andy Taylor wrote *Take It Easy* with Steve Jones, and he recorded the song for the soundtrack of the 1986 American film, *American Anthem*, which starred Mitch Gaylord as Steve Tevere, an American footballer turned gymnast (Mitch Gaylord was a member of America's gold medal winning gymnastics team at the 1984 Summer Olympics).

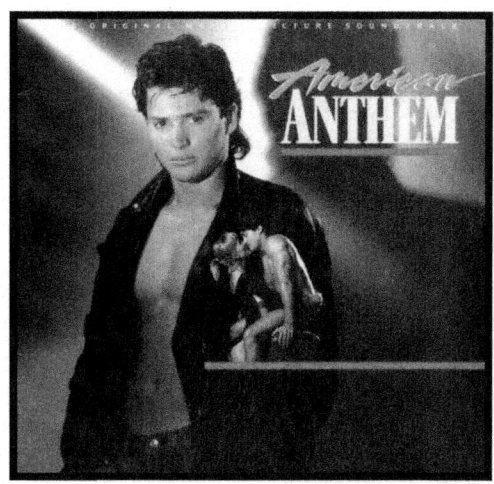

Andy Taylor became the second member of Duran Duran's classic five-man line-up to achieve a solo Top 40 single, when he took *Take It Easy* to no.19 in Canada, no.24 in the United States, no.30 in Australia and no.35 in Belgium. The single also spent a solitary week at a very lowly no.95 in the UK.

Take It Easy was one of three solo recordings Andy contributed to the *AMERICAN ANTHEM* soundtrack album, the other two being *Wings Of Love* and *Angel Eyes* ~ the latter featured as the B-side of *Take It Easy*.

22 ~ The Flame

UK: Parlophone Odeon Series NSR 3 (1986).
  B-side: *Flame Game (Yo Homeboy Mix)*.

26.07.86: **58**-72

Ireland
27.07.86: **29**

Netherlands
6.09.86: 42-**38**-44

The Flame was written by the three members of Arcadia, and was recorded at Paris's *Studio de la Grande Armée*, for the trio's *SO RED THE ROSE* album.

The Flame was the final single released from the album, and Arcadia promoted its release with a humorous music video directed by Russell Mulcahy, in which Nick Rhodes and Simon Le Bon played Abbott & Costello-like characters.

Arcadia's Roger Taylor didn't appear in the promo, but Duran Duran's John Taylor did ~ he made a cameo appearance, coming out of a wardrobe, or closet, with a contract for Nick Rhodes and Simon Le Bon to sign. This was an inside joke, as around this time Duran Duran were experiencing legal issues with Andy Taylor, as the band prepared to start work on the Duran Duran album that became *NOTORIOUS*.

The Flame was only a modest hit, charting at no.29 in Ireland, no.38 in the Netherlands and no.58 in the UK.

23 ~ Notorious

UK: EMI DDN 45 (1986).
  B-side: *Winter Marches On.*

1.11.86: 14-**7**-12-20-36-52-x-x-x-73-88-94

Australia
17.11.86: peaked at no.**17**, charted for 14 weeks

Austria
15.01.87: 16-**14**-16-22-24 (bi-weekly)

Belgium
8.11.86: 19-14-13-13-9-**6**-8-18-23-26

Canada
8.11.86: 80-64-45-32-21-17-15-15-15-15-**10-10**-15-17-30-32-39-52-64-82

Denmark
7.11.86: 6-**2-2-2**-4-5-8-8-14-x-14-13-14

Finland
11.86: peaked at no.**3**, charted for 8 weeks

France
24.01.87: 50-47-x-45-**37**-47-45-40-x-50

Germany
10.11.86: 69-19-19-13-14-**12**-20-25-26-34-43-56-66-67

Ireland
26.10.86: 25-7-**5**-8-23

Italy
1.11.86: peaked at no.**1** (4), charted for 17 weeks

Japan
21.11.86: peaked at no.**91**, charted for 3 weeks

Netherlands
1.11.86: 18-**6**-7-8-10-13-17-21-25-47

New Zealand
9.11.86: 27-8-**6**-8-9-15-8-8-8-8-18-18-33-36-47

Norway
15.11.86: 10-6-5-5-**4**-9-7-7-7-7-9

South Africa
14.12.85: peaked at no.**14**, charted for 9 weeks

Spain
2.02.87: peaked at no.**9**, charted for 16 weeks

Sweden
5.11.86: 15-7-**2-2**-3-5-16 (bi-weekly)

Switzerland
23.11.86: 17-10-6-5-5-5-**4**-9-9-17-30

USA

1.11.86: 56-43-30-21-16-11-8-4-3-3-**2**-3-13-24-38-62-81

Billboard Hot 100				AWARD ⓘ	LAST WEEK	PEAK POS.	WKS ON CHART
1		Walk Like An Egyptian The Bangles	+		1	1	16
2		Notorious Duran Duran	+		3	2	11
3		Shake You Down Gregory Abbott	+		4	3	13

WEEK OF JANUARY 10, 1987

Following The Power Station and Arcadia side-projects, and the James Bond theme *A View To A Kill*, Roger Taylor decided to retire from the music industry and, despite the band taking legal action against him, Andy Taylor stubbornly refused to re-join Duran Duran, to start working on the band's fourth studio album.

Having finally, reluctantly, agreed to let Andy go, the three remaining members of Duran Duran ~ John Taylor, Nick Rhodes and Simon Le Bon ~ decided to carry on as a trio. They wrote and recorded *Notorious* for their album with the same title, which was released in November 1986 ~ credited to 'Duran', as Andy Taylor threatened to sue if the three remaining members of the band called themselves Duran Duran.

Steve Ferrone played drums on the recording, and co-producer Nile Rodgers played guitar. The four backing vocalists on the track were Brenda White-King, Curtis King, Cindy Mizelle and Tessa Niles.

Notorious was the first single released by Duran Duran's new line-up, and the band promoted it with a music video directed by Paula Greif and Peter Kagan, which was shot in black and white on 23rd September 1986.

Despite losing two band members, *Notorious* continued Duran Duran's run of success, and it topped the singles chart in Italy for four weeks.

In the United States, the single was kept off the top spot by *Walk Like An Egyptian* by The Bangles. The single also achieved no.2 in Denmark and Sweden, and around the world it peaked at no.3 in Finland, no.4 in Norway and Switzerland, no.5 in Ireland, no.6 in Belgium, the Netherlands and New Zealand, no.7 in the UK, no.9 in Spain, no.10 in Canada, no.12 in Germany, no.14 in Austria and South Africa, no.17 in Australia and no.37 in France.

24 ~ Skin Trade

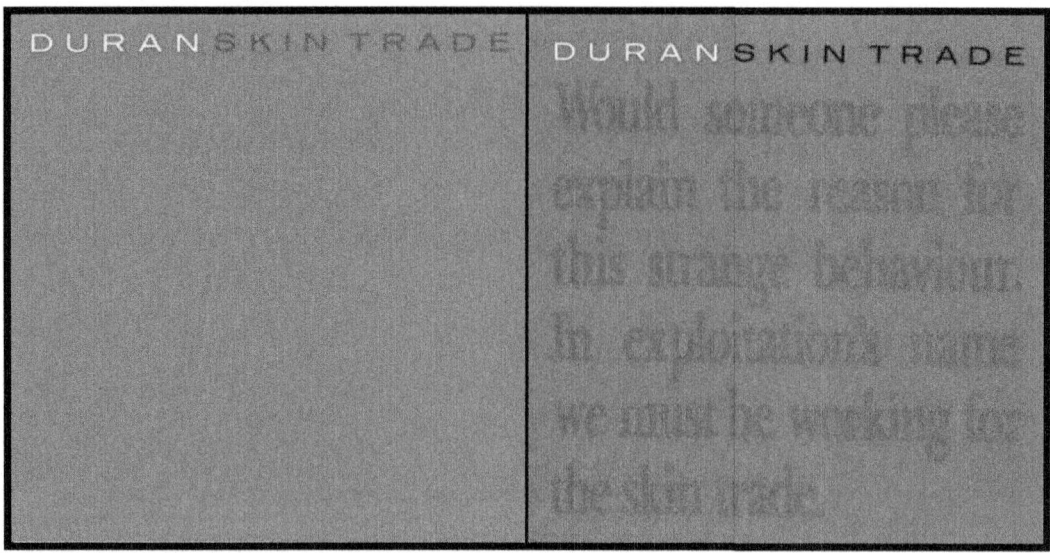

UK: EMI TRADE 1 (1987).
  B-side: *We Need You.*

21.02.87: 25-24-**22**-26-34-48

Belgium
28.02.87: 39-21-11-10-10-**9**-13-26

Canada
21.02.87: 95-92-87-79-72-**69**-71-77

Germany
23.02.87: 71-36-46-**35**-42-50-57-62-70

Ireland
22.02.87: 16-**10**-27

Italy
14.02.87: peaked at no.**8**, charted for 8 weeks

Netherlands
21.02.87: 64-25-15-**11-11**-19-18-29-40-54-98

New Zealand
8.03.87: **36**-41-46

Spain
30.03.87: peaked at no.**10**, charted for 8 weeks

USA
31.01.87: 83-65-57-53-49-43-**39**-46-70

The three remaining members of Duran Duran wrote *Skin Trade*, and the band recorded the song for their *NOTORIOUS* album. Once again, Steve Ferrone played drums on the recording, and Nile Rodgers and Warren Cuccurullo played guitar. The Borneo Horns were credited with playing horns, with backing vocals by Brenda White-King, Curtis King, Cindy Mizelle and Tessa Niles.

The song's title was inspired by a Dylan Thomas book, *Adventures In The Skin Trade*, which John Taylor happened to have with him when the band were working on their new album. Simon Le Bon wrote the lyrics, which revolved around how everybody is selling themselves.

Skin Trade was released as the second single from *NOTORIOUS*, but the original 'bum' sleeve design was withdrawn by the record company, as it was feared the risqué sleeve would result in some record stores refusing to stock the single. Instead, in most countries, the single was issued with a plain red sleeve.

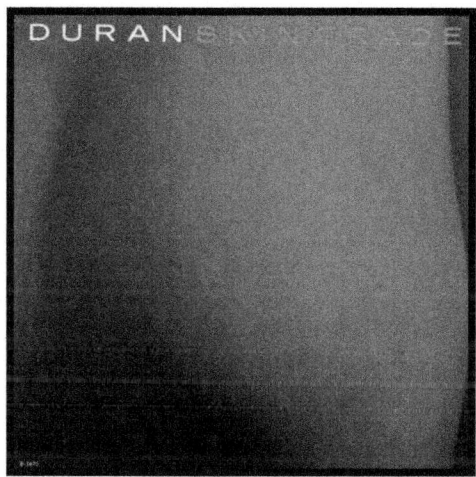

Duran Duran promoted *Skin Trade* with a music video directed by Paula Greif and Peter Kagan, which featured a rotoscope-like effect as the band performed the song. Both Steve Ferrone and Warren Cuccurullo appeared in the promo, as did the German supermodel, Tatjana Patitz.

'When we put out the *NOTORIOUS* album,' said Nick Rhodes, 'we thought, "Wow, we've got a song here, *Skin Trade*, that's probably the best thing we've ever written!" We put out *Notorious* as a single, which did extremely well, and we thought, "Great, now we will put out *Skin Trade*, it's going to do twice as well because it's a much better song."

And we put it out and it bombed, pretty much. From that moment onwards, I never second-guessed anything.'

Skin Trade was the first Duran Duran single to fail to achieve Top 20 success in both the UK and the United States, where it peaked at no.22 and no.39, respectively. The single also charted at no.8 in Italy, no.9 in Belgium, no.10 in Ireland and Spain, no.11 in the Netherlands, no.35 in Germany and no.36 in New Zealand.

The *Skin Trade* promo was nominated for two awards at the 1987 MTV Video Music Awards, but it lost out to Peter Gabriel's *Sledgehammer* in the Best Special Effects category, and to Robbie Nevil's *C'est La Vie* in the Best Cinematography category.

25 ~ Meet *El Presidente*

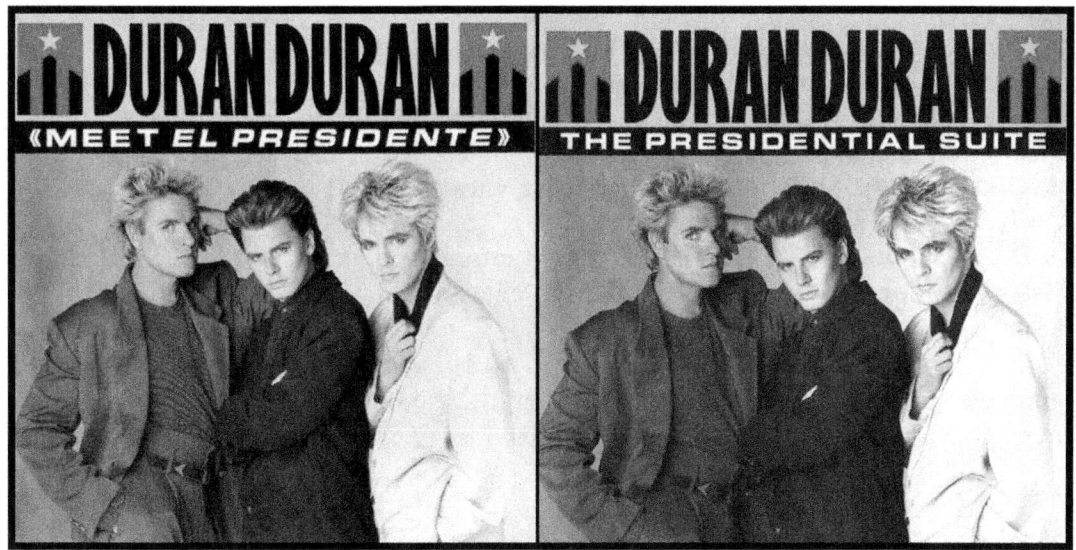

UK: EMI TOUR 1 (1987).
  B-side: *Vertigo (Do The Demolition)*.

25.04.87: 31-**24**-26-45-65

Belgium
2.05.87: 34-25-23-**13**-21

Germany
18.05.87: **54**-57-59-63-66

Ireland
19.04.87: 30-15-**13**-30

Italy
23.05.87: peaked at no.**10**, charted for 9 weeks

Netherlands
2.05.87: 61-49-**31-31**-36-46-62-71-87

Spain
25.05.87: peaked at no.**32**, charted for 2 weeks

USA
2.05.87: 86-74-**70**-77-92

Meet El Presidente was written by the three remaining members of Duran Duran, and they recorded the song for their *NOTORIOUS* album. As with the album's title track and *Skin Trade*, Steve Ferrone played drums on the recording, with Nile Rodgers playing guitar and horns credited to The Borneo Horns. The four backing vocalists were Brenda White-King, Curtis King, Cindy Mizelle and Tessa Niles.

Meet El Presidente, which was titled 'One Of The Faithful' in an earlier version that has appeared on a number of bootlegs, was issued as the third and last single from *NOTORIOUS*. Duran Duran promoted its release with a concert music video directed by Paula Greif and Peter Kagan.

Meet El Presidente, like *Skin Trade* before it, struggled to match the success of earlier Duran Duran singles, and once again it failed to enter the Top 20 in both the UK and the United States.

The single fared best in Italy, where it rose to no.10, and elsewhere it charted at no.13 in Belgium and Ireland, no.24 in the UK, no.31 in the Netherlands, no.32 in Spain, no.54 in Germany and a lowly no.70 in the United States.

Lost In You

UK: Warner Bros. Records W 7927 (1988).
  B-side: *Almost Illegal*.

28.05.88: 30-**21**-22-33-50-74

Australia
13.06.88: peaked at no.**22**, charted for 16 weeks

Belgium
28.05.88: **32**-38-38-34

Canada
28.05.88: 73-62-54-42-32-26-19-12-9-7-**6**-11-23-36-56-88

Germany
13.06.88: 32-31-**25**-27-28-32-37-47-54-59-58-58-68-65

Italy
21.05.88: peaked at no.**19**, charted for 6 weeks

Netherlands
4.06.88: 73-62-37-36-**34**-57-95

Switzerland
5.06.88: **30**

Andy Taylor wrote *Lost In You* with Rod Stewart, and Rod recorded the song for his *OUT OF ORDER* album, which was released in May 1988. The album was produced by Andy, Rod and Bernard Edwards.

'It was a Wednesday evening.' said Rod Stewart, 'and we'd been hard at it in the studio, coming up with nothing. I said to the assembled band that Wednesday evening was football practice night (and) asked Andy Taylor to experiment while I was gone, and maybe have something when I returned at 11pm … (*Lost In You*) was the result.'

Lost In You was released as the lead single from *OUT OF ORDER*, and achieved no.6 in Canada, no.12 in the United States, no.19 in Italy, no.21 in the UK, no.22 in Australia, no.25 in Germany, no.30 in Switzerland, no.32 in Belgium and no.34 in the Netherlands.

Lost In You was issued as a 12" picture disc single in the UK.

Forever Young

UK: Warner Bros. Records W 7796 (1988).
  B-side: *Days Of Rage*.

6.08.88: 78-62-**57**-73

Australia
3.10.88: peaked at no.**94**, charted for 2 weeks

Canada
13.08.88: 78-62-52-33-29-15-9-6-**5**-6-8-12-16-17-20-26-31-36-46-67

New Zealand
16.10.88: **46**

USA
6.08.88: 92-65-53-48-41-35-30-24-21-14-**12**-13-15-25-34-44-57-67-68-73-71-71-85-91

Forever Young was written by Rod Stewart, Jim Cregan and Kevin Savigar, and also ~ with his approval ~ credited Bob Dylan as he has written a similarly titled song. Rod recorded the song for his *OUT OF ORDER* album ~ the recording was produced by Rod and Andy Taylor.

    As the second single from the album, *Forever Young* charted at no.5 in Canada, no.12 in the United States, no.46 in New Zealand and no.57 in the UK.

    Days Of Rage, the B-side of *Forever Young*, was written by Andy Taylor.

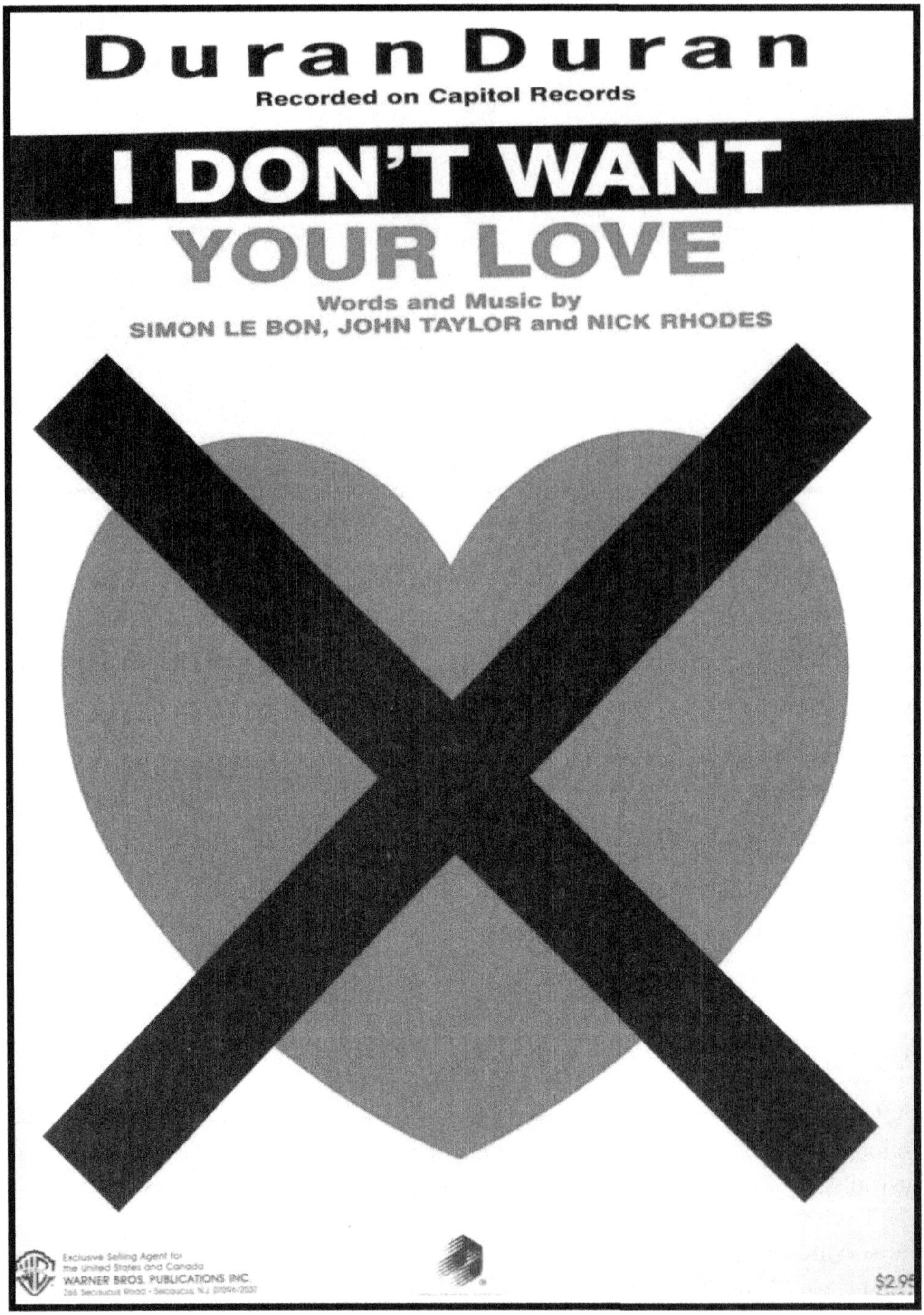
Duran Duran
Recorded on Capitol Records
I DON'T WANT
YOUR LOVE
Words and Music by
SIMON LE BON, JOHN TAYLOR and NICK RHODES
Exclusive Selling Agent for
the United States and Canada
WARNER BROS. PUBLICATIONS INC.

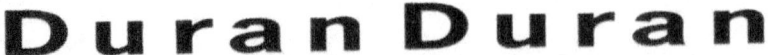

26 ~ I Don't Want Your Love

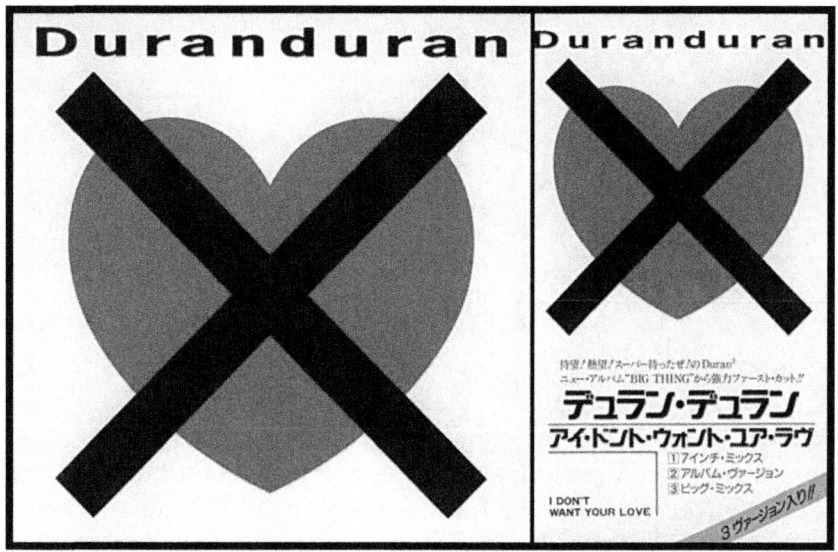

UK: EMI YOUR 1 (1988).
  B-side: *I Don't Want Your Love (Album Version).*

1.10.88: 20-**14**-18-28-67

Australia
13.11.88: peaked at no.**23**, charted for 6 weeks

Belgium
15.10.88: 40-20-**15**-18-22-32

Denmark
30.09.88: 14-9-9-8-**7**

Finland
10.88: peaked at no.**17**, charted for 4 weeks

Germany
31.10.88: **31**-36-37-47-52-59-64

Ireland
2.10.88: 11-**8**

Italy
24.09.88: peaked at no.**1** (7), charted for 17 weeks

Netherlands
1.10.88: 94-39-22-14-**11**-14-21-36-66-91

New Zealand
6.11.88: 27-15-21-**12**-21-45-37

Switzerland
23.10.88: 24-17-**15-15**-20-25-25-26

USA
15.10.88: 49-38-27-20-15-11-7-**4-4**-7-15-15-27-40-60-85

I Don't Want Your Love was written and recorded by Duran Duran ~ still a trio ~ for the band's fifth studio album, *BIG THING*, which was released in October 1988. The single and album were both credited to 'Duranduran'.

A number of musicians who weren't members of Duran Duran contributed to the recording, namely Steve Ferrone (drums), Chester Kamen (noise/rhythm guitar), Warren Cuccurullo (rhythm guitar), Patrick Bourgoin and Stan Harrison (saxophone), Mac Gollehon (trumpet) and Marc Chantereau (percussion), with Carole Fredericks and Joniece Jamison on backing vocals.

I Don't Want Your Love was released as the lead single from *BIG THING*, and Duran Duran promoted the single with a rowdy music video set in a courtroom, which was directed by Steve Lowe.

I Don't Want Your Love improved on the modest success of *Skin Trade* and *Meet El Presidente*, and topped the chart in Italy for an impressive seven weeks. The single also went to no.1 on Billboard's Hot Dance Club Play chart in the United States, and rose to no.4 on the Hot 100.

In other countries, *I Don't Want Your Love* achieved no.7 in Denmark, no.8 in Ireland, no.11 in the Netherlands, no.12 in New Zealand, no.14 in the UK, no.15 in Belgium and Switzerland, no.17 in Finland, no.23 in Australia and no.31 in Germany.

27 ~ All She Wants Is

UK: EMI DD 11 (1988).
  B-side: *I Believe/All I Need To Know (Medley)*.

7.01.89: 25-**9**-13-26-44

Australia
27.02.89: **98**

Germany
30.01.89: **28**-36-34-36-39-44-44-50-65-73

Ireland
15.01.89: **10-10**-28

Italy
24.12.88: peaked at no.**2**, charted for 10 weeks

Netherlands
7.01.89: 75-58-45-**44**-58-78

New Zealand
19.02.89: 49-**47**

USA
24.12.88: 85-85-62-53-40-32-26-26-**22**-28-43-67-99

Duran Duran wrote and recorded *All She Wants Is* for their *BIG THING* album, with Sterling Campbell playing drums on the recording, and Chester Kamen and Warren Cuccurullo playing guitars.

All She Wants Is was issued as the second single from the album, and the band promoted it release with a music video directed by Dean Chamberlain, which was filmed in London. However, as the members of Duran Duran were too busy promoting their new album to commit to a lengthy video shoot, they only appeared in brief scenes at the beginning and end of the promo. In between, the band consented to mannequins with latex masks of their faces being used, and Dean Chamberlin used these to film stop motion special effects which were incorporated into the music video.

All She Wants Is wasn't as successful as *I Don't Want Your Love* in most countries, but it did return Duran Duran to the Top 10 in the UK, where it peaked at no.9. The single also achieved no.2 in Italy, no.10 in Ireland, no.22 in the United States, no.28 in Germany, no.44 in the Netherlands and no.47 in New Zealand.

All She Wants Is, like *I Don't Want Your Love* before it, hit no.1 on Billboard's Hot Dance Club Play chart.

At the 1988 MTV Video Music Awards, the promo for *All She Wants Is* picked up an award for Innovation.

My Heart Can't Tell You No

UK: Warner Bros. Records W 7729 (1989).
  B-side: *The Wild Horse.*

22.04.89: 87-76-56-**49-49**-65

Canada
17.12.88: 80-70-70-70-61-47-24-19-17-14-10-6-**5**-7-11-14-16-27-41-48-71

USA
10.12.88: 92-80-61-61-54-50-41-33-32-27-21-18-13-9-7-5-**4**-7-17-30-43-56-68-79-96

My Heart Can't Tell Me No was written by Dennis Morgan and Simon Climie, and was recorded by Rod Stewart for his *OUT OF ORDER* album ~ Rod Stewart and Andy Taylor produced the recording.

  My Heart Can't Tell Me No, which was issued as a 12" picture disc in the UK, was the third single released from *OUT OF ORDER*. The single fared best in North America, where it rose to no.4 in the United States and no.5 in Canada.

  The single stalled at no.49 for two weeks in the UK, and it wasn't a hit anywhere else.

28 ~ Do You Believe In Shame?

UK: EMI DDA 12 (1989).
  B-side: *The Krush Brothers LSD Edit.*

22.04.89: **30**-31-35-66

Ireland
23.04.89: 20-**17**

Italy
8.04.89: peaked at no.**14**, charted for 7 weeks

Netherlands
6.05.89: 90-64-48-**41**-47-58-71-97

USA
18.03.89: 91-86-79-**72**-87

Duran Duran wrote and recorded *Do You Believe In Shame?* for their *BIG THING* album, with Sterling Campbell and Steve Ferrone playing drums on the recording, Warren Cuccurullo playing guitar and Daniel Abraham credited with playing primitive guitar.

  Legal action was subsequently taken against Duran Duran, as it was claimed the melody of *Do You Believe In Shame?* closely resembled that of Dale Hawkins's 1957 recording, *Susie-Q* (aka *Suzie Q*), which was later covered by Creedence Clearwater Revival and The Rolling Stones. The legal action was successful, which resulted in

Delmar Allen 'Dale Hawkins, Eleanor Broadwater and Stanley J. Lewis ~ the writers of *Susie-Q* ~ being added to the song-writing credits for *Do You Believe In Shame?*

Duran Duran dedicated *Do You Believe In Shame?* ~ the third and final single released from *BIG THING* ~ to three friends they had lost: artist Andy Warhol, record producer Alex Sadkin, and Simon Le Bon's childhood friend, David Miles, who died of an overdose in 1987. Simon Le Bon went on to write a further two songs in tribute to David Miles, namely *Ordinary World* and *Out Of My Mind*.

The music video for *Do You Believe In Shame?*, set in New York City, was directed by Chen Kaige, and featured different storylines for the three members of Duran Duran.

In the UK, the release of *Do You Believe in Shame?* was used to promote the band's Electric Theatre tour, with a triple single pack issued that included the tour dates.

Only a modest hit, *Do You Believe In Shame?* charted at no.14 in Italy, no.17 in Ireland, no.30 in the UK, no.41 in the Netherlands and no.72 in the United States.

Simon Le Bon, especially, was gutted by the lack of success of *Do You Believe In Shame?*

'That was one of the worst times for me personally,' he later admitted. '*Do You Believe In Shame?* was such a lovely song and it just fizzled away.'

Crazy About Her

UK: Not released.

USA: Warner Bros. Records 7-27657 (1988).
  B-side: *Dynamite (LP Version)*.

13.05.89: 74-60-48-43-35-30-24-21-18-15-15-**11**-12-28-42-65-91

Belgium
16.09.89: 50-32-34-22-22-**18**-19-25-41

Canada
5.06.89: 79-70-62-33-27-22-17-15-14-**12-12**-26-38-48-99

Germany
14.08.89: 98-x-64-**60**-64-67-71-81-91-91

Netherlands
2.09.89: 93-39-19-11-**10**-12-18-28-34-69-95

Crazy About Her was written by Duane Hitchings, Jim Cregan and Rod Stewart, and was recorded by Rod Stewart for his *OUT OF ORDER* album ~ the recording was produced by Rod with Andy Taylor and Bernard Edwards.
    Crazy About Her was issued as the fourth and final single from *OUT OF ORDER*, and it charted at no.10 in the Netherlands, no.11 in the United States, no.12 in Canada, no.18 in Belgium and no.60 in Germany.

29 ~ Burning The Ground

UK: EMI DD 13 (1989).
  B-side: *Decadance*.

16.12.89: 36-**31**-36-44-74

Ireland
7.01.90: **23**

Italy
6.01.90: peaked at no.**7**, charted for 9 weeks

Netherlands
23.12.89: 86-**75**-**75**-84

Burning The Ground was a one-off single that was created to promote Duran Duran's first greatest hits compilation, *DECADE*, which was released in November 1989.

The single, which didn't actually feature on *DECADE*, was created by producer John Jones, and featured snippets of the band's hits over the past ten years. Similarly the music video, directed by Adrian Martin, was essentially a montage of Duran Duran's old music videos, mixed with some live and other footage.

Burning The Ground, like many of Duran Duran's more recent singles, charted highest in Italy, where it was a no.7 hit. The single did much less well elsewhere, achieving no.23 in Ireland, no.31 in the UK and no.75 in the Netherlands, but missing the charts in most countries.

Dirty Love

UK: EMI EM 126 (1990).
  B-side: *Fired Up*.

17.02.90: 40-**32**-45-61

USA
1.06.91: 95-84-79-68-65-57-**55**-56-65-77-88-96-97

The rock band Thunder formed in London in 1989, and the five band members were Ben Matthews (guitar/keyboards), Danny Bowes (lead vocals), Gary 'Harry' James (drums), Luke Morley (guitar/backing vocals) and Mark 'Snake' Luckhurst (bass).

   The band's first chart success, *Dirty Love*, was written by Luke Morley, and Thunder recorded the song at the Great Linford Manor Studios in Milton Keynes, England, for their debut album, *BACK STREET SYMPHONY* (*aka BACKSTREET SYMPHONY*), which was released in March 1990 ~ the album was produced by Andy Taylor.

   Dirty Love was issued as the second single from the album, and gave Thunder their first hit single when it rose to no.32 in its second week on the chart in the UK. More than a year later, *Dirty Love* rose to no.55 on the Hot 100 in the United States.

Back Street Symphony

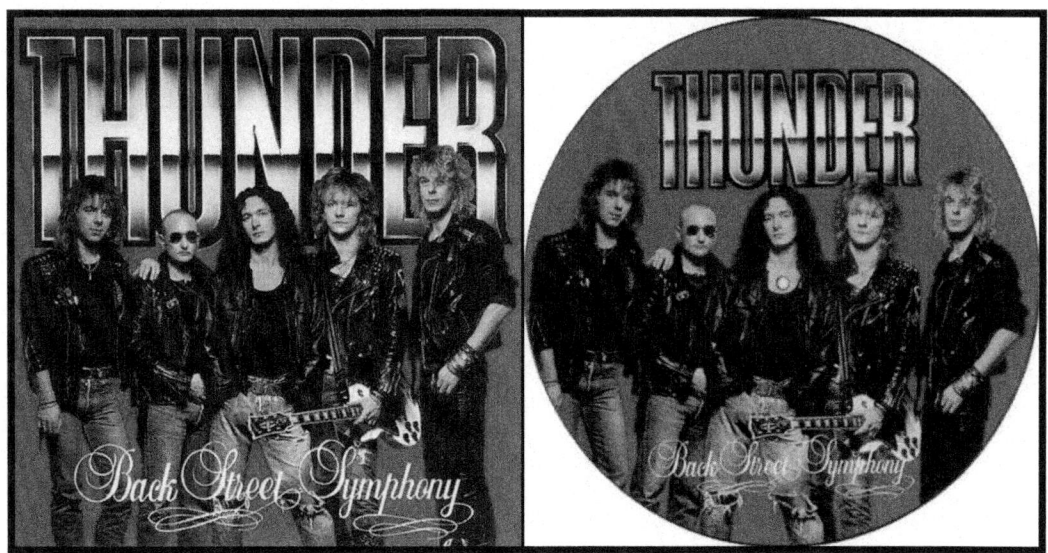

UK: EMI EM 137 (1990).
  B-side: *No Way Out Of The Wilderness*.

12.05.90: **25**-26-41-67

Back Street Symphony was written by Luke Morley, and was recorded by Thunder for their album with the same title, which Andy Taylor produced.
  Back Street Symphony gave Thunder their second hit in the UK, where it made its chart debut at no.25, but climbed no higher despite the single being issued as a shaped 7" picture disc, a 12" picture disc and a 12" clean vinyl single.

Gimme Some Lovin'

UK: EMI EM148 (1990).
  B-side: *I Wanna Be Her Slave*.

14.07.90: 38-**36**-56

Gimme Some Lovin' was written by Spencer Davis, Steve Winwood and Muff Winwood, and was originally recorded by The Spencer Davis Group in 1966 ~ they took the song to no.2 in the UK, no.6 in Australia, and no.7 in Ireland and the United States.

Thunder recorded a cover of *Gimme Some Lovin'* for their *BACK STREET SYMPHONY* album, which Andy Taylor produced ~ it was a no.36 hit in the UK.

30 ~ Violence Of Summer (Love's Taking Over)

UK: Parlophone DD 14 (1990).
  B-side: *Violence Of Summer (Love's Taking Over) (The Story Mix)*.

4.08.90: 23-**20**-32-54

Belgium
11.08.90: 48-44-48-**43**-48

Canada
8.09.90: 99-95-94-88-**82-82**

Germany
3.09.90: 97-x-**69**-75-76-77-76-94-89

Ireland
5.08.90: 23-**21-21**

Italy
14.07.90: peaked at no.**3**, charted for 17 weeks

Netherlands
11.08.90: 93-75-60-49-44-**43**-58-80

Switzerland
16.09.90: 30-x-**29**

Violence Of Summer (Love's Taking Over) was written by John Taylor, Nick Rhodes (credited as James Bates), Simon Le Bon, Sterling Campbell and Warren Cuccurullo, and it was recorded at London's Olympic Studios for Duran Duran's sixth studio album, *LIBERTY*, which was released in August 1990.

In recording *LIBERTY*, Duran Duran expanded from a trio to a quintet, with drummer Sterling Campbell and guitarist Warren Cuccurullo joining John Taylor, Nick Rhodes and Simon Le Bon, to become official members of the band.

'It just doesn't have a proper chorus,' acknowledged Simon Le Bon. 'Great verse though. Just not paying enough attention, we lost our concentration.'

Violence Of Summer (Love's Taking Over) was released as the lead single from *LIBERTY*, and the band promoted its release with a music video filmed in Paris and directed by Big TV! (*aka* Andy Delaney and Monty Whitebloom). The promo saw the new line-up playing the song on a bumper car set, which complimented the amusement park theme of the *LIBERTY* album sleeve.

However, Duran Duran had now been around for over ten years, and TV stations like MTV had moved on, with the focus shifting to younger acts, and stations like VH-1 were more interested in screening Duran Duran's classic promos. As a result, acts like Duran Duran found it increasingly difficult to effectively promote new material, and worse was to come, as charts around the world came to be dominated by first digital sales and then streaming 'sales'.

Violence Of Summer (Love's Taking Over) was a Top 3 hit in Italy, but it wasn't a Top 10 hit anywhere else. The single did achieve no.20 in the UK, no.21 in Ireland, no.29 in Switzerland, and no.43 in Belgium and the Netherlands. The single was also a minor hit in Canada, Germany and the United States.

She's So Fine

UK: EMI EM 111 (1989), EMI EM 158 (reissue, 1990).
  B-side (1989): *Girl's Going Out Of Her Head*.
  B-side (1990): *I Can Still Hear The Music*.

29.09.90: 38-**34**-60

She's So Fine was written by Andy Taylor and Luke Morley, and was recorded by Thunder for their *BACK STREET SYMPHONY* album, which Andy Taylor produced.

  She's So Fine was released as the lead single from the album, but it wasn't a hit. Then, on the back of three Top 40 singles from the album, *She's So Fine* was reissued and this time it did spend a couple of weeks in the Top 40 in the UK, peaking at no.34.

  She's So Fine was issued as a limited edition 10" blue vinyl single in the UK, and as a limited edition 12" single that featured live versions of *Back Street Symphony* and *Don't Wait For Me*, which were recorded at Donington '90.

31 ~ Serious

UK: Parlophone DD 15 (1990).
  B-side: *Yo Bad Azizi*.

17.11.90: 51-**48**-72

Germany
19.11.90: 99-x-**69**-x-94

Italy
13.10.90: peaked at no.**1** (1), charted for 15 weeks

Serious was written by Duran Duran's new five-man line-up, and was recorded at London's Olympic Studios for the band's *LIBERTY* album.

Serious was the second single issued from the album, and the band promoted it with a circus-themed music video shot in black and white, which was directed by Big TV! As well as Duran Duran, the promo featured the model, Tess Daly.

Serious hit no.1 in Italy, but it bombed everywhere else. The single peaked at no.48 in the UK, making it the band's lowest charting single to date, and was a minor no.69 hit in Germany, but that's it ~ it failed to chart anywhere else.

Duran Duran's record company planned to follow *Serious* with *Liberty* in Europe and *First Impression* in North America, but with *Serious* doing so badly both singles were cancelled.

Love Walked In

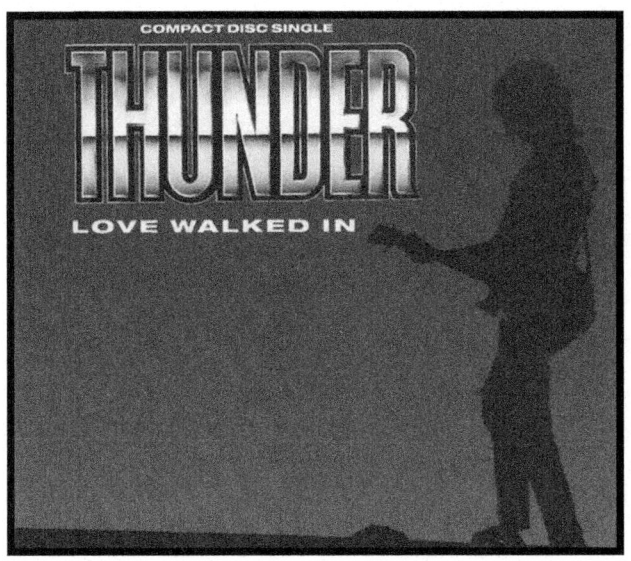

UK: EMI EM 175 (1991).
  B-side: *Flawed To Perfection (Demo).*

23.02.91: 22-**21**-30-55

Love Walked In was written by Luke Morley, and was recorded by Thunder for their *BACK STREET SYMPHONY* album, which Andy Taylor produced.

   Love Walked In was released as the fifth and final single from the album, and it gave Thunder their highest charting single in the UK to date, peaking at no.21 on its second week on the chart. The single was issued as a limited edition 12" picture disc.

Low Life In High Places

UK: EMI EM 242 (1992).
  B-side: *Baby I'll Be Gone*.

15.08.92: 25-**22**-33-49-75

Netherlands
29.08.92: 97-76-60-56-52-**47**-70

New Zealand
7.02.93: **44**

Low Life In High Places was written by Luke Morley, and was recorded by Thunder for their second album, *LAUGHING ON JUDGEMENT DAY*, which was released in August 1992 ~ the album was produced by Andy Taylor and Luke Morley.
   Low Life In High Places was released as the lead single from the album, and it continued Thunder's run of Top 40 singles in the UK, where it achieved no.22. The single also charted at no.44 in New Zealand and no.47 in the Netherlands.

Everybody Wants Her

UK: EMI EM249 (1992).
  B-side: *Dangerous Rhythm.*

10.10.92: 42-**36**-52-70

Everybody Wants Her was written by Ben Matthews, Danny Bowes, Gary 'Harry' James and Luke Morley, and was recorded by Thunder for their *LAUGHING ON JUDGEMENT DAY* album, which Andy Taylor and Luke Morley produced.

    Everybody Wants Her was released as the second single from the album, and spent a solitary week inside the Top 40 at no.36 in the UK, where a limited edition 12" picture disc single was issued.

32 ~ Ordinary World

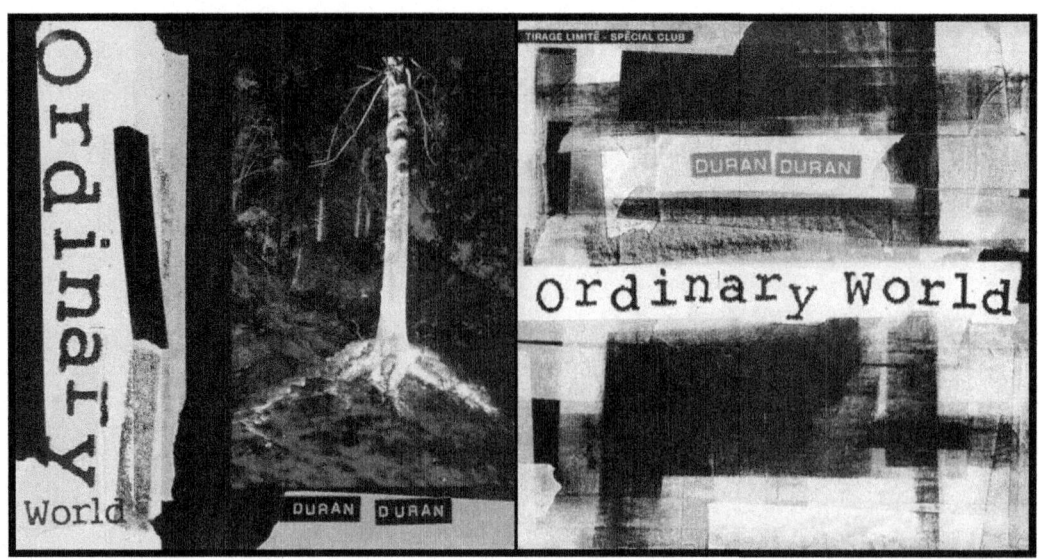

UK: Parlophone DD 16 (1993).
  B-side: *My Antarctica.*

30.01.93: 11-**6**-**6**-9-12-20-33-43-63

Australia
28.02.93: 42-37-30-31-28-24-22-20-22-**18**-19-29-33-38

Austria
14.03.93: 30-29-20-21-**15**-17-21-17-22-30-30

Canada
16.01.93: 85-66-44-11-9-7-2-**1**-**1**-**1**-**1**-**1**-5-15-30-56-71-87-97

Belgium
20.02.93: 49-47-42-50-29-29-37-23-22-**20**-23-26-26-36-46

Denmark
19.02.93: 10-8-16-6-6-**3**-4-9-5-12-20-20

France
10.04.93: 27-23-17-11-8-**6**-7-11-7-10-12-15-16-33-39-33

Germany
1.03.93: 53-52-30-24-19-17-**16**-18-17-21-23-27-30-31-34-41-71-76-78

Ireland
25.01.93: 25-7-4-**3**-5-10-10-12-13

New Zealand
28.02.93: 9-6-**3**-13-22-21-25-27-43

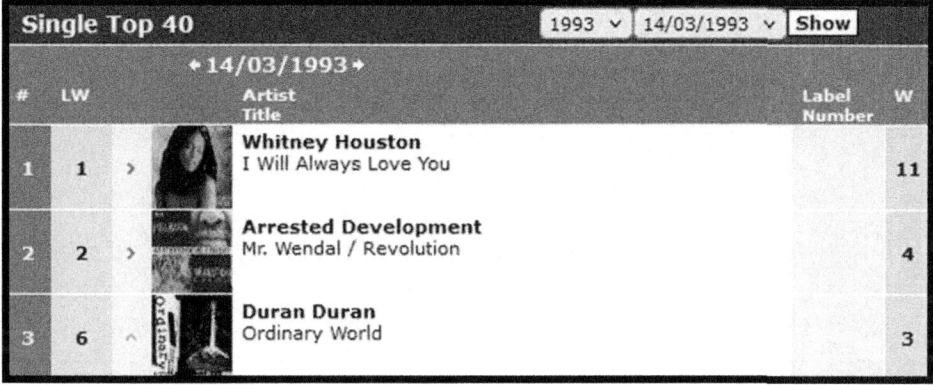

Sweden
24.02.93: 20-9-5-**2**-4-9-18-28 (bi-weekly)

Italy
23.01.93: peaked at no.**1** (1), charted for 18 weeks

Netherlands
6.03.93: 42-31-24-20-**16-16**-27-34-39

Norway
6.03.93: 10-7-7-**5**-9-9-7-10

Switzerland
28.02.93: 27-22-22-22-13-13-**11-11**-13-21-20-22-24-25-33-33-31

USA
9.01.93: 67-51-23-21-7-5-**3-3-3**-4-6-5-7-12-15-17-26-30-34-38-43-49

Billboard Hot 100				WEEK OF FEBRUARY 20, 1993

THIS WEEK		AWARD ⓘ	LAST WEEK	PEAK POS.	WKS ON CHART
1	**I Will Always Love You** Whitney Houston ✛		**1**	**1**	**15**
2	**A Whole New World (Aladdin's Theme)** Peabo Bryson & Regina Belle ✛	★	2	2	10
3	**Ordinary World** Duran Duran ✛	★	5	3	7

Ordinary World was written by Duran Duran, with Warren Cuccurullo joining John Taylor, Nick Rhodes and Simon Le Bon as an official member of the band. The song was recorded at London's Privacy Studios for Duran Duran's second self-titled album which, due to the cover design, is commonly known as 'The Wedding Album'. The album was released in February 1993.

The lyrics for *Ordinary World* were penned by Simon Le Bon, and it was the second of three songs he wrote as a tribute to his late childhood friend, David Miles.

'(I was) trying to get over the death of a best friend,' he said, 'and putting it into words freed me, absolutely. It really worked for me emotionally and mentally. Everyone who heard it could apply it to something in their life, but for a different reason.'

'I think Simon just felt our world was a malaise of complete chaos,' said Nick Rhodes. '*Ordinary World* was written from a heartfelt point of view.'

At the same time, the rest of the band weren't keen to see the word 'Ordinary' used in a Duran Duran song title, but Simon fought his corner and the word stayed.

Ordinary World was issued as the lead single from *DURAN DURAN (THE WEDDING ALBUM)*, and the band promoted its release with a wedding-themed music video filmed at Huntington Gardens in San Marino, California, which was directed by Nick Egan.

Ordinary World gave Duran Duran their biggest hit for seven years ~ it hit no.1 in Canada and Italy, and achieved no.2 in Sweden, no.3 in Denmark, Ireland, New Zealand and the United States, no.5 in Norway, no.6 in France and the UK, no.11 in Switzerland, no.15 in Austria, no.16 in Germany and the Netherlands, no.18 in Australia and no.20 in Belgium.

Simon Le Bon was one of Luciano Pavarotti's 'friends', who guested at a War Child charity concert staged at Parco Novi Sad in Modena, Italy, on 12th September 1995. The aim of the concert was to raise funds to benefit children in war-torn Bosnia.

During the concert, Simon performed *Ordinary World* ~ featuring new Italian lyrics written by the show's producer Michele Centonze ~ with the show's host. He also performed the 1993 Cranberries hit *Linger* with Dolores O'Riodan of the Cranberries, and as a finale all the show's guests joined Pavarotti to sing *Nessum Dorma*, including Simon, Bono, The Edge, Brian Eno, Dolores O'Riodan, Meat Loaf, Michael Bolton and Zucchero.

Credited to Luciano Pavarotti & Friends, an album of the concert titled *TOGETHER FOR CHILDREN OF BOSNIA* was released in 1996. It featured all three of Simon Le Bon's performances, and charted at no.4 in the Netherlands, no.5 in Austria, no.7 in Belgium, Germany and Switzerland, no.9 in New Zealand and no.11 in the UK.

A Better Man

UK: EMI BETTER 1 (1993).
  B-side: *New York, New York (Harry's Theme) (Live).*

13.02.93: **18**-20-47-62

Luke Morley wrote *A Better Man*, and Thunder recorded the song for their *LAUGHING ON JUDGEMENT DAY* album, which Andy Taylor and Luke Morley produced.
  A Better Man gave Thunder their highest charting single to date, when it was issued as the third single from the album ~ it made its chart debut in the UK at no.18, but the following week it slipped back to no.20 and climbed no higher.

33 ~ Come Undone

UK: Parlophone DD 17 (1993).
  B-side: *Ordinary World (Acoustic Version)*.

10.04.93: 17-**13**-17-15-26-35-51-72

Australia
8.08.93: 44-41-42-33-31-25-20-**19**-24-28-28-35-41

Belgium
22.05.93: **42**

Canada
24.04.93: 78-30-13-12-8-4-**2-2-2-2**-3-3-5-8-8-23-57-63-75-96

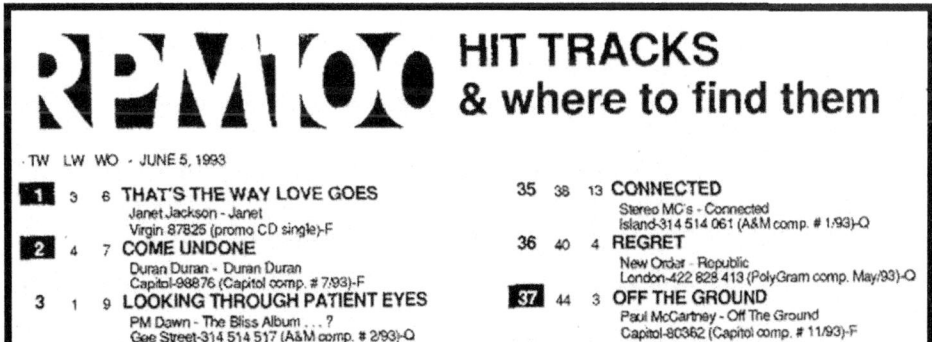

France
28.08.93: 49-45-x-x-49-46-x-x-x-47-48-42-**26-26**-31-42-48

Germany
7.06.93: 56-60-**42**-47-**42**-70-70-83-80-77

Ireland
11.04.93: 14-**9**-15-12-15-30

Italy
8.05.93: peaked at no.**8**, charted for 9 weeks

New Zealand
6.06.93: 40-39-32-33-**16-16**-21-34-21-48-35-33-43-44

Sweden
19.05.93: 27-**21**-24-31 (bi-weekly)

USA
17.04.93: 86-59-42-32-24-17-15-11-10-**7-7**-9-10-13-17-19-23-34-35-42-41-45-48-49-49

Come Undone was written by Duran Duran, and they recorded the song at London's Privacy Studios for *DURAN DURAN (THE WEDDING ALBUM)*, with Tessa Niles on backing vocals.

'It was something that Warren and I started writing alongside some other stuff that we'd been playing around with,' said Nick Rhodes, 'and Simon came in and heard what we were doing. He said, "Wow, I love that!" And so it became a Duran Duran song. He came up with a really great melody ~ we already had the "can't ever keep from falling apart" section ~ and he very quickly made it his, or himself part of it,'

Duran Duran was already working on their covers album, *THANK YOU*, with John Jones when *Come Undone* was written and recorded, so it was a late addition to *THE WEDDING ALBUM*. The band's John Taylor didn't play on the recording, but John Jones did ~ he was credited with playing bass, drums and keyboards, as well as singing background vocals.

Come Undone was released as the follow-up to the album's successful lead single, *Ordinary World*, and Duran Duran ~ including John Taylor ~ promoted its release with a music video directed by Julian Temple.

In Canada, *Come Undone* spent four straight weeks at no.2, behind Janet Jackson's *That's The Way Love Goes*. The single didn't do quite so well in other countries, but it did achieve no.7 in the United States, no.8 in Italy, no.9 in Ireland, no.13 in the UK, no.16 in New Zealand, no.19 in Australia, no.21 in Sweden, no.26 in France, and no.42 in Belgium and Germany.

Like A Satellite EP

UK: EMI CDEM 272 (1993).
Tracks: *Like A Satellite (LP Version)/(Live Version)/Gimme Shelter/The Damage Is Done.*

19.06.93: **28**-52

Like A Satellite was written by Luke Morley, and was recorded by Thunder for their *LAUGHING ON JUDGEMENT DAY* album, which Andy Taylor and Luke Morley produced.

Like A Satellite was released as a 4-track EP, which made its chart debut in the UK at no.28, to give Thunder their ninth Top 40 single in a row from their first two albums. However, the EP fell to no.52 the following week, and only managed two weeks on the chart.

Like A Satellite was the final Andy Taylor related release by Thunder.

34 ~ Too Much Information

UK: Parlophone CDDDS 18 (1993).
   Tracks: *Drowning Man (D:Ream 12")/Too Much Information (Ben Chapman 12" Mix)/*
      Too Much Information (Deptford Dub).

4.09.93: 43-**35**-49

Australia
8.11.93: peaked at no.**83**, charted for 2 weeks

Canada
14.08.93: 82-66-64-54-52-44-43-48-47-46-36-**26**-60-96

New Zealand
21.11.93: **48**

USA
4.09.93: 94-69-62-59-54-54-**45**-46-58-76-88

Too Much Information was written by Duran Duran, and was recorded by the band for *DURAN DURAN (THE WEDDING ALBUM)* ~ John Jones was credited with playing keyboards on the recording, and Steve Ferrone played drums.
   The general theme of the song's lyrics was commercialisation, especially in the music industry.

'We're living in a decadent society,' said John Taylor. 'There's too much television, too much media. I don't know whether we're in our last throes, but it's like the rise and fall of the Roman Empire.'

Too Much Information was issued as the third single from *THE WEDDING ALBUM*, and Duran Duran promoted its release with another music video directed by Julian Temple, which featured the band's stage designed for their Dilate Your Mind tour.

Too Much Information, following the success of *Ordinary World* and *Come Undone*, was only a modest hit. The single charted at no.26 in Canada, no.35 in the UK, no.45 in the United States and no.48 in New Zealand. It was also a minor no.83 hit in Australia, but it failed to chart in many countries.

The disappointing sales of *Too Much Information* resulted in the planned follow-up, *Femme Fatale*, being cancelled in most countries, although it was issued as a single in France.

35 ~ Perfect Day

UK: Parlophone CDDDS 20 (1995).
   Tracks: *Love Voodoo (Remix)/Needle And The Damage Done/911 Is A Joke (Alternative Version).*

25.03.95: **28-28**-46-67-91

Perfect Day was written and originally recorded by Lou Reed, for his 1972 album, *TRANSFORMER* ~ it was also released as the flip-side of the more popular *Walk On The Wild Side*.

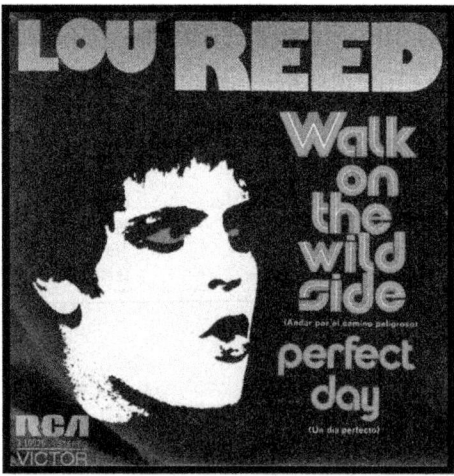

Duran Duran recorded a version of *Perfect Day* for their covers album, *THANK YOU*, which was released in April 1995.

Initially, Simon Le Bon couldn't help himself from doing an imitation of Lou Reed's voice, which was never going to work.

'So I had to invent a new picture in my head and a new story,' he said. 'I imagined I was singing it to my daughter Amber and suddenly the song became mine. It's just a beautiful song, it doesn't have to be about heroin.'

Lou Reed approved Duran Duran's cover of his song.

'It's the best cover ever completed of one of my songs,' he stated. 'He sings it better, they recorded it the way I meant it, so thank you Duran.'

Duran Duran took *Perfect Day* to no.28 in the UK, and the single spent three weeks at no.1 on the 'Bubbling Under' chart in the United States, but it failed to enter the Hot 100 and, surprisingly, it wasn't a hit anywhere else.

There have been numerous other covers of *Perfect Day* over the years. Also in 1995, Kirsty MacColl & Evan Dando scored a minor no.75 hit in the UK with their duet version of the song.

Two years later, a host of well-known artists ~ including writer Lou Reed ~ recorded *Perfect Day*, to raise funds for the British charity, BBC Children in Need. Artists who participated in the recording included Bono, Boyzone, David Bowie, Elton John, Emmylou Harris, Gabrielle, Heather Small, Joan Armatrading, Laurie Anderson, Robert Cray, Shane MacGowan, Suzanne Vega, Tammy Wynette and Tom Jones.

The charity cover of *Perfect Day* hit no.1 in Ireland, Norway and the UK, and charted at no.4 in Finland, no.6 in the Netherlands, no.7 in Belgium, no.24 in Austria, no.25 in New Zealand, no.31 in Sweden and no.37 in Switzerland.

Susan Boyle planned to perform *Perfect Day* on *America's Got Talent*, and record the song for her 2010 album, *THE GIFT*. However, due to a 'licensing glitch', she was told she couldn't perform the song and, as she had no time to rehearse a different song, her appearance on *America's Got Talent* was cancelled.

Lou Reed made amends for the glitch by not only giving his consent for Susan Boyle to go ahead and record Perfect Day for her *THE GIFT* album, he directed the accompanying music video ~ which was filmed on the shores of Scotland's Loch Lomond ~ himself.

Susan Boyle's cover of *Perfect Day* was released as a promo CD single in the UK only, and her recording was a very minor no.124 hit on the strength of download sales.

36 ~ White Lines (Don't Do It)

UK: Parlophone CDDDS 19 (1995).
   Tracks: *None Of The Above (Drizabone Mix)/Ordinary World (Acoustic Version)/Save A Prayer.*

17.06.95: 25-27-**17**-26-48-93
8.07.95: 94 (4th Format)

Australia
30.04.95: 43-25-26-23-22-**20**-35

Canada
20.03.95: 82-63-59-57-54-38-37-31-**28**-39-39-45-56-69

Italy
18.02.95: peaked at no.**22**, charted for 3 weeks

New Zealand
9.04.95: **31**-38-49

White Lines (Don't Do It) was written by Melvin 'Melle Mel' Glover and Sylvia Robinson, and was recorded by Melle Mel in 1983. The single also credited Grandmaster (Flash) ~ at the time, Melle Mel and Grandmaster Flash were no longer working together, and the latter was suing their record company for back royalties.
   The song, as the title suggests, was written about a cocaine-fuelled lifestyle, with 'Don't Do It' added to the song's title to make the recording more acceptable. The single

achieved no.7 in the UK, no.22 in Ireland, no.27 in Australia and Belgium, no.40 in the Netherlands and no.45 in New Zealand, but it failed to enter the Hot 100 in the United States.

Duran Duran recorded a cover of *White Lines (Don't Do It)* for their *THANK YOU* album ~ the recording featured both Melle Mel and Grandmaster Flash.

White Lines (Don't Do It) was released as the follow-up to *Perfect Day* in most countries (it was released before *Perfect Day* in North America), which it out-performed, rising to no.17 in the UK, no.20 in Australia, no.22 in Italy, no.28 in Canada and no.31 in New Zealand.

Duran Duran's cover, like Melle Mel's original, failed to enter the Hot 100 in the United States.

'It was a disaster,' said Warren Cuccurullo, 'because US alternative radio didn't want to play a song which had a black rapper on it, so an edit was done without the rap, but the trouble is that once you get a negative reaction to something it's pretty much over.'

You're The Star

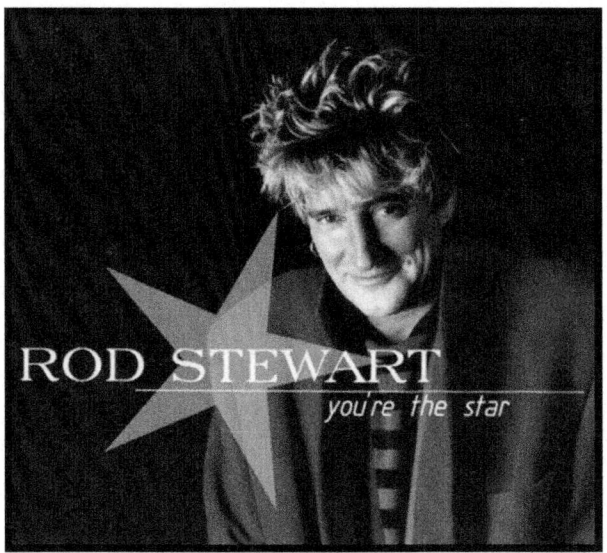

UK: Warner Bros. Records W0296CD (1995).
  Tracks: *Shock To The System (Album Version)/Have I Told You Lately (Album Version).*

20.05.95: **19**-26-39-60-75-95

Germany
15.05.95: 93-65-54-**53**-55-58-58-62-64-68

New Zealand
16.07.95: **42**-46

You're The Star was written by Billy Livsey, Frankie Miller and Graham Lyle, and was recorded by Rod Stewart for his album, *A SPANNER IN THE WORKS*, which was released in May 1995.

Andy Taylor played guitar on *You're The Star*, and he also wrote the single's B-side, *Shock To The System*, with Rod Stewart.

You're The Star was only released as a single in the UK, Australasia and mainland Europe, and achieved no.19 in the UK, no.42 in New Zealand and no.53 in Germany.

37 ~ Lay Lady Lay

UK: Not released.

Italy: Parlophone 7243 8 82247 2 7 (1995).
    Tracks: *Femme Fatale (Alternative Mix)/Diamond Dogs/Ordinary World (Acoustic Version Live Radio One).*

8.07.95: peaked at no.**18**, charted for 2 weeks

Lay Lady Lay was written and originally recorded by Bob Dylan, for his 1969 album, *NASHVILLE SKYLINE*.

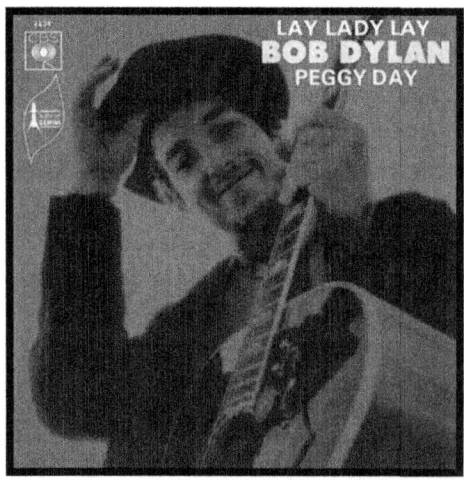

As a single, Bob Dylan took *Lay Lady Lay* to no.5 in the UK, no.7 in New Zealand and the United States, no.8 in Canada, no.13 in Ireland and no.18 in Australia.

Duran Duran recorded a cover of *Lay Lady Lay* for their *THANK YOU* album, and it was issued as a single in only two countries, Italy and Spain.

Lay Lady Lay was a no.18 hit in Italy, spending just two weeks on the chart, but it wasn't a hit in Spain.

38 ~ Out Of My Mind

UK: Virgin VSCDT 1639 (1997).
  Tracks: *Silva Halo/Sinner Or Saint/Out Of My Mind (Electric Remix).*

24.05.97: **21**-47-76

Canada
7.04.97: 93-84-70-61-55-**51**-75-97

Italy
17.05.97: peaked at no.**14**, charted for 4 weeks

Out Of My Mind was written by Duran Duran ~ now a trio again comprising Nick Rhodes, Simon Le Bon and Warren Cuccurullo. It was the third and final song Simon Le Bon wrote lyrics to as a tribute to his late childhood friend, David Miles, following *Do You Believe In Shame?* and *Ordinary World.* Dave DiCenso played drums on the recording, and Talvin Singh was credited with playing tabia and santoor.
  Out Of My Mind made its first appearance on the soundtrack album to the 1997 film, *The Saint*, which starred Val Kilmer as Simon 'The Saint' Templar. The soundtrack was released in March 1997, the same month as *Out Of My Mind*, and was Duran Duran's only contribution to the soundtrack.

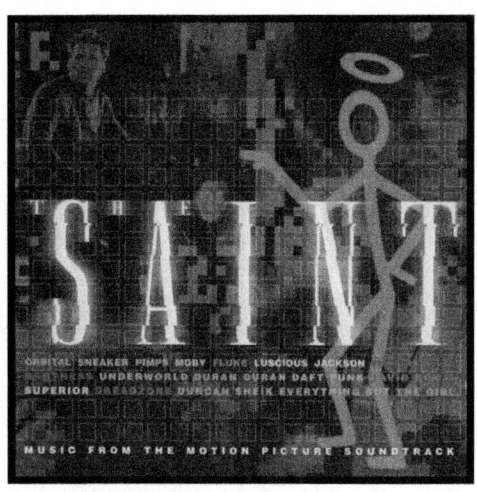

Duran Duran promoted the release of *Out Of My Mind* as a single with a music video directed by Dean Karr, which was shot at Krumlov Castle in Český Krumlov, Czech Republic, in February 1997. In the promo, thanks to the use of prosthetics and other special effects, Simon Le Bon is seen to age as the music video progresses.

Out Of My Mind was only a modest hit, rising at no.14 in Italy, no.21 in the UK and no.51 in Canada, but in most countries it failed to chart.

Later the same year, *Out Of My Mind* featured on Duran Duran's ninth studio album, *MEDAZZALAND*, which was released in October 1997.

39 ~ Electric Barbarella

UK: EMI TCELEC 2000 (1999).
Tracks: *Girls On Film (Tin Tin Out Radio Mix)/Electric Barbarella (Tee's Radio Mix).*

30.01.99: **23**-44-67-80

USA
11.10.97: 65-61-57-**52**-59-59-72-86-100

Electric Barbarella was written by Duran Duran, and was recorded by the trio ~ with Anthony J. Resta playing drums ~ for their *MEDAZZALAND* album. The band wrote the song as a tribute to Roger Vadim's 1967 film, *Barbarella*, which is where the name 'Duran Duran' originated.

Electric Barbarella was released as the follow-up to *Out Of My Mind* in North America, and Duran Duran promoted its release with a music video directed by Ellen von Unwerth. The promo featured a robotic sex doll played by the American model Myka Dunkle, which both MTV and VH-1 refused to play until a censored version was made available.

'She's young, she's beautiful, she's nearly naked and she's hovering!' said Simon Le Bon, speaking about the promos robotic sex doll. 'We're taking the piss out of ourselves and out of men's ideas of women, out of cyber-sex and technology.'

Electric Barbarella was a minor no.51 hit in the United States, its performance hampered by the fact by the time the modified music video was made available, the single had already fallen off the Hot 100.

Electric Barbarella wasn't issued as a single in the UK and Europe until January 1999, when it was released to promote Duran Duran's compilation album, *GREATEST*. The single made its chart debut in the UK at no.23, but it climbed no higher and it wasn't a hit anywhere else.

40 ~ Someone Else Not Me

UK: Hollywood Records 0108845HWR (2000).
  Tracks: *Someone Else Not Me (Album Version)/Starting To Remember*.

10.06.00: **53**

Italy
18.05.00: **26**

Someone Else Not Me was written by Duran Duran, and was recorded by the band ~ still a trio ~ for their tenth studio album, *POP TRASH*, which was released in June 2000.

A ballad, *Someone Else Not Me* was issued as the lead single from the album, and was promoted with a ground-breaking music video ~ the first to be created entirely in Macromedia Flash animation by Fullerene Productions.

Someone Else Not Me, like the singles that preceded it, struggled to find success. The single was a Top 40 hit in Italy only, where it spent a solitary week at no.26. *Someone Else Like Me* only managed one week on the UK chart as well, at no.53, but it bombed everywhere else.

We Used To Be Friends

UK: Capitol Records CL 843 (2003).
  B-side: *Minnesoter (Thee Slayer Hippie Mix)*.

17.05.03: **18**-44-72

Australia
19.05.03: peaked at no.**38**, charted for 14 weeks

We Used To Be Friends was written by Bjorn Thorsrud, Courtney Taylor-Taylor and Grant Nicholas, and was recorded by the American alternative rock band The Dandy Warhols for their 2003 album, *WELCOME TO THE MONKEY HOUSE*. Grant Nicholas was credited to avoid a lawsuit, as the song bore a number of similarities to the Feeder song, *Day In Day Out*, which he wrote.

  As well as producing the recording, Nick Rhodes was credited with playing additional synthesizer on the track, which was released as the album's lead single.

  We Used To Be Friends achieved no.18 in the UK and no.38 in Australia, but it wasn't a hit anywhere else.

You Were The Last High

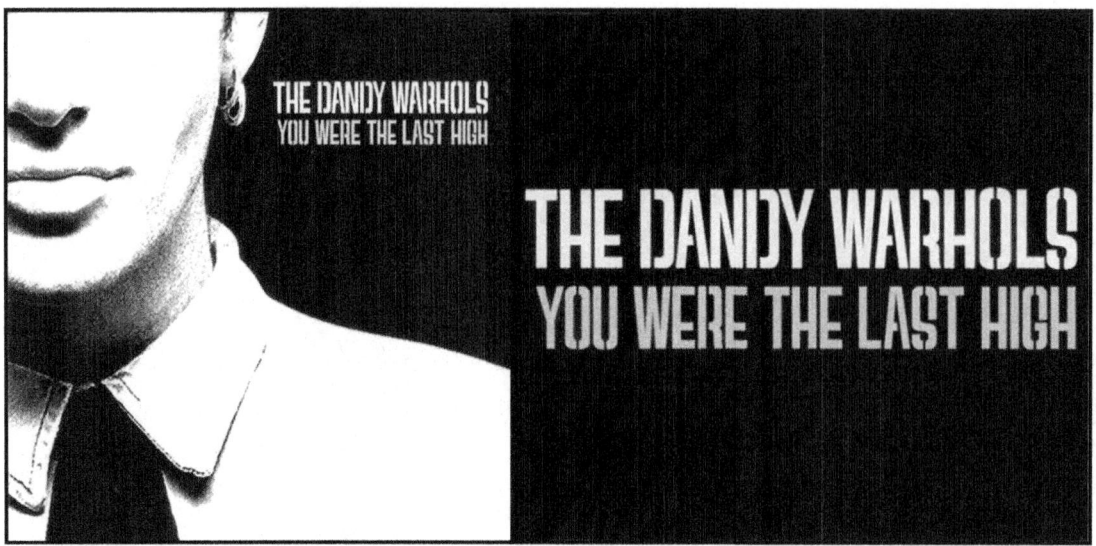

UK: Capitol Records CL 845 (2003).
  B-side: *We Used To Be Friends (Kenn Richards Remix)*.

9.08.03: **34**-68

Australia
13.10.03: peaked at no.**65**, charted for 4 weeks

You Were The Last High was written by Courtney Taylor-Taylor and Evan Dando, and was recorded by The Dandy Warhols for their *WELCOME TO THE MONKEY HOUSE* album. As with *We Used To Be Friends*, Nick Rhodes was credited with playing additional synthesizer and having a hand in producing *You Were The Last High*.

  You Were The Last High was released as the follow-up to *We Used To Be Friends*, and The Dandy Warhols promoted the single with a music video bearing an uncanny resemblance to Duran Duran's *Planet Earth* promo.

  Like *We Used To Be Friends* before it, *You Were The Last High* only achieved chart success in two countries, peaking at no.34 in the UK and no.65 in Australia.

41 ~ The Singles 1986-1995

Box-set of 14 CD Singles:

Notorious: *Notorious (45 Mix)/Winter Marches On/Notorious (Extended Mix)/(Latin Rascals Mix)*

Skin Trade: *Skin Trade (Radio Cut)/We Need You/Skin Trade (Stretch Mix)/(Album Version)*

Meet El Presidente: *Meet El Presidente (7" Remix)/Vertigo (Do The Demolition)/Meet El Presidente/(Meet El Beat)*

I Don't Want Your Love: *I Don't Want Your Love (Shep Pettibone 7" Mix)/(Album Version)/(Big Mix)*

All She Wants Is: *All She Wants Is (45 Mix)/I Believe All/I Need To Know/All She Wants Is (US Master Mix)/(Euro Dub Mix)/Skin Trade (Parisian Mix)*

Do You Believe In Shame?: *Do You Believe In Shame? (The Krush Brothers LSD Edit)/God (London)/This Is How A Road Gets Made/Palomino (Edit)/Drug (Original Version)/Notorious (Live)*

Burning The Ground: *Burning The Ground/Decadance/Decadance (2 Risk E Remix 12")*

Violence Of Summer (Love's Taking Over): *Violence Of Summer (Love's Taking Over) (7" Mix)/(The Story Mix)/(Power Mix)/(Album Version)/(The Rock Mix)/(The Dub Sounds Of A Powerful Mix)/(Power Cut Down)/Throb*

Serious: *Serious (Single Version)/Yo Bad Azizi/Water Babies/All Along The Water*

Ordinary World: *Ordinary World (Single Version)/My Antarctica/Ordinary World/Save A Prayer (Single Version)/Skin Trade/The Reflex (7" Version)/Hungry Like The Wolf/Girls On Film*

Come Undone: *Come Undone (Edit)/Ordinary World (Acoustic Version)/Come Undone (FGI Phumpin' 12")/(La Fin De Siecle)/(Album Version)/Rio (Album Version)/Is There Something I Shuld Know?/A View To A Kill*

Too Much Information: *Too Much Information (Album Version)/Come Undone (Live)/ Notorious (Live)/Too Much Information (Ben Chapman 12" Mix)/Drowning Man (D:Ream 12" Mix)/(D:Ream Ambient Mix)/Too Much Information (Ben Chapman Instrumental 12" Mix)/(Deptford Dub)/(Album Version Edit)/Come Undone (12" Mix Comin' Together)*

Perfect Day: *Perfect Day/Femme Fatale (Alternative Mix)/Love Voodoo (Remix)/The Needle And The Damage Done/911 Is A Joke (Alternate Version)/Make Me Smile (Come Up And See Me)/Perfect Day (Acoustic Version)*

White Lines (Don't Do It): *White Lines (Don't Do It (Album version)/Save A Prayer (Single Version)/None Of The Above (Drizabone Mix)/White Lines (Don't Do It) (70's Club Mix)/(Oakland Fonk Mix)/(Junior Vasquez Miz)/Ordinary World (Acoustic Version Simon Mayo Show)*

UK: EMI 549 8922 (2004).

The Singles 1986-1995 wasn't a hit in the UK.

Italy
23.09.04: peaked at no.**19**, charted for 3 weeks

This box-set of 14 CD singles, covering the period 1986-1995, would have been classed as an album in most countries, had it sold well enough to chart.

However, in the one country where the box-set did chart ~ Italy ~ it was placed on the singles chart, and achieved a very creditable no.19 during a three week chart run.

42 ~ (Reach Up For The) Sunrise

UK: Epic 675353 1 (2004).
  Tracks: *(Reach Up For The) Sunshine (Alex G Cosmic Mix).*

16.10.04: **5**-15-34-54-94

Australia
3.10.04: **22**-35-39-45-47

Italy
23.09.04: peaked at no.**2**, charted for 21 weeks

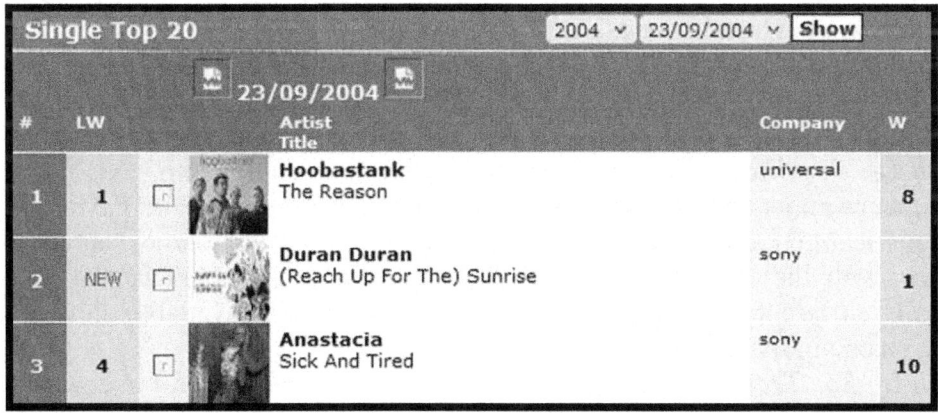

Austria
10.10.04: **50**-70-56-60-69

Belgium
9.10.04: 46-**42**-45

Denmark
15.10.04: **6**-10-12-17

Germany
11.10.04: **39**-51-61-62-84-97

Netherlands
2.10.04: **25**-28-28-46-63-78

New Zealand
1.11.04: **37**

Spain
3.10.04: **6**-14-9-18-16
30.01.05: 20

Switzerland
3.10.04: 71-**61**-81-74-80-79-85-96-96-94

USA
6.11.04: 95-**89-89**-96-100

Duran Duran wrote and recorded *(Rise Up For The) Sunrise* at London's Sphere Studios, for their *ASTRONAUT* album, which was released in September 2004 ~ Sally Boyden was credited with singing backing vocals on the recording.

Significantly, with Warren Cuccurullo leaving and the three Taylors ~ Andy, John and Roger ~ re-joining, the album saw the band's classic five man line-up restored for the first time since they recorded the *A View To A Kill* single in 1985 ~ nearly twenty years ago.

(Reach Up For The) Sunrise was issued as the lead single from *ASTRONAUT*, and Duran Duran promoted its release with a music video directed by Mark & Michael Polish. The promo featured each member of the band on the own journey across different landscapes, with the five of them meeting up on stage, for a brilliant sunrise finale. Additionally, different versions of the music video were made available online, each one focussing on one individual member of the band.

(Reach Up For The) Sunrise gave Duran Duran their biggest hit for over a decade, and achieved no.2 in Italy, no.5 in the UK, no.6 in Denmark and Spain, no.22 in Australia, no.25 in the Netherlands, no.37 in New Zealand, no.39 in Germany, no.42 in Belgium and no.50 in Austria.

The single was a minor no.61 hit in Switzerland, and stalled at no.89 for two weeks in the United States. However, *(Rise Up For The) Sunrise* did give Duran Duran their third and final no.1 on Billboard's Hot Dance Club Songs chart.

43 ~ What Happens Tomorrow

UK: Epic 675632 2 (2005).
   Tracks: *Silent Icy River/What Happens Tomorrow (Harry Peat Mix)*.

12.02.05: **11**-33-45

Germany
21.02.05: **80**

Italy
3.02.05: peaked at no.**2**, charted for 14 weeks

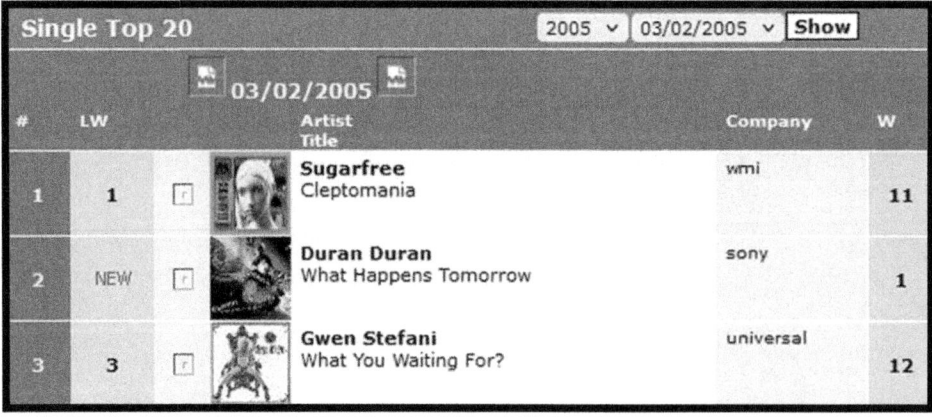

What Happen Tomorrow was written by Duran Duran, and the band recorded the song at London's Sphere Studios for their *ASTRONAUT* album.

What Happens Tomorrow was issued as the second single from the album, and Duran Duran promoted its release with a music video directed by Smith'n'Borin (*aka* Ryan Smith and Frank Buff Borin). In the promo, the five members of the band are depicted as constellations. Two former Playboy playmates, Nicole Marie Lenz and Steve Talley, also appeared in the music video.

Like so many of Duran Duran's recent singles, *What Happens Tomorrow* charted highest in Italy, where it achieved no.2 ~ kept out of the top spot by Sugarfree's *Cleptomania*. The single charted at a respectable no.11 in the UK, and was a minor no.80 hit in Germany, but it failed to chart anywhere else.

44 ~ Falling Down

UK: Epic 88697 19130 2 (2007).
  Tracks: *(Reach Up For The) Sunrise (Live)*.

17.11.07: **52**

Germany
30.11.07: **79**

Italy
8.11.07: peaked at no.**2**, charted for 8 weeks

Switzerland
25.11.07: 77-78-**60**-80-78-94

Duran Duran wrote *Falling Down* with Dominic 'Dom' Brown and Justin Timberlake, and they recorded the song at London's Sarm Studios and Manchester's Blueprint Studios, for their album *RED CARPET MASSACRE*, which was released in November 2007.

Duran Duran later confirmed the song had been written about Justin Timberlake's former girlfriend Britney's Spears's mental issues, with the band's Nick Rhodes describing the song as a 'satirical, social, pop cultural commentary.'

'I suppose it's loosely based on her,' Roger Taylor admitted, 'but not on one celebrity ~ just celebrity culture in general.'

Falling Down was released as the lead single from *RED CARPET MASSACRE*, and Duran Duran promoted the single with a music video filmed in Los Angeles, which was directed by Anthony Mandler. The promo featured models in rehab, two of them played by Allie Crandell and Tatiana Kovylina, with the members of Duran Duran dressed up as doctors and therapists. The band stated Britney Spears was the inspiration for the lead model in the music video.

'She (Kate Moss) doesn't appear in the video,' Nick Rhodes commented, 'but she and Lindsay (Dee Lohan) and Britney and Amy (Winehouse) have all provided us with inspiration.'

An X-rated version of the promo, featuring topless models, is known to have been filmed, but it remains unreleased.

Falling Down gave Duran Duran a hat-trick of no.2 singles in Italy, but it was much less successful in other countries. The single charted at no.52 in the UK, no.60 in Switzerland and no.79 in Germany, but it wasn't a hit anywhere else and, largely thanks to streaming 'sales' starting to dominate charts around the world, it proved to be the band's last Top 40 success.

THE ALMOST TOP 40 SINGLES

No singles by Duran Duran have made the Top 50 in one or more countries, but failed to enter the Top 40 in any. However, one box-set of singles did narrowly fail to enter the Top 40 in one country.

The Singles 81-85

This box-set featured 13 singles released between 1981 and 1985, namely: *Planet Earth, Careless Memories, Girls On Film, My Own Way, Hungry Like The Wolf, Save A Prayer, Rio, Is There Something I Should Know?, Union Of The Snake, New Moon On Monday, The Reflex, The Wild Boys* and *A View To A Kill.*

The Singles 81-85 was issued in Europe only, and it spent a solitary week at no.42 on the singles chart in Italy. In the UK, where the box-set was classed as an album, *The Singles 81-85* was a very minor no.183 hit, but it failed to chart anywhere else.

The Singles 81-85 was reissued in Europe and Japan in 2009, but it wasn't a hit anywhere.

Note: No albums by Duran Duran have entered the Top 50 in one or more countries, but failed to enter the Top 40 anywhere.

DURAN DURAN'S TOP 30 SINGLES

In this Top 30, each of Duran Duran's singles (including The Power Station & Arcadia) has been scored according to the following points system.

Points are given according to the peak position reached on the singles chart in each of the countries featured in this book:

No.1:   100 points for the first week at no.1, plus 10 points for each additional week at no.1.

No.2:   90 points for the first week at no.2, plus 5 points for each additional week at no.2.

No.3:   85 points.
No.4-6:   80 points.
No.7-10:   75 points.

No.11-15:   70 points.
No.16-20:   65 points.
No.21-30:   60 points.
No.31-40:   50 points.

No.41-50:   40 points.
No.51-60:   30 points.
No.61-70:   20 points.
No.71-80:   10 points.
No.81-100:   5 points.

Total weeks charted in each country are added, to give the final points score.

Reissues, remixes, re-entries and re-recordings of a single are counted together.

1   *A View To A Kill* ~ 2,166 points

2   *The Wild Boys* ~ 2,014 points

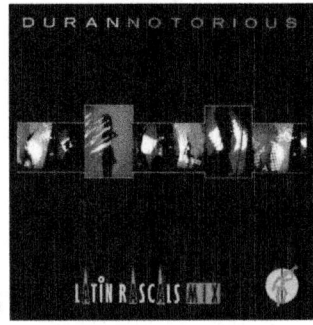

3   *Notorious* ~ 1,778 points

4   *The Reflex* ~ 1,673 points

5   *Ordinary World* ~ 1,538 points

6   *Union Of The Snake* ~ 1,502 points

7   *Election Day* | Arcadia ~ 1,332 points

8   *Some Like It Hot* | The Power Station ~ 1,270 points

9   *Is There Something I Should Know?* ~ 1,253 points

10 *I Don't Want Your Love* ~ 1,008 points

11. *Come Undone* ~ 856 points
12. *Hungry Like The Wolf* ~ 822 points
13. *(Reach Up For The) Sunrise* ~ 737 points
14. *Save A Prayer* ~ 673 points
14. *Skin Trade* ~ 673 points

16. *New Moon On Monday* ~ 607 points
17. *Get It On* | The Power Station ~ 539 points
18. *Girls On Film* ~ 511 points
19. *Rio* ~ 507 points
20. *All She Wants Is* ~ 495 points

21. *Meet El Presidente* ~ 468 points
22. *Violence Of Summer (Love's Taking Over)* ~ 455 points
23. *My Own Way* ~ 399 points
24. *White Lines (Don't Do It)* ~ 334 points
25. *Planet Earth* ~ 289 points

26. *Do You Believe In Shame?* ~ 271 points
27. *Too Much Information* ~ 226 points
28. *Burning The Ground* ~ 214 points
29. *What Happens Tomorrow* ~ 188 points
30. *Serious* ~ 181 points

In terms of chart success around the world, Duran Duran's James Bond theme song *A View To A Kill* is their most successful single, narrowly ahead of *The Wild Boys*. *Notorious* is ranked at no.3, with *The Reflex* and *Ordinary World* rounding off the Top 5.

The Top 30 features 27 singles by Duran Duran, plus two by The Power Station and one by Arcadia. The latter's *Election Day* is at no.7, one place ahead of The Power Station's *Some Like It Hot*, with The Power Station's cover of Marc Bolan's *Get It On* at no.17.

The most recent single to feature in the Top 30 is *What Happens Tomorrow*, which is ranked at no.29.

SINGLES TRIVIA

To date, Duran Duran has achieved 35 Top 40 singles in one or more of the countries featured in this book. Additionally, Arcadia achieved four Top 40 hits and The Power Station scored three Top 40 hits, with Andy Taylor and John Taylor on one Top 40 success each.

There follows a country-by-country look at Duran Duran's most successful hits, starting with their homeland.

Note: in the past, there was often one or more weeks over Christmas and New Year when no new chart was published in some countries. In such cases, the previous week's chart has been used to complete chart runs. Similarly, where a bi-weekly or monthly chart was in place, for chart runs these are counted as two and four weeks, respectively.

DURAN DURAN IN THE UK

Most Hits

33 hits	Duran Duran
4 hits	The Power Station
3 hits	Arcadia
3 hits	Andy Taylor
1 hit	John Taylor

Andy's cover the of Kinks hit *Lola* and *Stone Cold Sober* both missed the Top 40, peaking at no.60 and no.94, respectively.

Most Weeks

239 weeks	Duran Duran
17 weeks	The Power Station
13 weeks	Arcadia
6 weeks	Andy Taylor
4 weeks	John Taylor

No.1 Singles

1983	*Is There Something I Should Know?*
1984	*The Reflex*

Most weeks at No.1

4 weeks	*The Reflex*
2 weeks	*Is There Something I Should Know?*

Singles with the most weeks

16 weeks	*A View To A Kill*
14 weeks	*The Reflex*
14 weeks	*The Wild Boys*
12 weeks	*Hungry Like The Wolf*
11 weeks	*Planet Earth*
11 weeks	*Girls On Film*
11 weeks	*My Own Way*
11 weeks	*Rio*
11 weeks	*Union Of The Snake*
9 weeks	*Save A Prayer*
9 weeks	*Is There Something I Should Know?*
9 weeks	*Notorious*
9 weeks	*Ordinary World*

The Brit Certified/BPI (British Phonographic Industry) Awards

The BPI began certifying Silver, Gold & Platinum singles in 1973. From 1973 to 1988: Silver = 250,000, Gold = 500,000 & Platinum = 1 million. From 1989 onwards: Silver = 200,000, Gold = 400,000 & Platinum = 600,000. Awards are based on shipments, not sales; however, in July 2013 the BPI automated awards, based on actual sales since February 1994.

Gold   *Is There Something I Should Know?* (April 1983) = 500,000

Gold	*Hungry Like The Wolf* (February 2021) = 400,000
Gold	*Ordinary World* (June 2022) = 400,000
Silver	*Save A Prayer* (September 1982) = 250,000
Silver	*Rio* (January 1983) = 250,000
Silver	*Union Of The Snake* (October 1983) = 250,000
Silver	*The Reflex* (May 1984) = 250,000
Silver	*The Wild Boys* (November 1984) = 250,000
Silver	*A View To A Kill* (June 1985) = 250,000
Silver	*Girls On Film* (April 2021) = 200,000

DURAN DURAN IN AUSTRALIA

Most Hits

22 hits	Duran Duran
3 hits	The Power Station
3 hits	Arcadia
1 hit	John Taylor
1 hit	Andy Taylor

Most Weeks

271 weeks	Duran Duran
36 weeks	The Power Station
18 weeks	Arcadia
15 weeks	Andy Taylor
9 weeks	John Taylor

Duran Duran's highest charting single in Australia is *The Wild Boys*, which peaked at no.3.

Singles with the most weeks

34 weeks	*Planet Earth*
30 weeks	*Girls On Film*
20 weeks	*Some Like It Hot* ~ The Power Station
18 weeks	*Hungry Like The Wolf*
18 weeks	*The Reflex*
17 weeks	*The Wild Boys*
16 weeks	*My Own Way*
16 weeks	*Union Of The Snake*
15 weeks	*Is There Something I Should Know?*

14 weeks	*A View To A Kill*
14 weeks	*Notorious*

DURAN DURAN IN AUSTRIA

Most Hits

6 hits	Duran Duran
1 hit	The Power Station

Most Weeks

62 weeks	Duran Duran
8 weeks	The Power Station

Duran Duran's highest charting single in Austria is *The Wild Boys*, which peaked at no.2.

Singles with the most weeks

14 weeks	*The Wild Boys*
14 weeks	*A View To A Kill*
11 weeks	*Ordinary World*
10 weeks	*Notorious*
8 weeks	*The Reflex*
8 weeks	*Some Like It Hot* ~ The Power Station

DURAN DURAN IN BELGIUM (Flanders)

Most Hits

15 hits	Duran Duran
1 hit	The Power Station
1 hit	Arcadia
1 hit	Andy Taylor

Most Weeks

113 weeks	Duran Duran
8 weeks	The Power Station
7 weeks	Arcadia
1 weeks	Andy Taylor

No.1 Singles

1984   *The Reflex*

The Reflex topped the chart for four weeks.

Singles with the most weeks

15 weeks   *The Reflex*
15 weeks   *Ordinary World*
14 weeks   *The Wild Boys*
13 weeks   *A View To A Kill*
10 weeks   *Notorious*
 8 weeks   *Skin Trade*
 8 weeks   *Some Like It Hot* ~ The Power Station

DURAN DURAN IN CANADA

Most Hits

17 hits   Duran Duran
 3 hits   The Power Station
 2 hits   Arcadia
 1 hit   John Taylor
 1 hit   Andy Taylor

Most Weeks

265 weeks   Duran Duran
 54 weeks   The Power Station
 28 weeks   Arcadia
 19 weeks   Andy Taylor
 15 weeks   John Taylor

No.1 Singles

1983   *Hungry Like The Wolf*
1985   *A View To A Kill*
1993   *Ordinary World*

Ordinary World topped the chart for five weeks, and *Hungry Like The Wolf* and *A View To A Kill* for one week each.

Singles with the most weeks

23 weeks	*The Reflex*
23 weeks	*Some Like It Hot* ~ The Power Station
22 weeks	*A View To A Kill*
20 weeks	*Notorious*
20 weeks	*Come Undone*
19 weeks	*Hungry Like The Wolf*
19 weeks	*The Wild Boys*
19 weeks	*Save A Prayer*
19 weeks	*Ordinary World*
19 weeks	*Get It On* ~ The Power Station

DURAN DURAN IN DENMARK

Most Hits

7 hits	Duran Duran
1 hit	The Power Station
1 hit	Arcadia

Most Weeks

70 weeks	Duran Duran
5 weeks	Arcadia
4 weeks	The Power Station

No.1 Singles

1985	*A View To A Kill*

A View To A Kill topped the chart for seven weeks.

Singles with the most weeks

18 weeks	*A View To A Kill*
16 weeks	*The Wild Boys*
12 weeks	*Notorious*
12 weeks	*Ordinary World*

DURAN DURAN IN FINLAND

Most Hits

11 hits	Duran Duran
1 hit	Arcadia

Most Weeks

88 weeks	Duran Duran
8 weeks	Arcadia

No.1 Singles

1983	*Union Of The Snake*

Union Of The Snake topped the chart for seven weeks.

Singles with the most weeks

16 weeks	*Union Of The Snake*
12 weeks	*The Reflex*
8 weeks	*My Own Way*
8 weeks	*Hungry Like The Wolf*
8 weeks	*Is There Something I Should Know?*
8 weeks	*The Wild Boys*
8 weeks	*A View To A Kill*
8 weeks	*Election Day* ~ Arcadia
8 weeks	*Notorious*

DURAN DURAN IN FRANCE

Duran Duran achieved seven hits in France, which spent 8 weeks on the chart.

The band's highest charting single is *Ordinary World*, which peaked at no.6.

Singles with the most weeks

20 weeks	*A View To A Kill*
16 weeks	*The Wild Boys*
16 weeks	*Ordinary World*
12 weeks	*Come Undone*
11 weeks	*The Reflex*

DURAN DURAN IN GERMANY

Most Hits

18 hits	Duran Duran
2 hits	The Power Station
2 hits	Arcadia
1 hit	John Taylor

Most Weeks

186 weeks	Duran Duran
20 weeks	The Power Station
15 weeks	Arcadia
5 weeks	John Taylor

No.1 Singles

1984	*The Wild Boys*

The Wild Boys topped the chart for three weeks.

Singles with the most weeks

21 weeks	*A View To A Kill*
19 weeks	*Ordinary World*
17 weeks	*The Reflex*
17 weeks	*The Wild Boys*
16 weeks	*Union Of The Snake*
14 weeks	*Notorious*
13 weeks	*Some Like It Hot* ~ The Power Station
12 weeks	*Election Day* ~ Arcadia
11 weeks	*Is There Something I Should Know?*
11 weeks	*Save A Prayer (Special Edited Version)*

DURAN DURAN IN IRELAND

Most Hits

22 hits	Duran Duran
3 hits	Arcadia
2 hits	The Power Station

Most Weeks

108 weeks	Duran Duran
7 weeks	The Power Station
7 weeks	Arcadia

No.1 Singles

| 1984 | *The Reflex* |

The Reflex topped the chart for three weeks.

Singles with the most weeks

9 weeks	*A View To A Kill*
9 weeks	*Ordinary World*
8 weeks	*Hungry Like The Wolf*
8 weeks	*The Reflex*
7 weeks	*Rio*
6 weeks	*My Own Way*
6 weeks	*Save A Prayer*
6 weeks	*Come Undone*

DURAN DURAN IN ITALY

Most Hits

24 hits	Duran Duran
1 hit	The Power Station
1 hit	Arcadia
1 hit	John Taylor

Most Weeks

271 weeks	Duran Duran
18 weeks	Arcadia
12 weeks	John Taylor
7 weeks	The Power Station

No.1 Singles

| 1985 | *A View To A Kill* |

1985	*Election Day* ~ Arcadia
1986	*Notorious*
1988	*I Don't Want Your Love*
1990	*Serious*
1993	*Ordinary World*

Most weeks at No.1

7 weeks	*I Don't Want Your Love*
6 weeks	*A View To A Kill*
6 weeks	*Election Day* ~ Arcadia
4 weeks	*Notorious*

Singles with the most weeks

30 weeks	*The Wild Boys*
23 weeks	*A View To A Kill*
21 weeks	*(Reach Up For The) Sunrise*
18 weeks	*Election Day* ~ Arcadia
18 weeks	*Ordinary World*
17 weeks	*Notorious*
17 weeks	*I Don't Want Your Love*
17 weeks	*Violence Of Summer (Love's Taking Over)*
15 weeks	*The Reflex*
15 weeks	*Serious*

DURAN DURAN IN JAPAN

Duran Duran achieved eight hits singles in Japan, which spent 78 weeks on the chart.

The band's highest charting single is *A View To A Kill*, which peaked at no.28.

Singles with the most weeks

18 weeks	*Union Of The Snake*
15 weeks	*The Wild Boys*
14 weeks	*Is There Something I Should Know?*
14 weeks	*A View To A Kill*
12 weeks	*The Reflex*

DURAN DURAN IN THE NETHERLANDS

Most Hits

18 hits	Duran Duran
2 hits	Arcadia
1 hit	The Power Station

Most Weeks

154 weeks	Duran Duran
11 weeks	Arcadia
8 weeks	The Power Station

No.1 Singles

1984	*The Reflex*

The Reflex topped the chart for five weeks.

Singles with the most weeks

16 weeks	*The Reflex*
16 weeks	*A View To A Kill*
14 weeks	*The Wild Boys*
11 weeks	*Skin Trade*
10 weeks	*Notorious*
10 weeks	*I Don't Want Your Love*
9 weeks	*Meet El Presidente*
9 weeks	*Ordinary World*
8 weeks	*Union Of The Snake*
8 weeks	*Some Like It Hot* ~ The Power Station
8 weeks	*Election Day* ~ Arcadia
8 weeks	*Do You Believe In Shame?*
8 weeks	*Violence Of Summer (Love's Taking Over)*

DURAN DURAN IN NEW ZEALAND

Most Hits

20 hits	Duran Duran
2 hits	The Power Station
1 hit	Arcadia

Most Weeks

196 weeks   Duran Duran
23 weeks   The Power Station
14 weeks   Arcadia

Duran Duran's highest charting singles in New Zealand are *Union Of The Snake* and *Ordinary World*, which both peaked at no.3.

Singles with the most weeks

33 weeks   *Girls On Film*
16 weeks   *Is There Something I Should Know?*
16 weeks   *Union Of The Snake*
15 weeks   *The Reflex*
15 weeks   *The Wild Boys*
15 weeks   *Notorious*
14 weeks   *Hungry Like The Wolf*
14 weeks   *Come Undone*
14 weeks   *Election Day* ~ Arcadia
12 weeks   *A View To A Kill*
12 weeks   *Get It On* ~ The Power Station

DURAN DURAN IN NORWAY

Most Hits

6 hits   Duran Duran
1 hit   Arcadia

Most Weeks

38 weeks   Duran Duran
4 weeks   Arcadia

Duran Duran's highest chart single in Norway is *A View To A Kill*, which peaked at no.2.

Singles with the most weeks

13 weeks   *A View To A Kill*
11 weeks   *Notorious*
8 weeks   *Ordinary World*

| 4 weeks | *Union Of The Snake* |
| 4 weeks | *Election Day* ~ Arcadia |

DURAN DURAN IN SOUTH AFRICA

Most Hits

| 4 hits | Duran Duran |
| 1 hit | The Power Station |

Most Weeks

| 48 weeks | Duran Duran |
| 10 weeks | The Power Station |

No.1 Singles

| 1985 | *The Wild Boys* |

The Wild Boys topped the chart for one week.

Singles with the most weeks

14 weeks	*Hungry Like The Wolf*
14 weeks	*The Wild Boys*
11 weeks	*A View To A Kill*
10 weeks	*Some Like It Hot* ~ The Power Station
9 weeks	*Notorious*

DURAN DURAN IN SPAIN

Most Hits

| 8 hits | Duran Duran |

| 1 hit | The Power Station |
| 1 hit | Arcadia |

Most Weeks

| 101 weeks | Duran Duran |

| 13 weeks | Arcadia |
| 11 weeks | The Power Station |

Duran Duran's highest charting single in Spain is *The Wild Boys*, which peaked at no.3.

Singles with the most weeks

25 weeks	*A View To A Kill*
22 weeks	*The Wild Boys*
17 weeks	*The Reflex*
16 weeks	*Notorious*
13 weeks	*Election Day* ~ Arcadia
11 weeks	*Some Like It Hot* ~ The Power Station

DURAN DURAN IN SWEDEN

Duran Duran achieved eight hits in Sweden, which spent 70 weeks on the chart.

No.1 Singles

| 1985 | *A View To A Kill* |

A View To A Kill topped the chart for two weeks.

Singles with the most weeks

16 weeks	*A View To A Kill*
16 weeks	*Ordinary World*
14 weeks	*Notorious*
8 weeks	*Come Undone*
6 weeks	*Is There Something I Should Know?*

DURAN DURAN IN SWITZERLAND

Most Hits

10 hits	Duran Duran
1 hit	The Power Station
1 hit	Arcadia

Most Weeks

101 weeks   Duran Duran
  7 weeks   The Power Station
  6 weeks   Arcadia

Duran Duran's highest chart single in Switzerland is *The Wild Boys*, which peaked at no.2 for five weeks.

Singles with the most weeks

17 weeks   *A View To A Kill*
17 weeks   *Ordinary World*
13 weeks   *The Wild Boys*
12 weeks   *The Reflex*
11 weeks   *Notorious*
10 weeks   *(Reach Up For The) Sunshine*
 8 weeks   *I Don't Want Your Love*

DURAN DURAN IN THE UNITED STATES

Most Hits

21 hits   Duran Duran
 3 hits   The Power Station
 2 hits   Arcadia
 2 hits   Andy Taylor
 1 hit   John Taylor

Most Weeks

300 weeks   Duran Duran
 43 weeks   The Power Station
 26 weeks   Arcadia
 23 weeks   Andy Taylor
 12 weeks   John Taylor

No.1 Singles

1984   *The Reflex*
1985   *A View To A Kill*

Both singles topped the Hot 100 for two weeks.

Singles with the most weeks

25 weeks	*Come Undone*
23 weeks	*Hungry Like The Wolf*
22 weeks	*Ordinary World*
21 weeks	*The Reflex*
18 weeks	*The Wild Boys*
18 weeks	*Some Like It Hot* ~ The Power Station
17 weeks	*Is There Something I Should Know?*
17 weeks	*Union Of The Snake*
17 weeks	*A View To A Kill*
17 weeks	*Take It Easy* ~ Andy Taylor
17 weeks	*Notorious*

RIAA (Recording Industry Association of America) Awards

The RIAA began certifying Gold singles in 1958 and Platinum singles in 1976. From 1958 to 1988: Gold = 1 million, Platinum = 2 million. From 1988 onwards: Gold = 500,000, Platinum = 1 million. Awards are based on shipments, not sales (unless the award is for digital sales).

Gold	*Hungry Like The Wolf* (March 1993) = 500,000
Gold	*The Wild Boys* (March 1993) = 500,000
Gold	*The Reflex* (March 1993) = 500,000
Gold	*Ordinary World* (March 1993) = 500,000

DURAN DURAN IN ZIMBABWE

Duran Duran achieved two hit singles in Zimbabwe, which spent 19 weeks on the chart.

The band's highest charting single is *Union Of The Snake*, which peaked at no.2.

Singles with the most weeks

10 weeks	*Union Of The Snake*
9 weeks	*A View To A Kill*

All The Top 40 Albums

THE OFFICIAL UK CHARTS·GOSSIP·PERSONAL ADVICE·DISCO·REVIEWS

record

mirror

CROSSRHODES We give Duran Duran a hard time

Sex in pop – a frank investigation   **Grandmixer D.ST**

1 ~ DURAN DURAN

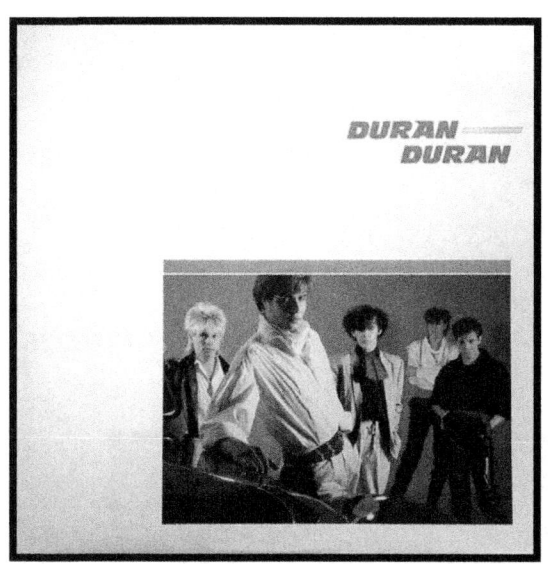

Girls On Film/Planet Earth/Anyone Out There/To The Shore/Careless Memories/Night Boat/Sound Of Thunder/Friend Of Mine/Tel Aviv

North America: *To The Shore* omitted.

Produced by Colin Thurston.

UK: EMI EMC 3372 (1981).

27.06.81: 9-13-11-10-7-10-6-4-4-5-**3**-7-12-19-23-25-28-44-38-45-53-64-73-72-65-44-48-
48-24-17-19-32-37-51-74-51-44-46-50-60-76-72-72-67-78-x-98-x-73-74-54-49-52-64-
75-84-69-68-70-84-84-78-61-50-56-76-79-86

Pos	LW	Title, Artist		Peak Pos	WoC
1	1	**TIME** ELECTRIC LIGHT ORCHESTRA	JET	1	5
2	2	**LOVE SONGS** CLIFF RICHARD	EMI	1	10
3	5 ↑	**DURAN DURAN** DURAN DURAN	EMI	3	11

4.12.82: 94-80-83-75-75-55-38-60-51-65-92-55-81-58-83-92-70-40-42-34-51-57-52-38-
67-89-94-79-83-x-66-77-62-73-47-41-52-44-47-54-38-63-82-74-82-94-66-x-67-95-71-

76-85
4.08.84: 93
22.10.20: 71

Australia
14.09.81: peaked at no.**9**, charted for 52 weeks

Canada
11.06.83: 94-69-43-45-39-32-33-30-28-**27-27-27**-32-33-35-43-43-50-48-55-55-57-63-77

New Zealand
29.11.81: 46-9-10-15-15-15-15-12-9-9-9-**2-2**-3-3-5-3-5-6-7-8-7-12-16-10-6-6-7-12-18-26-29-39-23-26-26-36-34-29-26-45-49-26-49-44-45

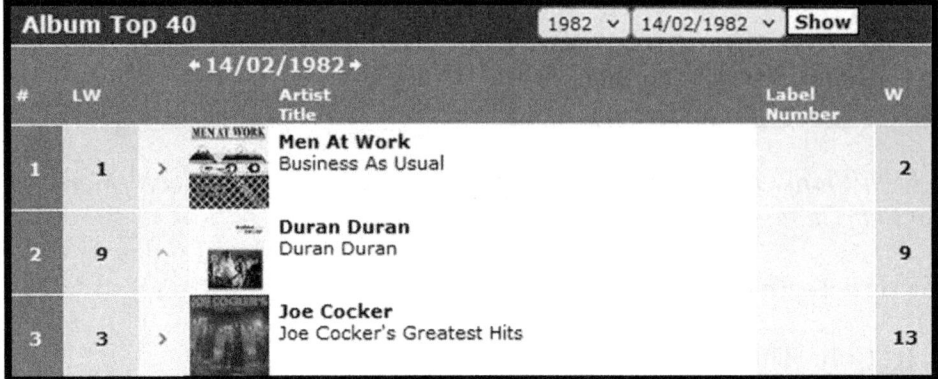

10.07.83: 42-x-49
4.04.93: 43
11.07.93: 47-x-x-38-40-32-32-38

Sweden
28.08.81: 25-43-x-28-28-30-26-15-16-13-6-**3**-6-8-14-26 (bi-weekly)

Japan
5.07.81: peaked at no.**25**, charted for 26 weeks

USA
26.02.83: 76-69-69-69-67-67-67-63-65-92-89-88-91-90-x-97-84-48-35-30-27-22-16-14-11-**10**-11-25-28-31-34-37-47-48-64-73-80-84

Duran Duran's self-titled debut album was recorded at three different studios, London's Red Bus and Utopia, and Chipping Norton Recording Studios in Chipping Norton, Oxfordshire.

The album was recorded in December 1980 and January 1981, and the instrumental tracks for the album were laid down relatively quickly. The vocals took longer, not least because Simon Le Bon wasn't used to singing in a studio setting and, initially, he found it difficult to adjust. There was even talk of replacing him as the band's lead singer, before EMI's A&R director Dave Ambrose intervened, and ~ a definite plus ~ Simon Le Bon quickly emerged as the band's best lyric writer.

'Simon came in with this book of poetry,' said Andy Taylor, 'and kept coming up with these ideas and melodies. We were like, "This guy doesn't even know what his potential is".'

Prior to starting work on recording their debut album, the five members of Duran Duran spent two months working on songs. It was during this period that an agreement was reached to credit all songs to all five members of the band, and to split all the royalties equally.

Dave Ambrose recommended Colin Thurston, who had worked with the likes of David Bowie, Iggy Pop, the Human league and Bow Wow Wow, as producer for the project

'Colin was absolutely the right producer for us,' John Taylor later acknowledged. 'He knew how to take what was best about us and magnify it, and boy, did he take our sound to another level.'

In writing and recording their debut album, Duran Duran was influenced by numerous artists around at the time, including David Bowie, Chic, Giorgio Moroder, the Human League, Japan, Roxy Music and Ultravox.

'We wrote the first album,' said Andy Taylor, 'to kind of make up what we were going to be, what this futuristic sound was.'

Three singles were released from *DURAN DURAN*:

- *Planet Earth*
- *Careless Memories*
- *Girls On Film*

All three singles were hits, with *Girls On Film* giving the band their first Top 10 success in the UK.

DURAN DURAN rose to no.3 in the UK, and to date the album has logged an impressive 119 weeks on the chart. The album was a no.2 hit in New Zealand, and charted at no.3 in Sweden, no.9 in Australia and no.25 in Japan.

When it was first released, the album failed to chart in North America. However, when the album was reissued in early 1983 with the hit *Is There Something I Should Know?* added to the end of side one, the album rose to no.10 in the United States and no.27 in Canada.

In 2010, *DURAN DURAN* was remastered by Andrew Walter at Abbey Road Studios, and reissued as:

- a vinyl album with bonus 12" single.
- a 2 x CD edition with bonus tracks.
- a box-set comprising the 2 x CD edition, plus a DVD.

The tracks on the 12" single were as follows:

Planet Earth (Night Version)/Girls On Film (Extended Night version)/Planet Earth (Night Mix)/Girls On Film (Night Mix)

The 2 x CD edition featured the following bonus tracks:

CD1:
   The B-sides: *Late Bar/Khanada/Fame/Faster Than Light*

CD2:
   The AIR Studio Demos: *Girls On Film/Tel Aviv*
   Manchester Square Demos: *Anyone Out There/Planet Earth/Friends Of Mine/Late Bar*
   BBC Radio 1 Session (mono): *Night Boat/Girls On Film/Anyone Out There/Like An Angel*
   The Night Versions: *Planet Earth (Night Version/Girls On Film (Extended Night Version)/Planet Earth (Night Mix)/Girls On Film (Night Mix)*

The DVD featured the following videos and performances:

The Videos: *Planet Earth/(Club Version)/Careless Memories/Girls On Film (Long Uncensored Version)/(Short Censored Version)/Night Boat/A Day In The Life Featurette*
Top Of The Pops: *Planet Earth/Careless Memories/Girls On Film*
Old Grey Whistle Test: *Night Boat/Anyone Out There*
Get Set For Summer: *Girls On Film*
Multi-Coloured Swop Shop: *Friend Of Mine/Girls On Film*

2 ~ RIO

Rio/My Own Way/Lonely In Your Nightmare/Hungry Like The Wolf/Hold Back The Rain/New Religion/Last Chance On The Stairway/Save A Prayer/The Chauffeur

Produced by Colin Thurston.

UK: EMI EMC 3411 (1982).

22.05.82: 4-**2**-3-4-5-6-7-9-15-15-19-20-21-15-8-5-4-10-8-9-16-19-27-30-24-23-16-6-5-3-5-4-4-4-3-11-12-15-17-12-11-13-21-23-20-11-7-9-12-14-17-20-23-26-31-37-40-43-36-29-27-23-25-23-24-26-26-25-23-27-30-38-52-40-48-57-44-43-41-42-47-55-61-71-71-63-43-68-62-76-87-75-91-88-78-83

Pos	LW	Title, Artist		Peak Pos	WoC
1	1	**COMPLETE MADNESS** MADNESS	STIFF	1	5
2	4 ↑	**RIO** DURAN DURAN	EMI	2	2
3	7 ↑	**CHARTBUSTERS** VARIOUS ARTISTS	RONCO	3	3

5.05.84: 88-93-x-79-75-85-x-x-87-94-82-89-x-63-83-90
12.01.85: 90
17.09.15: 28

Australia
14.06.82: peaked at no.**1** (1), charted for 27 weeks

Canada
12.06.82: 49-44-43-50-50
2.10.82: 54-52-67-87
19.02.83: 93-60-44-28-22-14-7-3-**1**-2-3-2-2-4-5-7-7-8-11-12-14-16-22-26-26-29-31-37-38-38-41-44-43-49-57-54-61-61-62-70-75-78

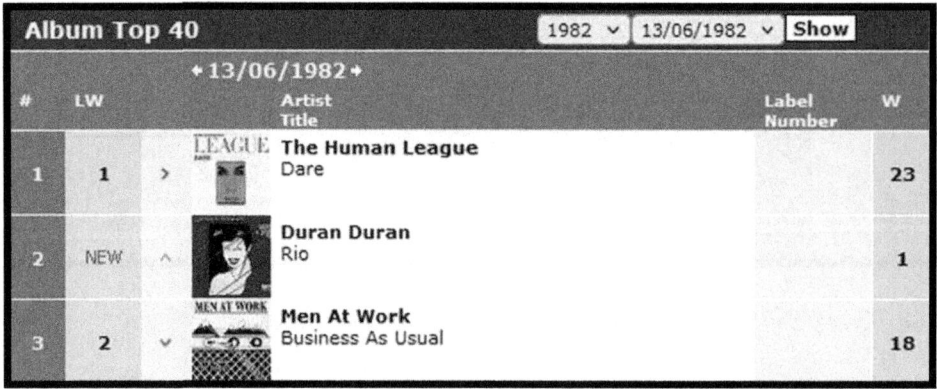

Finland
05.82: peaked at no.**3**, charted for 36 weeks

Japan
21.05.82: peaked at no.**27**, charted for 25 weeks

Netherlands
29.05.82: **40**

New Zealand
13.06.82: **2-2**-6-10-7-7-9-6-7-10-8-8-4-9-10-12-14-15-13-22-21-30-34-34-44-49-x-49-49-49-49-49-39-36-37-35-43-x-x-x-48-40-38-32-31-33-24-23-22-23-21-50-42-31-39-24-12-25-37-41-37-47-38-43-39

13.11.83: 42

Norway
5.06.82: 40-35-34-x-**13**-25-25-23

South Africa
18.09.82: peaked at no.**7**, charted for 13 weeks

Sweden
1.06.82: 12-**9**-10-29-37-42 (bi-weekly)

USA
23.12.82: 95-95-80-66-43-28-22-15-12-7-7-**6-6-6-6-6-6-6**-9-9-11-12-16-18-23-27-41-59-
   66-74-82-88-96-x-99

Duran Duran wrote and recorded their second album between January and March 1982 at London's AIR Studios.

'When we started the *RIO* album in January 1982,' said Nick Rhodes, 'we were all terrified of the success of the first LP and we thought, "How on earth are we going to top that?".'

The pressure the band felt in England saw them briefly fleeing to a château in France, to work on some new songs.

'We'd already moved on (from the first album).' said Nick Rhodes, 'and we'd got some songs that we thought were as good, if not better, that some of the songs on the first album already.'

The album's title was John Taylor's idea, and the band loved it because they felt it represented the exotic and optimistic tone of the album.

'The word looks great,' said Simon Le Bon, 'sounds great and makes people think of parties, rivers ~ it's Spanish for river! ~ foreign places and sunshine.'

RIO's iconic sleeve was designed by Malcolm Garrett, and was painted by Patrick Nagel ~ the design paid homage to the 1950s packaging for cigars.

'It's a much more inward looking album that the first album,' said John Taylor. 'I think that *RIO* was much more about ourselves responding to each other, and the experiences that we were having, rather than what was going on outside us.'

Duran Duran promoted *RIO* with a tour of Europe and the United States in the second half of 1982, and three singles ~ all hits ~ were released from the album:

- *Hungry Like The Wolf*
- *Save A Prayer*
- *Rio*

RIO rose to no.2 in the UK, kept off the top spot by the Madness compilation, *COMPLETE MADNESS*. The album did hit no.1 in Australia, and achieved no.2 in New

Zealand, no.3 in Finland, no.7 in South Africa, no.9 in Sweden, no.13 in Norway, no.27 in Japan, no.40 in the Netherlands, no.43 in Canada and a hugely disappointing no.122 in the United States.

Following the album's relative failure in the United States, Capitol Records commissioned several remixes, to make the album more accessible to American radio. David Kershenbaum remixed four of the songs on the album, namely *Rio*, *Lonely In Your Nightmare*, *Hungry Like The Wolf* and *Hold Back The Rain*.

John Taylor, especially, was unhappy with the remixes.

'That was the end of Duran Duran,' he complained, 'our original idea ~ an underground club band.'

Despite whatever misgiving members of the band had, the remixes were effective, with the new version of *RIO* hitting no.1 in Canada and spending seven straight weeks at no.6 in the United States, where it logged over two years on the Billboard 200 chart.

RIO has been reissued a number of times over the years.

In 2001, the album was remastered and reissued with three music videos added: *Rio*, *Hungry Like The Wolf* and *Save A Prayer*.

In 2009, a 2 x CD edition of *RIO* was released:

CD1 ~ Original album with the following bonus tracks:
Rio (US Album Remix)/My Own Way (Carnival Remix)/Lonely In Your Nightmare (US Album Remix)/Hungry Like The Wolf (US Album Remix)/Hold Back The Rain (US Album Remix)

CD2:
The Manchester Square Demos (Recorded 28th August 1981): *Last Chance On The Stairway/My Own Way/New Religion/Like An Angel*
Non Album Singles & B-Sides: *My Own Way (Original 7" Version)/Like An Angel/ Careless Memories (Live)/The Chauffeur (Blue Silver) (Early Version)*
Versions & Mixes: *My Own Way (Night Version)/Hungry Like The Wolf (Night Version)/Rio (Night Version)/New Religion (Carnival Version)/Hold Back The Rain (Carnival Version)*

The 2009 edition was repackaged and reissued in 2015.

3 ~ CARNIVAL EP

Europe: *Hungry Like The Wolf (Night Version)/Rio (Night Version)/Planet Earth (Night Version)/Girls On Film (Night Version)*

North America: *Hungry Like The Wolf/Girls On Film/Hold Back The Rain/My Own Way*

Japan: *Rio (Part II)/Hold Back The Rain (Remix)/My Own Way/Hungry Like The Wolf (Night Version)/New Religion*

UK: Not released.

USA: Harvest DLP-15006 (1982).

13.11.82: **98-98-98**

Japan
1.02.83: peaked at no.**25**, charted for 18 weeks

This EP was released to promote Duran Duran's *RIO* album, and featured a different track listing in Europe (Netherlands and Spain), North America and Japan.

 CARNIVAL was most successful in Japan, where it rose to no.25 on the album chart. The EP also spent three weeks at a lowly no.98 in the United States, but it wasn't a hit anywhere else.

WHITE FEATHERS

White Feathers/Too Shy/Lies And Promises/Magician Man/Kajagoogoo (Instrumental)/
Ooh To Be Ah/Ergonomics/Hang On Now/This Car Is Fast/Frayo

Produced by Nick Rhodes & Colin Thurston, except *Kajagoogoo (Instrumental)*, which
Kajagoogoo produced with Tim Palmer.

UK: EMI EMC 3433 (1983).

30.04.83: **5**-9-15-20-23-29-14-23-29-32-35-36-39-45-37-45-54-72-71-72

Australia
23.05.83: peaked at no.**53**, charted for 11 weeks

Austria
1.06.83: 17-x-x-**15** (bi-weekly)

Canada
28.05.83: 98-93-88-72-59-56-52-49-47-**46**-56-56-69-77-83-89-90

Finland
04.83: peaked at no.**3**, charted for 17 weeks

Germany
16.05.83: 26-**7**-9-**7**-8-11-14-12-14-13-17-13-23-16-17-20-17-22-34-45-59-60-56-54-61-
   59-62

Netherlands
21.05.83: **36**-42

New Zealand
15.05.83: **17**-23-22-28-45

Sweden
17.05.83: 15-**7**-12-26

USA
18.06.83: 56-50-41-**38-38**-58-58-57-54-56-54-72-93-94

Zimbabwe
21.08.83: peaked at no.**5**

Originally known as Art Nouveau, the band that became Kajagoogoo formed in Leighton Buzzard, England, in 1978. The four members were Jez Strode, Nick Beggs, Steve Askew and Stuart Neale.

The band advertised for a lead singer in 1981, and recruited Christopher 'Limahl' Hamill (Limahl was an anagram of his surname). Around the same time, the band changed their name to Kajagoogoo.

Kajagoogoo were struggling to get a recording contract when, working as a waiter at London's Embassy Club, Limahl happened to meet Nick Rhodes. After listening to it, and liking what he heard, Nick took Kajagoogoo's demo tape to Duran Duran's record company, EMI ~ just one of the record companies that had already rejected it.

'Nick made them listen to it again,' said Nick Beggs, 'and they changed their minds. There's no doubt about it, we were signed because of Nick Rhodes, and we hadn't even written *Too Shy* at that point.'

Nick went on to produce Kajagoogoo's debut album, *WHITE FEATHERS*, with Colin Thurston. The album was released in April 1983, and generated three Top 40 singles:

- *Too Shy*
- *Ooh To Be Ah*
- *Hang On Now*

WHITE FEATHERS achieved no.3 in Finland, no.5 in the UK and Zimbabwe, no.7 in Germany and Sweden, no.15 in Austria, no.17 in New Zealand, no.36 in the Netherlands, no.38 in the United States, no.46 in Canada and no.53 in Australia.

DURAN DURAN

Seven and the Ragged Tiger

デュラン・デュラン／セブン＆・ザ・ラグド・タイガー

RittorMusic

4 ~ SEVEN AND THE RAGGED TIGER

The Reflex/New Moon On Monday/(I'm Looking For) Cracks In The Pavement/I Take The Dice/Of Crime And Passion/Union Of The Snake/Shadows On Your Side/Tiger Tiger/The Seventh Stranger

Produced by Alex Sadkin, Ian Little & Duran Duran.

UK: EMI EMC 1654541 (1983).

3.12.83: **1**-5-6-8-8-16-19-22-27-29-26-22-25-17-27-31-40-51-55-54-63-47-25-20-19-17-19-15-30-28-35-40-39-36-45-39-53-41-60-49-70-80-90-93

Pos	LW	Title, Artist			Peak Pos	WoC
1	New	**SEVEN AND THE RAGGED TIGER** DURAN DURAN		EMI	1	1
2	New	**UNDER A BLOOD RED SKY** U2		ISLAND	2	1
3	1 ↓	**COLOUR BY NUMBERS** CULTURE CLUB		VIRGIN	1	7

12.01.85: 66-63-x-86

Australia
28.11.83: peaked at no.**2**, charted for 30 weeks

Austria
15.07.84: 19-**11**-12-18-20-19 (bi-weekly)

Canada
26.11.83: 77-44-27-20-16-15-15-12-9-8-8-8-9-12-12-11-10-9-**7**-**7**-8-12-14-16-16-13-13-
   10-9-9-**7**-8-9-9-9-8-17-17-17-18-19-23-27-33-33-42-43-58-73

Finland
11.83: peaked at no.**3**, charted for 19 weeks

France
11.03.84: peaked at no.**20**, charted for 16 weeks

Germany
26.12.83: 64-x-62-63-43-48-45-46-49-44-46-53-53-50-57-53-55-57-53-54-55-61-44-39-
   37-27-24-21-**17**-18-20-29-28-35-40-37-34-44-51-58-62

Italy
14.01.84: peaked at no.**12**, charted for 18 weeks

Japan
16.12.83: peaked at no.**6**, charted for 47 weeks

Netherlands
17.12.83: 42-22-40-x-x-x-48-45-33-43-26-15-20-22-32-37-50
19.05.84: 32-13-4-**1-1-1-1-1**-3-5-4-6-8-8-13-18-22-13-24-38-46

Norway
17.12.83: 19-x-x-16-**14-14**

New Zealand
18.12.83: **1-1-1-1-1**-7-14-25-26-35-40-38-50-40-43-41-38-34-44-x-x-49-x-47-35-40-35-
32-32-26-11-15-10-12-5-4-5-7-10-12-17-25-24-28-38-39-43-46

South Africa
31.12.83: peaked at no.**7**, charted for 11 weeks

Sweden
13.12.83: **19**-27-42-39-47 (bi-weekly)

Switzerland
22.07.84: 17-20-19-**16**-22-23-26-23-28

USA
10.12.83: 30-17-12-12-12-11-10-10-10-**8-8-8-8**-10-10-11-13-14-14-19-21-20-22-18-17-
15-14-10-10-10-10-**8**-11-13-17-17-26-27-31-33-40-42-48-59-62-69-88-94-98-97

Duran Duran recorded their third studio album between April and October 1983. For tax
reasons, the band chose to record the album outside the UK, and they moved into a
château in Valbonne, on France's popular *Côte d'Azur*, in April. Here, they installed a 24-
track mobile studio rented from London's RAK Studios.

'We were recording in the south of France,' said John Taylor, 'and pretending we were
the Rolling Stones when we were only making our third record. We'd just barely moved
out of our parents' homes. We didn't know anything about tax years but our managers did,
and that's why we were there, and that really began a negative roll of publicity.'

No new songs were written ahead of the move to France, which meant the band were
starting from scratch, but big egos and a partying lifestyle led to growing tensions within
the band.

'We were living the high life to the full,' Andy Taylor later admitted, 'and soon we
were partying in Cannes every night.'

Although not as productive as the band had hoped, their time in France did yield a
demo of *Union Of The Snake*, a song titled *Seven And The Ragged Tiger* (which evolved

into *The Seventh Stranger*), plus a few other ideas including a track titled *Spidermouse*, which became *New Moon On Monday*.

From France, Duran Duran jetted to AIR Studios on the Caribbean island of Montserrat, before they relocated again, this time to 301 Studios in Sydney, Australia, where the album was finally completed.

'I thought the thing was never going to get finished,' said Nick Rhodes. 'Everybody was pulling and tugging in different directions. To me that album, more than any of them, on the surface of it, there's a lot of pretty songs on there but then underneath there's this sort of not quite controllable hysteria.'

'It took seven or eight months to record,' added Andy Taylor, 'which was too long. The LP involved a set of compromises, we were too careful. It was like we were saying, "Hey, guys, we've made it to the top now, so let's be careful now and not spoil it".'

Duran Duran did write and record a song titled *Seven And The Ragged Tiger*, with the 'seven' a reference to the five band members and their two managers Michael and Paul Berrow, and the 'ragged tiger' denoting success.

'Seven people running after success,' said Simon Le Bon, who came up with the title. 'It's ambition. That's what it's about.'

'I didn't like it,' admitted Nick Rhodes, referring to the song. 'I thought it was too naïve and throwaway. I've always enjoyed Simon's more obscure lyrics.'

Seven And The Ragged Tiger failed to make the final track listing of the album named after it, and not all members of Duran Duran were on board with the chosen title.

'It seems to me like the name of a kids' book,' said Nick Rhodes, 'not so much the Famous Five, more sort of piratey.'

Duran Duran released three successful singles from *SEVEN AND THE RAGGED TIGER*:

- *Union Of The Snake*
- *New Moon On Monday*
- *The Reflex*

The single version of *The Reflex* was remixed by Chic's Nile Rodgers.

Duran Duran promoted the *SEVEN AND THE RAGGED TIGER* with an extensive global tour, which took in England, Australia, Japan and North America. The Sing Blue Silver Tour kicked off in Canberra, Australia, in November 1983, and concluded in San Diego, California, the following April. The continental Europe leg of the tour was cancelled, as members of the band were all suffering from exhaustion.

Despite the growing tensions within the band, *SEVEN AND THE RAGGED TIGER* made its chart debut in the UK at no.1, ahead of U2's new album, *UNDER A BLOOD RED SKY*. It spent just one week at the top, and proved to be Duran Duran's only chart-topping album in the UK.

Around the world, *SEVEN AND THE RAGGED TIGER* hit no.1 in the Netherlands and New Zealand, and achieved no.2 in Australia, no.3 in Finland, no.6 in Japan, no.7 in Canada and South Africa, no.8 in the United States, no.11 in Austria, no.12 in Italy, no.14

in Norway, no.16 in Switzerland, no.17 in Germany, no.19 in Sweden and no.20 in France.

SEVEN AND THE RAGGED TIGER was reissued in two formats in 2010, a 2 x CD edition, plus a box-set comprising the same 2 x CD edition with a DVD.

CD1: Original album.

CD2: Non Album Singles And B-Sides, Mixes: *Is There Something I Should Know?/ Faith In This Colour/(Alternate Slow Mix)/Secret Oktober/Tiger Tiger (Ian Little Remix)/The Reflex (Single Version)/Make Me Smile (Come Up And See Me) (Live)/New Religion (Live at the LA Forum 9/2/84)/The Reflex (Live at the LA Forum 9/2/84)/Is There Something I Should Know? (Monster Mix)/Union Of The Snake (Monkey Mix)/New Moon On Monday (Dance Mix)/The Reflex (Dance Mix)*

DVD: As The Lights Go Down: A Film Conceived By Duran Duran And Russell Mulcahy: *Intro: Tiger Tiger/Is There Something I Should Know?/Hungry Like The Wolf/Union Of The Snake/New Religion/Save A Prayer/Rio/The Seventh Stranger/The Chauffeur/Planet Earth/Careless Memories/Girls On Film*
The Videos: *Is There Something I Should Know?/Union Of The Snake/New Moon On Monday (EP Version)/The Reflex/New Moon On Monday (Movie Version)*
Top Of The Pops Performances: *Is There Something I Should Know?/The Reflex*

As The Lights Go Down was recorded live at California's Oakland Coliseum in April 1984 ~ in 2019, it was released as a limited edition pink and blue vinyl album in Europe only.

5 ~ TIGER! TIGER! EP

The Reflex (Dance Mix)/Union Of The Snake (The Monkey Mix)/New Moon On Monday/Is There Something I Should Know? (Monster Mix)/Tiger Tiger

Japan
5.06.84: peaked at no.**4**, charted for 21 weeks

This 5-track EP was released exclusively in Japan, where it rose to no.4 on the album chart during a lengthy five month chart run.

6 ~ ARENA

Is There Something I Should Know?/Hungry Like The Wolf/New Religion/Save A Prayer/
The Wild Boys/The Seventh Stranger/The Chauffeur/Union Of The Snake/Planet Earth/
Careless Memories

Produced by Duran Duran & Nile Rodgers.

UK: Parlophone DD2 (1984).

24.11.84: **6**-7-9-10-15-11-9-7-11-14-16-20-25-33-31-42-43-56-65-67-62-57-74-x-98-x-
95-x-75-100-x-75-86-78-x-x-90

Australia
19.11.84: peaked at no.**8**, charted for 18 weeks

Austria
1.01.85: 15-11-**7**-8-12 (bi-weekly)

Canada
17.11.84: 61-40-25-18-14-**10-10-10**-13-12-12-19-24-33-33-33-32-38-41-41-41-44-48-62-
72-77-78

Finland
11.84: peaked at no.**8**, charted for 14 weeks

Germany
26.11.84: 42-31-9-4-**1-1-1-1**-2-5-8-10-15-14-18-24-20-30-42-50-49-55-57-65-64

Italy
17.11.84: peaked at no.**1** (2), charted for 35 weeks

Japan
16.11.84: peaked at no.**3**, charted for 18 weeks

Netherlands
24.11.84: 47-**5**-9-10-10-14-12-11-6-6-10-17-19-12-16-14-21-23-30-38-41-42
3.08.85: 47-42-48-48-40

New Zealand
25.11.84: 15-8-6-**3-3-3-3-3**-7-12-12-18-16-22-25-30-50-46

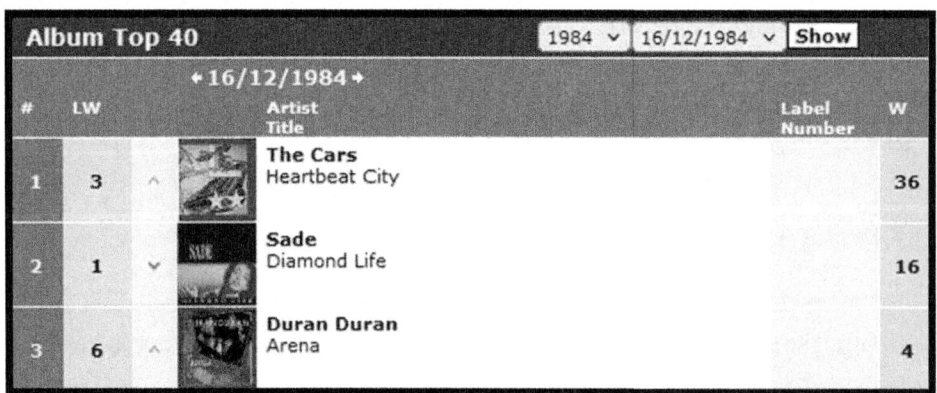

16.06.85: 11-17-19-26-25-27-29-31-42-35-38-36-31-37-35-41-42-50-x-x-44

Norway
1.12.84: 18-**16**-18-18-17-17-17-17

DURAN DURAN
arena

recorded around the world

1984

gatefold sleeve includes
8 page full colour booklet

record: EX 26 0308 1
tape: EX 26 0308 4
UK DD2

is there something I should know?

hungry like the wolf

new religion

save a prayer

the wild boys

the chauffeur

the seventh stranger

union of the snake

planet earth

careless memories

includes the smash hit single 'the wild boys'

major tv campaign
commences December 8 until December 21
london ITV1, london channel 4, Central ITV1, Central channel 4, TVS ITV1
plus
full page ads in the key music papers, including: Smash Hits, No 1, Just 17, NME
plus
650 3D indoor window displays
and advertising throughout the national press

South Africa
8.12.84: peaked at no.**4**, charted for 17 weeks

Sweden
23.11.84: 30-37-49-45-22-**16**-21-48 (bi-weekly)
9.08.85: 38 (bi-weekly)

Switzerland
9.12.84: 11-14-11-11-9-7-6-**4**-11-13-15-22-25

USA
1.12.84: 49-9-7-5-5-**4-4-4**-5-11-16-16-23-25-27-43-40-54-62-93

Duran Duran's first live album, *ARENA* was recorded during the band's concerts at California's Oakland Coliseum between the 12th and 15th April 1985. The album also featured one new studio recording, *The Wild Boys*.

ARENA was released on the back of Duran Duran's hugely successful 1983-84 world tour, and yielded two singles, *The Wild Boys* and *Save A Prayer*. The latter was issued as the 'US Single Version' in North America, while a slightly longer edit known as the 'Special Edited Version' was released in mainland Europe.

ARENA continued Duran Duran's run of success, and topped the album chart for four weeks in Germany. The album also hit no.1 in Italy, and achieved no.3 in Japan and New Zealand, no.4 in South Africa, Switzerland and the United States, no.5 in the Netherlands, no.6 in the UK, no.7 in Austria, no.8 in Australia and Finland, no.10 in Canada, and no.16 in Norway and Sweden.

'I hope it's a reflection of our ability to play live,' said Andy Taylor, speaking about the success of *ARENA*. 'We played to at least a million people on the world tour and some of them obviously liked us. *ARENA* broke us in both Italy and Germany.'

In 1985, two Arena-related home videos were released, *Arena* and *The Making Of Arena*. The *Arena* home video featured the following performances:

Tiger Tiger/Is There Something I Should Know?/Hungry Like The Wolf/Union Of The Snake/Save A Prayer/The Wild Boys (Music Video)/Planet Earth/Careless Memories/ Girls On Film/The Reflex/Rio

ARENA was remastered and reissued in 2004 with two bonus tracks:

- *Girls On Film*
- *Rio*

7 ~ MIXING EP

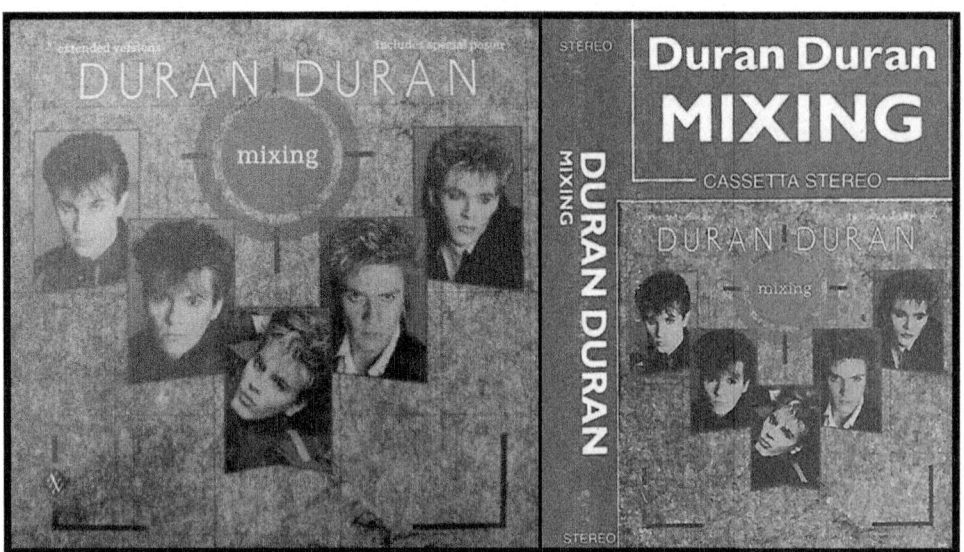

Save A Prayer (Night Version)/Careless Memories (From The Arena)/The Reflex (Dance Mix)/The Wild Boys (Wilder Than Wild Boys) (Extended Mix)

Italy: Parlophone 50 2403081 (1985)

23.03.85: peaked at no.**3**, charted for 13 weeks.

This 4-track remix EP was released exclusively in Italy, where it rose to no.3 on the albums chart.

8 ~ THE POWER STATION

*Some Like It Hot/Murderess/Lonely Tonight/Communication/Get It On (Bang A Gong)/
Go To Zero/Harvest For The World/Still In Your Heart*

Produced by Bernard Edwards.

UK: Parlophone CDP 7 46127 2 (1985).

6.04.85: **12**-13-**12**-18-21-19-19-28-20-20-29-30-45-70-72-75-63-76-90-78-91-96-x-96

Australia
13.05.85: peaked at no.**15**, charted for 20 weeks

Canada
13.04.85: 63-34-19-17-17-16-14-**12**-**12**-17-17-18-19-24-24-25-25-30-29-28-28-26-26-26-
31-32-41-56-63-76-78

Germany
22.04.85: 55-**23**-**23**-26-26-29-36-26-27-37-44-53-58-65-63-x-61

Netherlands
20.04.85: **13**-18-21-27-x-50

New Zealand
28.04.85: 39-**23**-36-31-30-32-44-35-45-49-36-44-37-39-29-27-34-34-32-36-41

Sweden
3.05.85: **38** (bi-weekly)

Switzerland
21.04.85: 22-28-19-**16**-27

USA
13.04.85: 64-35-26-17-13-13-12-12-12-10-9-9-8-7-7-**6**-7-**6**-8-8-15-22-26-28-31-32-41-41-
47-44-55-86

Needing a break from Duran Duran after the band's world tour and *SEVEN AND THE RAGGED TIGER* album, Andy Taylor and John Taylor joined forces with Chic's drummer, Tony Thompson, to form a side project which also involved Chic's Bernard Edwards on the production side of things.

Initially, the plan was for a different singer to perform each song, and several well-known artists including Mick Jagger, Billy Idol and Mick Ronson were approached. However, the first singer to actually meet and work with the trio was Robert Palmer.

'Robert came in,' said Tony Thompson, 'sang the track *Some Like It Hot*, and then asked us what else we had. Then he did *Get It On*, and we said, "To heck with Jagger, this is it!" It's kind of a Chic funk foundation with a Duran Duran rock 'n' roll top and R&B feel courtesy of Palmer.'

The new supergroup planned to call themselves 'Big Brother' but, while working together at New York City's The Power Station recording studios, they decided to go with 'The Power Station' instead.

Three hit singles were released from The Power Station's self-titled debut album:

- *Some Like It Hot*
- *Get It On* ~ titled *Get It On (Bang A Gong)* in North America
- *Communication*

THE POWER STATION charted highest in the United States, where it spent two non-consecutive weeks at no.6. Elsewhere, the album achieved no.12 in Canada and the UK, no.13 in the Netherlands, no.15 in Australia, no.16 in Switzerland, no.23 in Germany and New Zealand, and no.38 in Sweden.

THE POWER STATION was reissued in 2005 with seven bonus tracks:

Someday, Somehow, Someone's Gotta Pay/The Heat Is On/Communication (Long Remix)/Get It On (Bang A Gong) (7")/Some Like It Hot And The Heat Is On/ Communication (Remix)/Some Like It Hot (7")

The Power Station reformed in 1996, originally with the same four-man line-up, to record a new album. However, although he was involved in writing songs for the album, John Taylor was going through a divorce and entering drug rehab at the time, so he pulled out of actually recording the new album, and his place was taken by producer Bernard Edwards. John Taylor was credited with co-writing nine of the eleven songs The Power Station recorded for the album, which was titled *LIVING IN FEAR*.

Sadly, before *LIVING IN FEAR* was released at the end of September 1996, Bernard Edwards contracted pneumonia and died, which resulted in the album being dedicated to him.

Only one single, *She Can Rock It*, was released from *LIVING IN FEAR* ~ it was a minor no.63 hit in the UK, but it failed to chart anywhere else.

LIVING IN FEAR, perhaps surprisingly, wasn't a hit anywhere.

9 ~ SO RED THE ROSE

*Election Day/Keep Me In The Dark/Goodbye Is Forever/The Flame/Missing/Rose Arcana/
The Promise/El Diablo/Lady Ice*

Produced by Arcadia & Alex Sadkin.

UK: Parlophone Odeon Series PCSD 101 (1985).

7.12.85: **30**-37-57-70-79-68-69-73-78-88

Australia
23.12.85: peaked at no.**35**, charted for 10 weeks

Canada
7.12.85: 77-59-46-23-23-23-15-**14**-22-25-32-36-40-50-55-60-85-100

Finland
12.85: peaked at no.**20**, charted for 10 weeks

Germany
13.01.86: **55**-64

Italy
30.11.85: peaked at no.**1** (1), charted for 14 weeks

Netherlands
14.12.85: 46-**34**-45-48-62-65-69-75

New Zealand
15.12.85: **22-22-22-22-22**-28-33-38-44-x-50-x-x-36-29

Sweden
13.12.85: **48** (bi-weekly)

USA
21.12.85: 35-25-25-24-**23-23**-25-28-36-44-48-49-62-85

With Andy Taylor and John Taylor busy with The Power Station, the three remaining members of Duran Duran ~ Nick Rhodes, Roger Taylor and Simon Le Bon ~ decided to work together as a trio. Inspired by Nicolas Poussin's painting *Et In Arcadia Ego* ('The Arcadian Shepherds'), the trio decided to call themselves Arcadia.

'Arcadia was actually a great time for Simon and me,' said Nick Rhodes, 'because we managed to escape from the craziness. We fled to Paris, which became our sort of second home.'

Arcadia recorded their one and only album, titled *SO RED THE ROSE*, at Paris's *Studio de la Grande Armée* between April and June 1985. The album featured a number of guest musicians, including David Gilmour, Grace Jones, Herbie Hancock and Sting. Roger Taylor was involved with the recording of the album, but less so with the promotional sides of things.

SO RED THE ROSE produced four Top 40 singles:

- *Election Day*
- *The Flame*
- *Goodbye Is Forever*
- *The Promise*

The album itself went all the way to no.1 in Italy, and charted at no.14 in Canada, no.20 in Finland, no.22 in New Zealand, no.23 in the United States, no.30 in the UK, no.34 in the Netherlands, no.35 in Australia, no.48 in Sweden and no.55 in Germany.

SO RED THE ROSE was reissued as a box-set comprising 2 x CDs and a DVD in 2010, as follows:

CD1 Bonus Tracks: *Say The Word (7" Edit)/Election Day (Single Version)/Goodbye Is Forever (Single Mix)/The Promise (7" Mix)/The Flame (7" Remix)/Say The Word/ She's Moody And Grey, She's Mean And Restless*

CD2: *Election Day (Consensus Mix)/Goodbye Is Forever (12" Extended Mix)/The Promise (Instrumental)/Rose Arcana/The Flame (Extended Remix)/Say The Word (Extended Vocal Remix)Election Day (Cryptic Cut)/The Promise (12" Mix)/Goodbye Is Forever (Dub Mix)/Say The Word (Extended Instrumental Remix)/Election Day (Early Rough Mix)/Flame Game (Yo Homeboy Mix)*

DVD: *Introduction/Filming Election Day/Election Day/Filming The Promise/The Promise/Filming Goodbye Is Forever/Goodbye Is Forever/Filming The Flame/The Flame/Filming Missing/Missing/Credits*

Arcadia wrote and recorded *Say The Word* as the theme song for the 1986 film, *Playing For Keeps* ~ it was issued as a single in North America only, but it wasn't a hit.

10 ~ NOTORIOUS

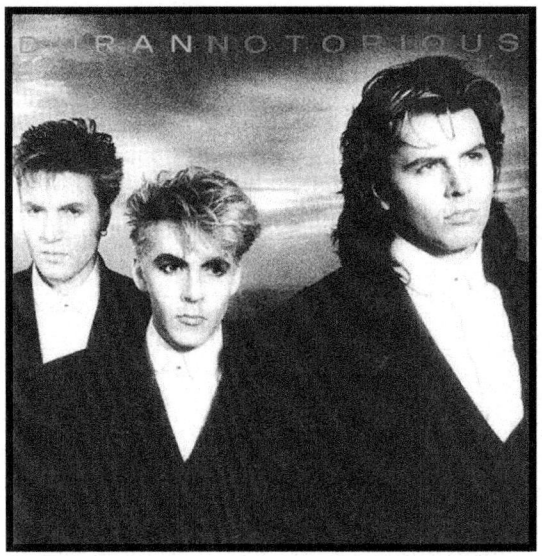

Notorious/American Science/Skin Trade/A Matter Of Feeling/Hold Me/Vertigo (Do The Demolition)/So Misled/Meet El Presidente/Winter Marches On/Proposition

Produced by Duran Duran & Nile Rodgers.

UK: EMI CDP 7 46415 2 (1986).

6.12.86: **16**-53-56-75-75-69-70-74-x-x-x-80-64-53-75-78
9.05.87: 74-96-95

Australia
22.12.86: peaked at no.**30**, charted for 9 weeks

Austria
1.01.87: 27-22-**20**-25-26 (bi-weekly)

Canada
6.12.86: 74-44-36-31-31-31-20-**19-19-19**-25-24-28-31-31-37-38-63-63-79-97

Finland
12.86: peaked at no.**23**, charted for 9 weeks

France
15.03.87: peaked at no.**30**, charted for 2 weeks

Germany
15.12.86: 64-**22**-37-39-39-43-56-58-58-59

Italy
29.11.86: peaked at no.**2**, charted for 20 weeks

Japan
6.12.86: peaked at no.**9**, charted for 20 weeks

Netherlands
6.12.86: 17-**11**-23-31-63-45-55-74-x-67-x-x-72-55-49-61-43-54-71-66-x-x-x-63-54-75

New Zealand
21.12.86: 17-17-17-17-**15**-20-23-31-35-x-48

Norway
13.12.86: 13-9-10-10-10-10-10-**8**-10-14-20

Sweden
3.12.86: 25-**8**-11-13-20-29 (bi-weekly)

Switzerland
4.01.87: **19**-28-22-23

USA
20.12.86: 24-19-19-16-14-13-**12**-13-14-15-20-23-29-33-43-57-70-79-98-x-99-98-98

Following the *SEVEN AND THE RAGGED TIGER* album and their world tour, the five members of Duran Duran concentrated on two side projects, Arcadia and The Power Station. They did reunite long enough to write and record the theme song for the 1985 James Bond film, *A View To A Kill*, but that's it.

The following year, Roger Taylor had had enough, and decided to retire from the music business. Then, later the same year, Andy Taylor signed a solo deal with MCA in Los Angeles, and started work on a solo album.

The three remaining members of Duran Duran took legal action against Andy, to try to force him to join them in the studio to work on a new album, but not only did he refuse to comply, he threatened to sue the remaining trio if they carried on using the name Duran Duran. Simon Le Bon complained of too many lawyers and too many accountants getting involved.

'It got quite nasty,' he admitted. 'It was quite difficult to make an album, going to the lawyers mornings and laying down tracks in the afternoons. Thank God for Nile Rodgers, he held it all together.'

Having given up on trying to force Andy to join them, John Taylor, Nick Rhodes and Simon Le Bon wrote and recorded a new album between June and September 1986, working at a number of different studios in London, Paris and New York City. Andy Taylor, although he had quit the band, was credited with playing guitar on four tracks on the album, namely *American Science*, *Skin Trade*, *A Matter Of Feeling* and *Proposition*.

The album, which was titled *NOTORIOUS*, featured numerous other musicians, including producer Nile Rodgers and Warren Cuccurullo on guitar, drummer Steve Ferrone, Jimmy Maelen on percussion, and Mac Gollehon and The Borneo Horns on horns. Four backing vocalists were also credited: Brenda White-King, Curtis King, Cindy Mizelle and Tessa Niles.

NOTORIOUS featured a number of songs titled after Alfred Hitchcock films, including the title track (a 1946 Hitchcock film), *Vertigo* (a 1958 film) and *Rope* (a 1948 film) ~ the latter was the original title for the song *Hold Me*.

Perhaps mindful of Andy Taylor's threat to sue, *NOTORIOUS* and the three singles released from it were all credited to 'Duran', as opposed to Duran Duran. The three singles, all hits, were:

- *Notorious*
- *Skin Trade*
- *Meet El Presidente*

NOTORIOUS charted at no.2 in Italy, no.8 in Norway and Sweden, no.9 in Japan, no.11 in the Netherlands, no.12 in the United States, no.15 in New Zealand, no.16 in the UK, no.19 in Canada and Switzerland, no.20 in Austria, no.22 in Germany, no.23 in Finland, and no.30 in Australia and France.

NOTORIOUS was remastered and reissued in 2010 as:

- 2 x CDs
- a box-set featuring the same 2 x CDs plus a DVD
- a digital only remix EP
- a digital only live album

The track listings were as follows:

CD1 Bonus Tracks ~ Single Versions And B-Sides: *We Need You/Notorious (45 Mix)/ Skin Trade (Radio Cut)/Meet El Presidente (7" Mix)*

CD2 ~ Mixes: *Notorious (Extended Mix)/Meet El Presidente (Presidential Suite Mix)/ Skin Trade (Parisian Mix)/American Science (Chemical Reaction Mix)/Vertigo (Do The Demolition) (Mantronix Mix)/Skin Trade (Stretch Mix)/Notoriousaurus Rex*
Duran Goes Dutch EP (Recorded at The Ahoy, Rotterdam on 7th May 1987): *Notorious (Live)/Vertigo (Do The Demolition (Live)/New Religion (Live)/American Science (Live)/Hungry Like The Wolf (Live)*

DVD ~ Working For The Skin Trade (Recorded during the Strange Behaviour Tour in Rio de Janeiro, Brazil): *Intro/A View To A Kill/Notorious/New Religion/Vertigo (Do The Demolition)/The Chauffeur/Save A Prayer/Skin Trade/Hungry Like The Wolf/The Wild Boys/Credits*
The Videos: *Notorious/Skin Trade/Meet El Presidente*
Top Of The Pops: *Notorious*

Remix EP (digital): *Skin Trade (S.O.S Dub)/Meet El Presidente (Meet El Beat)/ American Science (Meltdown Dub)/Vertigo (Do The Demolition) 9B-Boy Mix)/ Notorious (Latin Rascals Mix)*

Live Album (digital): *Introduction/A View To A Kill/Notorious/American Science/ Union Of The Snake/Vertigo (Do The Demolition)/New Religion/Meet El Presidente/ Election Day/Some Like It Hot/The Chauffeur/Skin Trade/Hold Me (incorporating. Dance To The Music)/Is There Something I Should Know?/Hungry Like The Wolf*

The live album was recorded at New York City's The Beacon Theater on 31st August 1987.

11 ~ STRANGE BEHAVIOR EP

Notorious (Extended Mix)/Skin Trade (Stretch Mix)/We Need You/Notorious (Little Rascals Mix)/Skin Trade (Album Version)/A View To A Kill

UK: Not released.

Japan: EMI S18-5008 (1987).

21.03.87: peaked at no.**9**, charted for 9 weeks

This 6-track EP was released exclusively in Italy and Japan, and was a no.9 hit in Japan. The EP was issued as a 12" picture disc in Italy.

12 ~ THUNDER

I Might Lie/Don't Let Me Die Young/Life Goes On/Thunder/Night Train/Tremblin'/Bringin' Me Down/Broken Window/French Guitar

Produced by Andy Taylor & Steve Jones.

UK: MCA Records DMCG 6018 (1987).

30.05.87: **61**

Canada
4.04.87: 96-94-91-88-**85-85-85-85**-95

Sweden
8.04.87: **31** (bi-weekly)

Having quit Duran Duran, Andy Taylor recorded his debut solo album *THUNDER* during the summer of 1986. The album was recorded at The Record Plant in Los Angeles, California, and Andy produced the album with Steve Jones (ex-Sex Pistols).

Andy wrote one track, *Broken Window*, himself, and he co-wrote the other eight songs on the album with Steve Jones. Andy and Steve played guitar on the album, which also featured:

- Patrick O'Hearn on bass guitar
- Mickey Curry on drums

- Brett Tuggle on keyboards
- Paulinho Da Costa on percussion
- Howard Kaylan & Mark Volman on backing vocals

Three singles ~ which all failed to chart ~ were issued from *THUNDER*:

- *Don't Let Me Die Young*
- *I Might Lie*
- *Life Goes On*

THUNDER owes its Top 40 status to its performance in Sweden, where it made its chart debut at no.31. Elsewhere, the album spent a single week at no.61 in the UK and was a minor no.85 hit in Canada, but it failed to chart in most countries.

In 2010, Andy released *THUNDER IN TOKYO – JULY 8, 1987*, originally as a free download made available via his official website. The release featured six songs recorded live at the NHK Hall in Tokyo, Japan, during Andy's Thunder Tour:

When The Rain Comes Down/I Might Lie/Brinin' Me Down/Tremblin'/Take It Easy/
You Really Got Me

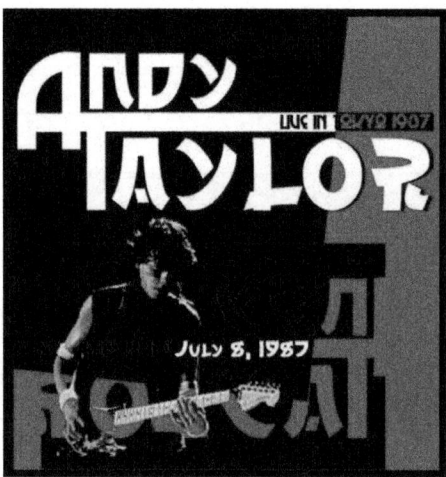

OUT OF ORDER

Lost In You/Lethal Dose Of Love/The Wild Horse/Forever Young/My Heart Can't Tell Me No/Dynamite/Nobody Knows You When You're Down And Out/Crazy About Her/Try A Little Tenderness/When I Was Your Man

Produced by Rod Stewart, Andy Taylor & Bernard Edwards.

UK: Warner Bros. Records WX 152 (1988).

4.06.88: **11**-13-24-30-51-59-77-x-x-x-x-100

Canada
28.05.88: 80-50-25-18-14-12-10-10-10-7-4-5-4-4-3-**2**-3-4-6-6-7-8-8-9-7-10-7-9-8-12-11-11-11-12-12-16-20-19-18-17-19-20-27-23-29-38-41-38-42-48-46-42-35-30-26-21-24-27-35-34-31-40-35-34-33-30-33-31-31-45-48-51-50-60-61-66-79-95

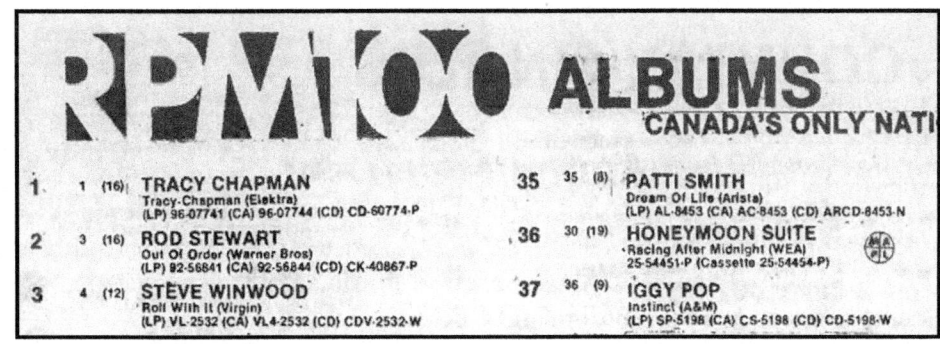

225

Australia
27.06.88: peaked at no.**26**, charted for 17 weeks

Austria
15.06.88: **10**-18-18-22 (bi-weekly)

Germany
6.06.88: 20-16-8-**6-6-6**-9-13-15-16-17-21-28-27-29-34-37-50-53-52-55

Netherlands
18.06.88: **37**-45-57-73

New Zealand
3.07.88: **47**-49

Norway
28.05.88: 19-14-**11**-19

Sweden
8.06.88: 3-**1-1-1**-5-8-16-35

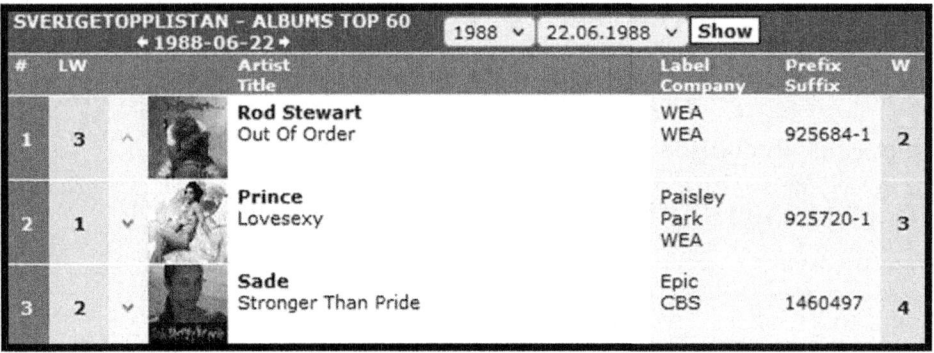

Switzerland
5.06.88: 24-29-**7**-10-**7**-13-16-27-27-29

USA
4.06.88: 83-53-40-38-35-33-32-30-31-31-30-31-31-31-30-30-26-26-23-22-21-22-23-24-26-28-30-32-44-45-45-49-47-46-45-56-51-39-37-29-26-23-23-**20-20**-22-21-22-27-26-29-30-29-29-33-36-36-44-47-46-47-45-43-50-63-72-89-95

Andy Taylor co-produced Rod Stewart's *OUT OF ORDER* album with Rod Stewart and Bernard Edwards. The album, which was released in May 1988, was recorded at two Los Angeles studios, Ocean Way Recording and Record Plant.

Andy played guitar on seven of the eleven tracks on the album, and he co-wrote five of them with Rod Stewart, namely *Lost In You*, *The Wild Horse*, *Lethal Dose Of Love*, *Dynamite* and *Almost Illegal*. Tony Brock was also credited with co-writing *Lethal Dose Of Love*.

Four hit singles were released from *OUT OF ORDER*:

- *Lost In You*
- *Forever Young*
- *My Heart Can't Tell You No*
- *Crazy About Her*

OUT OF ORDER hit no.1 for three weeks in Sweden, and achieved no.2 in Canada, no.6 in Germany, no.7 in Switzerland, no.10 in Austria, no.11 in Norway and the UK, no.20 in the United States, no.26 in Australia, no.37 in the Netherlands and no.47 in New Zealand.

13 ~ BIG THING

Big Thing/I Don't Want Your Love/All She Wants Is/Too Late Marlene/Drug (It's Just A State Of Mind)/Do You Believe In Shame?/Palamino/Interlude One/Land/Flute Interlude One/The Edge Of America/Lake Shore Driving

Japan Bonus EP (1989): *Notorious (Live)/Vertigo (Do The Demolition) (Live)/New Religion (Live)/Hungry Like The Wolf (Live)/American Science (Live)*

Produced by Duran Duran, Daniel Abraham & Jonathan Elias.

UK: EMI CD DDB 33 (1988).

29.10.88: **15**-49-72
21.01.89: 58-66

Australia
20.11.88: **46**-47-49

Germany
7.11.88: 48-**31**-45-52-57-60-66

Italy
15.10.88: peaked at no.**5**, charted for 19 weeks

Japan
16.10.88: peaked at no.**9**, charted for 7 weeks

Netherlands
5.11.88: **18**-19-36-51-71-78-78
13.05.89: 92-81-79-77-90

New Zealand
27.11.88: **34**-38

Sweden
2.11.88: **27**-39 (bi-weekly)

Switzerland
13.11.88: **19**-21

USA
12.11.88: 31-25-**24-24**-25-29-30-30-35-36-32-37-40-40-43-52-57-77-81-97-92

Duran Duran ~ still a trio ~ recorded their fifth studio album at Paris's Davout Studios, and mixed the album at New York's Soundworks. As well as the three official members of the band the album, titled *BIG THING*, credited Chester Kamen and Warren Cuccurullo on guitars, and drummers Steve Ferrone and Sterling Campbell.

'We dispensed with the politeness of *NOTORIOUS*,' said Nick Rhodes, 'and we could scream at each other again. We like tension, we have disagreements, I think that's how we create.'

Duran Duran dedicated *BIG THING* to three people who died in 1987:

- Producer Alex Sadkin, who was killed in a car crash.
- Artist Andy Warhol, who died following gallbladder surgery.
- Simon Le Bon's childhood friend, David Miles, who died of a drugs overdose.

Like *NOTORIOUS*, *BIG THING* was credited to 'Duran' on the album sleeve, rather than Duran Duran. Three singles were released from the album, and all became Top 40 hits in at least one country:

- *I Don't Want Your Love*
- *All She Wants Is*
- *Do You Believe In Shame?*

The three singles were credited to 'Duranduran'.

Big Thing was issued as a promotional single in the UK and Mexico, while *Too Late Marlene* was released as a promotional single in Brazil, but neither track was given a full release anywhere.

Duran Duran promoted *BIG THING* with a global Electric Theatre Tour ~ at the end of the tour, both Sterling Campbell and Warren Cuccurullo became full-time members of the band, thus making Duran Duran a quintet again.

BIG THING achieved no.5 in Italy, no.9 in Japan, no.15 in the UK, no.18 in the Netherlands, no.19 in Switzerland, no.24 in the United States, no.27 in Sweden, no.31 in Germany, no.34 in New Zealand and no.46 in Australia.

BIG THING was reissued on CD with one bonus track in 2006: *Drug (It's Just A State Of Mind (Daniel Abraham Mix)*.

Four years later, the album was remastered and reissued as a box-set featuring 2 x CDs and a DVD, as follows:

CD1: Original album, but with the Daniel Abraham Mix of *Drug (It's Just A State Of Mind)*, as was originally intended.

CD2 ~ Singles And B-Sides: *I Don't Want Your Love (7" Mix)/All She Wants Is (45 Mix)/I Believe/All I Need To Know (Full Version)/The Krush Brothers LSD Edit/God (London)/This Is How A Road Gets Made/Palomino (Edit)/Drug (It's Just A State Of Mind) (Remix)/Big Thing (7" Mix)*
Mixes: *I Don't Want Your Love (Big Mix)/All She Wants Is (US Master Mix)/Big Thing (12" Mix)/All She Wants Is (Eurohouse Mix)*

DVD ~ Big Thing Live at Palatrussardi, Milan, Italy, on 12th December 1988:
Introduction/God/Big Thing/I Don't Want Your Love/Hungry Like The Wolf/Do You Believe In Shame?/All She Wants Is/Planet Earth/This Is How A Road Gets Made/ Winter Marches On/Palomino/Too Late Marlene/Girls On Film/Notorious/Skin Trade/Is There Something I Should Know?/The Wild Boys/Drug/Save A Prayer/The Reflex/Rio/The Edge Of America
The Videos: *I Don't Want Your Love/All She Wants Is/Do You Believe In Shame?*

14 ~ DECADE

*Planet Earth/Girls On Film/Hungry Like The Wolf/Rio/Save A Prayer/Is There Something
I Should Know?/Union Of The Snake/The Reflex/The Wild Boys/A View To A Kill/
Notorious/Skin Trade/I Don't Want Your Love/All She Wants Is*

Brazil: *A Matter Of Feeling* replaced *All She Wants Is*

UK: EMI CDDDX 10 (1989).

25.11.89: **5**-9-16-23-26-25-16-16-23-36-38-35-43-55-70
17.09.94: 76-66-96

Australia
25.12.89: peaked at no.**89**, charted for 6 weeks

Canada
9.12.89: 82-**81**-84-84-84-89-94

Italy
2.12.89: peaked at no.**22**, charted for 2 weeks

Japan
6.12.89: peaked at no.**76**, charted for 2 weeks

Netherlands
2.12.89: 97-89-**84**

Duran Duran's first compilation album, as per the title *DECADE*, celebrated the band's first ten years.

To promote the album, producer John Jones created a remix single titled *Burning The Ground*, which featured snippets of some of Duran Duran's biggest hits ~ however, *Burning The Ground* wasn't include on *DECADE* itself.

DECADE made its debut in the UK at no.5, but the compilation fared less well in other countries, achieving at no.22 in Italy but peaking well outside the Top 40 in Australia, Canada, Japan, the Netherlands and the United States.

DECADE was released as a 2 x VideoCD in Europe in 1995, which carried an '18' certificate.

The music videos featured were as follows:

VideoCD1: *Opening Titles/Planet Earth/Girls On Film/Hungry Like The Wolf/Rio/Save A Prayer/Is There Something I Should Know?/Union Of The Snake/The Reflex/The Wild Boys/A View To A Kill*

VideoCD2: *Notorious/Skin Trade/I Don't Want Your Love/All She Wants Is/Violence Of Summer (Love's Taking Over)/Serious/Ordinary World/Come Undone*

BACK STREET SYMPHONY

She's So Fine/Dirty Love/Don't Wait For Me/Higher Ground/Until My Dying Day/Back Street Symphony/Love Walked In/An Englishman On Holiday/Girl's Going Out Of Her Head/Gimme Some Lovin'

Cassette & CD Bonus Track: *Distant Thunder*

Japan Bonus CD (1991): *Another Shot At Love (Live at Opera on the Green, London, 16 July 1989)/Girl's Going Out Of Her Head (Live at Maritime Bar, Southend, 20 November 1989)/An Englishman On Holiday (Live at Maritime Bar, Southend, 20 November 1989)/ Until My Dying Day (Live at Town & Country Club, London, 7 March 1990)/Fired Up (Live at Town & Country Club, London, 7 March 1990)/Dirty Love (Live at Town & Country Love, London, 7 March 1990)/She's So Fine (Live at Monsters of Rock, Donington, 18 August 1990)/Back Street Symphony (Live at Monsters of Rock, Donington, 18 August 1990)/Higher Ground (Live at Monsters of Rock, Donington, 18 August 1990)/ Don't Wait For Me (Live at Monsters of Rock, Donington, 18 August 1990)*

Produced by Andy Taylor.

UK: EMI EMC/CDEMC 3570 (1990).

17.03.90: **21**-37-57-69
19.05.90: 59-62-73
28.07.90: 73
1.09.90: 45-71-66
2.03.91: 52-50-64-57-64

Andy Taylor was the solo producer of Thunder's debut album, *BACK STREET SYMPHONY* (*aka BACKSTREET SYMPHONY*).

The album was recorded during August and September 1989 at Great Linford Manor Studios in Milton Keynes, England, before being mixed at London's AIR Studios. As well as producing the album, Andy Taylor co-wrote two songs ~ *She's So Fine* and *Until My Dying Day* ~ with Luke Morley, and he played guitar on *Until My Dying Day*.

Five singles, all of which were Top 40 hits in the UK, were released from *BACK STREET SYMPHONY*:

- *She's So Fine*
- *Dirty Love*
- *Back Street Symphony*
- *Gimme Some Lovin'*
- *Love Walked In*

Thunder's debut single, *She's So Fine*, missed the chart when it was first released, but it was reissued as the follow-up to *Gimme Some Lovin'*, and second time around it was a hit.

BACK STREET SYMPHONY was a no.21 hit in the UK, and was a minor no.114 hit on the Billboard 200 in the United States, but the album failed to chart anywhere else.

BACK STREET SYMPHONY was remastered and reissued in 2009 as a 2 x CD edition:

CD1 Bonus Tracks: *Dirty Love (Extended Version)/Fired Up (Flexi-Disc 7")/I Wanna Be Her Slave/She's So Fine (Full Length Version)*

CD2: *Until The Night Is Through (Dance Dance Dance)/I Can Still Hear The Music/ No Way Out Of The Wilderness/Back Street Symphony (7" Version)/An Englishman On Holiday (Live)/Girl's Going Out Of Her Head (Live)/Another Shot Of Love (Live)/Back Street Symphony (Live)/She's So Fine (Live)/Until My Dying Day (Live)/Higher Ground (Live)/Don't Wait For Me (Live)/Fired Up (Live)/Dirty Love (Live)*

15 ~ LIBERTY

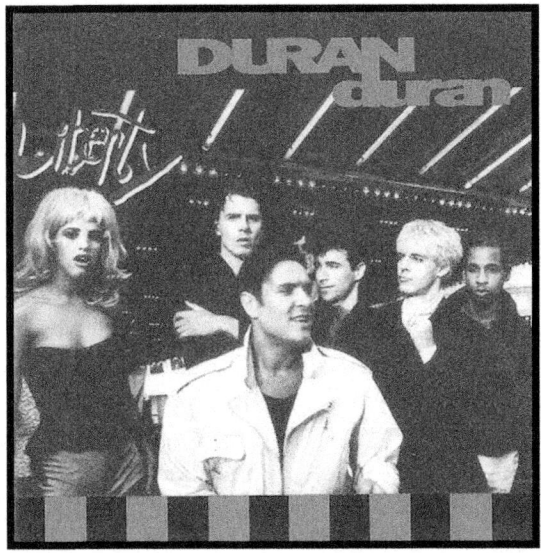

Violence Of Summer (Love's Taking Over)/Liberty/Hothead/Serious/All Along The Water/ My Antarctica/First Impression/Read My Lips/Can You Deal With It/Venice Drowning/ Downtown

Japan Bonus CD: *Yo Bad Azizi/Throb/Violence Of Summer (Love's Taking Over) (The Story Mix)*

Produced by Duran Duran & Chris Kimsey.

UK: Parlophone CDPCSCD 112 (1990).

1.09.90: **8**-29-49-71

Australia
8.10.90: peaked at no.**56**, charted for 7 weeks

Italy
1.09.90: peaked at no.**6**, charted for 6 weeks

Japan
22.08.90: peaked at no.**24**, charted for 4 weeks

Netherlands
1.09.90: 71-50-40-**37**-48-64-78

Switzerland
16.09.90: **36**-40

USA
8.09.90: 83-**46**-65-81-90

Duran Duran's new five-man line-up wrote and recorded the band's sixth studio album between May and October 1989, however, production of *LIBERTY* wasn't actually completed until the following March.

'We went into a barn in Sussex,' said Simon Le Bon, 'and started jamming away, and before we got finished it was like, "Right, we've got the album, let's go and record it now". And I don't think we got it right, I don't think we were paying enough attention … But out of that came two of the best songs Duran's ever come up with, *Serious* and *My Antarctica*, they're really, really beautiful songs. I don't think it's a bad album, but there are definitely weak spots on it, definitely.'

'*LIBERTY* was a bitch to make,' said John Taylor. 'It seemed the worst place you could be in the world was in Duran Duran. I wasn't strong enough to leave, so all I could do by that point was hang on by the skin of my teeth.'

Demo sessions for *LIBERTY*, titled 'Didn't Anybody Tell You?', surfaced as a bootleg in 1999, and featured half a dozen songs that didn't make the album:

Bottleneck/Money On Your Side/Dream Nation/In Between Woman/Worth Waiting For/ My Family

'I like coming across things that I've forgotten about,' said John Taylor, 'that I've forgotten we've recorded. That's why's really exciting about the *Didn't Anybody Tell You* bootleg, because there's so many songs on there that never got finished.'

Only two singles were released from *LIBERTY*, and while both gained Top 40 status in at least one country, neither was a sizeable hit:

- *Violence Of Summer (Love's Taking Over)*
- *Serious*

LIBERTY was a Top 10 hit in Italy and the UK, where it peaked at no.6 and no.8, respectively, but it only managed four weeks on the chart in both countries and was only a modest hit elsewhere. The album charted at no.24 in Japan, no.36 in Switzerland, no.37 in the Netherlands, no.46 in the United States and no.56 in Australia.

With hindsight, Duran Duran saw the *LIBERTY* album as something of a low point in their career.

'I don't think any of us were prepared for the duration of the low,' said Simon Le Bon. 'You feel that people have got a bit sick of you and we got a bit sick of it as well. There were times when everyone in the band felt like giving up.'

LAUGHING ON JUDGEMENT DAY

Does It Feel Like Love?/Everybody Wants Her/Low Life In High Places/Laughing On Judgement Day/Empty City/Today The World Stopped Turning/Long Way From Home/ Fire To Ice/Feeding The Flame/A Better Man/The Moment Of Truth/Flawed To Perfection/Like A Satellite/Baby I'll Be Gone

Produced by Andy Taylor & Luke Morley.

UK: EMI CD EMD 1035 (1992).

5.09.92: **2**-13-24-25-31-43-46-35-43-58

Pos	LW		Title, Artist		Peak Pos	WoC
1	New		**GREATEST HITS** KYLIE MINOGUE	POLYDOR	1	1
2	New		**LAUGHING ON JUDGEMENT DAY** THUNDER	EMI	2	1
3	1 ↓		**BEST 1** THE SMITHS	WEA	1	2

Germany
19.10.92: 97-x-**80**-87-95-87

Sweden
16.09.92: **37**-46 (bi-weekly)

Switzerland
27.09.92: **33**

Thunder's second album *LAUGHING ON JUDGEMENT DAY* was recorded between February and June 1992 at Outside Studios in Cleckendon, England, and was mixed at London's AIR Studios by David Bascombe.

This time, due to a busy schedule, Andy Taylor didn't have time to produce the whole album, so he produced some tracks and the band's lead singer Luke Morley produced the rest. Andy co-wrote two songs Thunder recorded for *LAUGHING ON JUDGEMENT DAY* with Luke Morley, *Empty City* and *Baby I'll Be Gone*.

Three singles, an EP and a promotional single were issued from the album:

- *Low Life In High Places*
- *Everybody Want Her*
- *A Better Man*
- *Like A Satellite* EP
- *Does It Feel Like Love?*

Does It Feel Like Love? was released as a promotional CD single in the United States and as a promotional 7" single in Spain, but it wasn't a hit in either country.

LAUGHING ON JUDGEMENT DAY debuted in the UK at no.2, behind Kylie Minogue's *GREATEST HITS*, and charted at no.33 in Switzerland and no.37 in Sweden. The album was also a minor no.80 hit in Germany, but it failed to chart in most countries.

16 ~ DURAN DURAN (THE WEDDING ALBUM)

Too Much Information/Ordinary World/Love Voodoo/Drowning Man/Shotgun/Come Undone/Breath After Breath/UMF/Femme Fatale/None Of The Above/Shelter/To Whom It May Concern/Sin Of The City

Japan Bonus Tracks: *Time For Temptation (Alternate Version)/Stop Dead (Edit)*

UK Tour Edition Bonus CD: *Falling Angel/Stop Dead/Time For Temptation/Come Undone (12" Mix – Comin' Together)/Ordinary World (Acoustic Version)/Too Much Information (David Richards 12" Mix)*

Produced by Duran Duran & John Jones.

UK: Parlophone CDDDB 34 (1993).

27.02.93: **4**-13-22-27-34-39-32-22-14-5-6-7-11-17-27-41-48-62-70-84-77-84-96-92-x-x-x-87-58-59-90
29.01.94: 53-71

Australia
16.05.93: **20**-38-39

Austria
14.03.93: 38-26-25-25-**12**-29-24-28-29

Canada

6.03.93: 10-14-23-22-23-24-26-25-29-28-27-16-12-9-10-**8**-9-**8**-**8**-10-15-17-20-33-37-51-61-64-80

Finland

02.93: peaked at no.**20**, charted for 12 weeks

France

25.04.93: peaked at no.**32**, charted for 8 weeks

Germany

8.03.93: 96-39-26-24-**22**-**22**-23-**22**-26-30-32-39-43-54-51-69-66-60-72-80-85

Italy

20.02.93: peaked at no.**6**, charted for 19 weeks

Japan

24.02.93: peaked at no.**24**, charted for 8 weeks

Netherlands

27.02.93: 98-60-35-25-**23**-**23**-25-30-33-34-39-50-72

South Africa

20.03.93: peaked at no.**8**, charted for 13 weeks

Sweden

10.03.93: 35-**21**-31-33-46-43-46-46 (bi-weekly)

Switzerland

14.03.93: 26-24-24-27-**23**-27-25-34-33-34

USA

13.03.93: **7**-11-21-21-25-28-26-30-29-23-20-22-19-20-21-17-15-18-20-21-23-26-30-34-34-36-43-54-67-73-89-97

With drummer Sterling Campbell having parted company with the band after just one album, Duran Duran were reduced to a quartet for their seventh studio album.

The band completed the recording of their second self-titled album in early 1992, however, influenced by the apparent lack of interest in the album, the band's management company Left Bank got cold feet, and pulled the album ~ this meant the album wasn't actually released until the following February, following the success of the lead single, *Ordinary World*.

The album's sleeve, designed by Nick Egan, featured wedding photographs of the parents of the four members of Duran Duran. The album, as per the promo cassette version released in the UK, was originally titled *DURAN DURAN (THE WEDDING ALBUM)*, but 'The Wedding Album' was dropped before the album was commercially released ~ however, the UK cassette version still maintained the album's original title, presumably in error.

Despite the change of title, the album still became known as '*THE WEDDING ALBUM*', which helped to distinguish it from the band's self-titled debut album.

'Bring(ing) Warren in and just giving full rein to his talents is really what *THE WEDDING ALBUM* was about,' said John Taylor. 'Rather than trying to control it, just acknowledge what Warren has to offer is what made that album work.'

With drummer Sterling Campbell gone, Duran Duran used three different drummers in recording *DURAN DURAN (THE WEDDING ALBUM)*: producer John Jones, Steve Ferrone and Vinnie Colaiuta.

Six singles were released from *DURAN DURAN (THE WEDDING ALBUM)* in various countries:

- *Ordinary World*
- *Come Undone*
- *Too Much Information*
- *Drowning Man*
- *Femme Fatale*
- *None Of The Above*

Ordinary World gave Duran Duran their biggest hit since *A View To A Kill* in 1985, and the follow-up *Come Undone* was a sizeable hit in many countries as well. *Too Much Information* was a more modest hit, but it still achieved Top 40 status in Canada and the UK.

A remixed version of *Drowning Man* was issued as a single in the United States, and as a promo 12" single in the UK, but it wasn't a hit. *Femme Fatale* was released exclusively in France, where it failed to chart. *None Of The Above* was released in Japan, and as a promo CD single in the United States, but like *Drowning Man* and *Femme Fatale* it failed to chart.

DURAN DURAN (THE WEDDING ALBUM) gave Duran Duran their most successful album for ten years in many countries. The album achieved no.4 in the UK, no.6 in Italy, no.7 in the United States, no.8 in Canada and South Africa, no.12 in Austria, no.20 in Australia and Finland, no.21 in Sweden, no.22 in Germany, no.23 in the Netherlands and Switzerland, no.24 in Japan and no.32 in France.

17 ~ THANK YOU

White Lines/I Wanna Take You Higher/Perfect Day/Watching The Detectives/Lay Lady Lay/911 Is A Joke/Success/Crystal Ship/Ball Of Confusion/Thank You/Drive By/I Wanna Take You Higher Again

Japan Bonus Tracks: *Diamond Dogs/Femme Fatale*

Produced by Duran Duran & John Jones.

UK: Parlophone CDDDB 36 (1995).

8.04.95: **12**-30-61

Australia
22.05.95: peaked at no.**64**, charted for 2 weeks

Austria
23.04.95: **25**-33-34

Belgium
22.04.95: **34**

Canada
17.04.95: 27-**15**-25-25-25-33-36-45-54-73-75-85-86-86-89-91-96

Germany
10.04.95: 96-x-**50**-75-70-88-93-93

Italy
1.04.95: peaked at no.**17**, charted for 2 weeks

Japan
12.04.95: peaked at no.**27**, charted for 6 weeks

Netherlands
8.04.95: 84-59-**34**-41-59-81-90

Switzerland
23.04.95: **44**-x-**44**

USA
22.04.95: **19**-41-50-56-64

Duran Duran started work on recording their eighth studio album ~ the band's first covers album ~ before their *DURAN DURAN (THE WEDDING ALBUM)* was released.

'The idea behind the *THANK YOU* album,' said Warren Cuccurullo, 'was to do it on tour. We intended to record it fast, keep it raw, get it out quick. That's what me and John wanted to do, but then Simon wanted to do more recording after the tour and they went to France in the summer. Time started going past and it ended up being presented as a follow-up to *THE WEDDING ALBUM*, which it was never intended to be.'

The album was titled after a Led Zeppelin song, and also featured covers of songs by Melle Mel, Sly & The Family Stone, Lou Reed, Elvis Costello, Bob Dylan, Public Enemy, Iggy Pop, The Doors and The Temptations. The album did feature one song Duran Duran wrote themselves, namely *Drive By*.

The Japanese edition of *THANK YOU* featured two bonus tracks, a cover of David Bowie's *Diamond Dogs* and the previously released *Femme Fatale*, which was originally recorded by The Velvet Underground & Nico.

Although he was no longer a member of Duran Duran, Roger Taylor was credited with playing drums on two tracks the band recorded for *THANK YOU*, namely *Perfect Day* and *Watching The Detectives*.

'We've always been cocky bastards,' said Simon Le Bon, 'and with this record we've got our balls back. The mere fact that we did those songs is quite an act of irreverence … You don't have to pass a test to be allowed to do a led Zeppelin or a Lou Reed song.'

Three singles were released from *THANK YOU*:

- *Perfect Day*
- *White Lines (Don't Do It)*
- *Lay Lady Lay*

Perfect Day and *White Lines (Don't Do It)* were moderately successful, while *Lay Lady Lay* was issued as a single exclusively in Italy, where it was a Top 20 hit.

Although not as successful as *DURAN DURAN (THE WEDDING ALBUM)*, *THANK YOU* did chart at no.12 in the UK, no.15 in Canada, no.17 in Italy, no.19 in the United States, no.25 in Austria, no.27 in Japan, no.34 in Belgium and the Netherlands, no.44 in Switzerland, no.50 in Germany and no.64 in Australia.

A SPANNER IN THE WORKS

Windy Town/The Downtown Lights/Leave Virginia Alone/Sweetheart Like You/This/Lady Luck/You're The Star/Muddy, Sam And Otis/Hang On St Christopher/Delicious/Soothe Me/Purple Heather

Produced by Rod Stewart, Andy Taylor, Bernard Edwards, James Newton-Howard, Lenny Waronker, Michael Oslin & Trevor Horn.

UK: Warner Bros. Records 9362-45867-2 (1995).

10.06.95: 5-**4**-6-11-26-30-45-54-54-60-59-70-79

Canada
19.05.95: 49-8-**2-2**-12-17-17-18-19-22-24-30-41-55-59-64-76-82-82-86-91-98

Australia
26.06.95: peaked at no.**31**, charted for 5 weeks

Austria
11.06.95: 31-**13**-29-23-22-18-25-39-35

Belgium
17.06.95: 32-**22**-30-41

Germany
12.06.95: 10-10-**9**-11-14-19-20-23-30-34-41-40-41-54-55-67

Netherlands
17.06.95: 67-26-**23**-36-58-92

New Zealand
2.07.95: **13**-19-22-20-31-31-47

Norway
10.06.95: 25-18-13-**6**-13-15-25-29-39

Sweden
2.06.95: 8-**2**-3-5-7-10-10-13-16-30-25-46-46-48

SVERIGETOPPLISTAN - ALBUMS TOP 60 ← 1995-06-09 →	1995 ∨	09.06.1995 ∨	Show

#	LW		Artist Title	Label Company	Prefix Suffix	W
1	1	>	**Gyllene Tider** Halmstads pärlor	Parlophone EMI	4751492	3
2	8	^	**Rod Stewart** A Spanner In The Works	Warner WMS	2458672	2
3	4	^	**Eric Gadd** Floating	Metronome WMS	0101592	9

Switzerland
11.06.95: **15**-16-17-24-25-33-27-32-33-50-49-x-49

USA
24.06.95: 36-**35**-43-59-64-65-82-86

A SPANNER ON THE WORKS, which was released in May 1995, was the second Rod Stewart album Andy Taylor worked on. The album was record at four different studios,

A&M Studios and Ocean Way Recording in Los Angeles, Hollywood's Herschel House, and Woodstock House in Wicker, Ireland.

Andy co-wrote one song on the album, *Delicious*, with Rod Stewart and Robin LeMesurier, and he co-produced the track with Rod Stewart. He also played guitar on *Delicious*, and on a further two tracks, *You're The Star* and Rod Stewart's cover of Sam Cooke's *Soothe Me*.

Five singles were released from *A SPANNER IN THE WORKS*, but only one of them ~ *You're The Star* ~ had a connection with Andy.

A SPANNER IN THE WORKS charted at no.2 in Canada and Sweden, no.4 in the UK, no.6 in Norway, no.9 in Germany, no.13 in Austria and New Zealand, no.15 in Switzerland, no.22 in Belgium, no.23 in the Netherlands, no.31 in Australia and no.35 in the United States.

18 ~ MEDAZZALAND

Medazzaland/Big Bang Generation/Electric Barbarella/Drums (Live)/Who Do You Think You Are?/Silva Halo/Be My con/Buried In The Sand/Michael You've Got A Lot To Answer For/Midnight Sun/So Long Suicide/Undergoing Treatment

Japan Bonus Track: *Ball And Chain*

Produced by TV Mania, Anthony J. Resta, Bob St. John & Syn Pro Tokyo.

UK & Europe: Tape Modern 538805881 (2022).

MEDAZZALAND wasn't released physically in the UK and Europe until 2022.

USA: Capitol Records CDP 7243 8 33876 2 (1997).

1.11.97: **58**

Canada
27.10.97: **66**

Japan
10.09.97: peaked at no.**37**, charted for 2 weeks

Duran Duran recorded their ninth studio album during 1996 and 1997 at a host of different studios in the UK and the United States. In January 1997, however, John Taylor decided to part company with the band, reducing Duran Duran to a trio again: Nick Rhodes, Simon Le Bon and Warren Cuccurullo.

The three remaining band members re-recorded most of the songs they had worked on with John, but he was credited with playing bass on four songs: *Medazzalin*, *Big Band Sensation*, *Be My Icon* and *So Long Suicide*.

The album's unusual title was inspired by the dental drug midazolam, which Simon Le Bon had been administered when he visited the dentists.

'It's the strangest thing,' he said, 'in dentistry you need to be awake so that you can respond to commands to keep your mouth open and move your jaw and things, so they give you this stuff and you go into this state where you are awake and you respond, but you don't really know what's going on.'

'I wanted *MEDDAZALAND* to capture the 1990s in the way *RIO* expressed the 1980s,' said Nick Rhodes. 'The day we make records that aren't as exciting as those we've done previously, we should stop making records.'

Only two singles were released from *MEDAZZALAND*, and both were modest hits:

- *Out Of My Mind*
- *Electric Barbarella*

Out Of My Mind originally featured on the soundtrack album to the 1997 film, *The Saint*.

MEDAZZALAND was released in Japan, Latin America and North America ahead of its planned release in Europe, and the album charted at no.37 in Japan, no.58 in the United States and no.66 in Canada.

This poor showing meant plans to release the album in the UK and Europe were pushed back and back, and eventually the album was shelved.

'It was pretty much a commercial disaster,' admitted Nick Rhodes, 'but I stand by it, absolutely. There are a few songs on there that are as good as anything we've ever done.'

Disappointing sales meant Duran Duran's contract with EMI was dissolved, following the release of *MEDAZZALAND*, and the record company passed ownership of the album's master tapes to the band, along with audio and video of Duran Duran's 1995 and 1997 concerts.

Duran Duran did consider releasing *MEDAZZALAND* in the UK themselves, but instead they signed with Hollywood Records, and began working on a new album.

MEDAZZALAND was released digitally in Europe in 2008, but the UK had to wait until 2021 for a digital release. The following year, to mark the album's 25th anniversary, *MEZZADALAND* was finally released physically in Europe, including the UK, as a CD and as a double neon pink vinyl album, which was also issued in North America.

19 ~ GREATEST

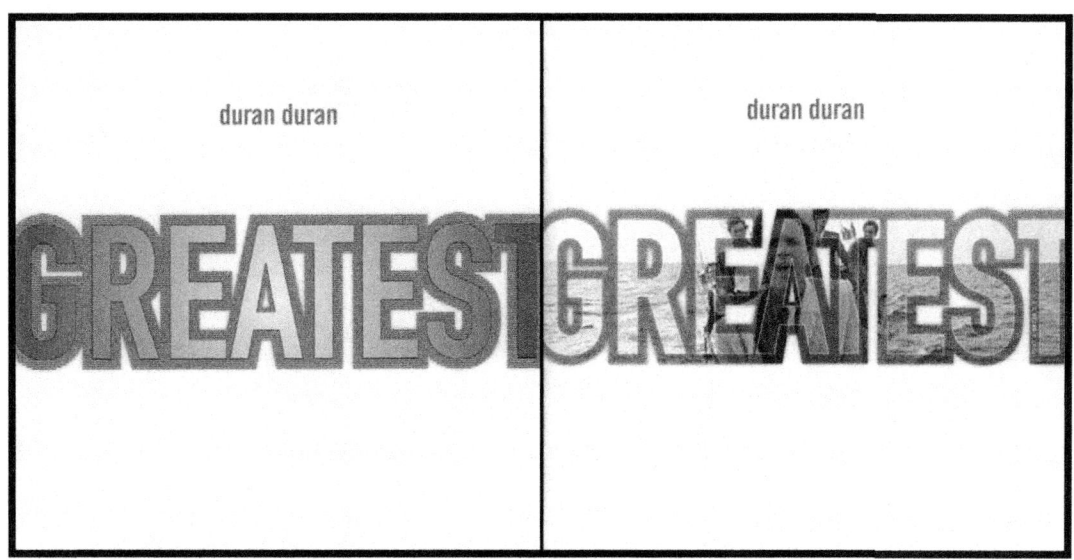

Is There Something I Should Know?/The Reflex/A View To A Kill/Ordinary World (Single Version)/Save A Prayer (US Single Version)/Rio (US Edit)/Hungry Like The Wolf/Girls On Film/Planet Earth (Single Version)/Union Of The Snake/New Moon On Monday/The Wild Boys/Notorious/I Don't Want Your Love (Shep Pettibone 7" Mix)/All She Wants Is (45 Mix)/Electric Barbarella (Edit)/Serious (Edit)/Skin Trade (Radio Cut)/Come Undone (Edit)

UK: EMI 496 2392 (1998).

21.11.98: 15-24-25-27-28-28-34-27-35-41-44-50-46-56-61-49-56-68-60-71-80-92-90-x-95-85-91
13.10.01: 32-29-39-65
12.01.02: 67-73-71-88
6.07.02: 83
28.02.04: **4-4**-9-24-24-40-46-59-50-46-58-69-86
25.09.04: 41-41-44-45-63-89-x-90
8.01.05: 77-69-77-85
5.11.05: 67-83
27.01.07: 59-54-81
21.07.07: 91
2.04.11: 37-57

Austria
7.02.99: **30**-46-48-50

Belgium
28.11.98: 44-31-23-20-**19-19**-20-24-25-31-33-42-50-50

Denmark
8.07.05: 39-29-25-**12**-33

Finland
7.11.98: 32-29-31-38
10.04.99: **13**-34

France
4.04.99: **23**

Italy
14.10.04: peaked at no.**22**, charted for 33 weeks

Netherlands
14.11.98: 92-86-97-43-29-27-26-**24**-25-31-38-49-64-75-82-90-90-40-37-89-x-98-97-97-
  97-93-84-100
22.09.01: 79-83-91-x-x-90-85
4.06.05: 43-31-61-69-82

New Zealand
15.11.98: 21-21-27-31-45-48
30.11.03: 28-25-**12**-22-38-34-45-x-x-x-49

Norway
27.12.97: 39
26.12.98: 40-27-27-**13**-35-34

Sweden
16.03.00: **38**-46

Having parted company with Duran Duran, EMI wasted no time in putting out a 'best of' compilation album, titled simply *GREATEST*.

In the UK, to promote the compilation, *Electric Barbarella* was issued as a single ~ this was the first time it was made available in the UK, as the *MEDAZZALAND* album was cancelled in the UK and mainland Europe.

When it was originally released, *GREATEST* achieved no.13 in Finland and Norway, no.15 in the UK, no.19 in Belgium, no.21 in New Zealand, no.23 in France, no.24 in the Netherlands, no.30 in Austria and no.38 in Sweden. The compilation was also a very minor no.170 hit in the United States.

GREATEST was released on VHS as a home video, which featured the following music videos:

Planet Earth/Girls On Film (Uncensored)/The Chauffeur (Uncensored)/Hungry Like The Wolf/Save A Prayer/Rio/Is There Something I Should Know?/Union Of The Snake/ New Moon On Monday/The Reflex/The Wild Boys (Extended Version)/A View To A Kill/Notorious/Skin Trade/I Don't Want Your Love/All She Wants Is/Serious/Burning Ground/Ordinary World/Come Undone/Electric Barbarella/My Own Way

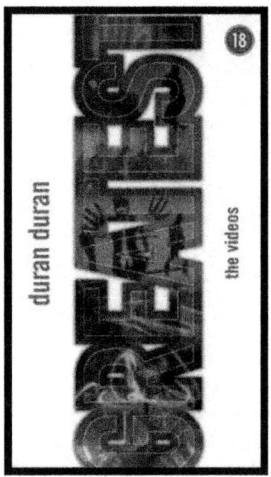

Duran Duran's classic five-man line-up reformed in 2001 and, frustrated by their inability to secure the kind of record contract they wanted, the band embarked on a world tour in 2003, as a way of proving they were still popular. The tour sold out, and helped to boost sales of *GREATEST*, which re-entered the charts and achieved a new peak in several countries. Second time around, the compilation charted at no.4 in the UK, no.12 in Denmark and New Zealand, and no.22 in Italy.

In 2003, *GREATEST* was released as 2 x DVDs, which as well as alternate versions of some music videos also included:

- *A Day In The Life* Featurette
- Midsummer Night's Tube Feature
- *A View To A Kill* Interview
- *The Wild Boys* Interview
- *SEVEN AND THE RAGGED TIGER* Interview
- Electronic Press Kit for *LIBERTY*
- TV Commercial for *DURAN DURAN (THE WEDDING ALBUM)*

20 ~ POP TRASH

Someone Else Not Me/Lava lamp/Playing With Uranium/Hallucinating Elvis/Starting To Remember/Pop Trash Movie/Fragment/Mars Meets Venus/Lady Xanax/The Sun Doesn't Shine Forever/Kiss Goodbye/Last Day On Earth

International Bonus Tracks: *Un Autre Que Moi* (French version of *Someone Else Not Me*)/*Alguien Que No Soy Yo* (Spanish version of *Someone Else Not Me*)/*Prototypes*

Produced by TV Mania & Syn Productions.

UK: Hollywood Records 0107512HWR (2000).

1.07.00: **53**

Germany
26.06.00: **80**

Italy
10.06.00: peaked at no.**23**, charted for 5 weeks

Japan
7.06.00: **76**

Having signed with Hollywood Records, the three remaining members of Duran Duran started working on what would be the band's tenth studio album immediately.

'To me,' said Warren Cuccurullo, '*POP TRASH* is all the stuff we're surrounded by. It's soundbites from television, it's things on the internet, it's displays in shop windows and new gadgets that we buy and packaging.'

But, following John Taylor quitting the band, Nick Rhodes and Simon Le Bon found it tough going.

'Things felt very different without John,' said Nick Rhodes. 'Although he had departed during *MEDAZZALAND*, he had been part of the initial writing sessions and played on several tracks of that album. Our writing process became very different for *POP TRASH*. Also, Simon was having difficulty with some of the lyrics at this time, so I ended up writing more of them that I would have anticipated. We had a new label, Hollywood Records, which proved to be, at best, exasperating.'

Andrew Day was responsible for the album sleeve of *POP TRASH*, which depicted a rhinestone-encrusted car once owned by Liberace.

Only one single was issued from *POP TRASH* in most countries, with a further two tracks promoted as singles in Germany and Japan, respectively.

- *Someone Else Not Me*
- *Playing With Uranium*
- *Last Day On Earth*

Someone Else Not Me was a Top 30 hit in Italy and charted at no.53 in the UK, but it wasn't a hit anywhere else. *Playing With Uranium* was released as a promotional CD single in Germany, while *Last Day On Earth* was issued as a single exclusively in Japan, but neither song was a hit.

POP TRASH only achieved Top 40 status in one country, Italy, where it peaked at no.23. The album spent a solitary week on the UK's album chart at no.53, and it was a minor hit in Japan and Germany. In the United States, the album stalled at a lowly no.135.

In March 2001, following poor sales of *POP TRASH*, Duran Duran announced their contract with Hollywood Records had been terminated.

'Never was there a place less like a record company,' said Nick Rhodes. 'You're listening to these people, and finally I had to say, "How funny that your corporate logo is a large pair of ears, yet not one of you in here happens to have any".'

Simon Le Bon admitted *POP TRASH* was a complete disaster.

'I was thinking, "How do I get out of this?",' he said. 'I missed John terribly. The reason we never got a permanent bass player was quite simply because the seat was still left there for him … We realised that Duran Duran without a single Taylor was pretty tricky and not something people would readily accept, no matter how good the album might have been. It was a marketing nightmare … morale in the band was at an all-time low.'

In August 2000, while on tour in the United States to promote *POP TRASH*, John Taylor invited Nick Rhodes and Simon Le Bon to his home for lunch.

'Simon started talking about he'd been unhappy for some time,' said Nick, 'and wanted to move on. The background to this is that as far as Simon was concerned his relationship with Warren had come to an end … It wasn't anything personal, but Simon wasn't happy and didn't want to make another Duran Duran album with Warren.'

There was talk of the band's classic five-man line-up reuniting and, as Nick and Simon continued the band's tour, John contacted the other two Taylors, Andy and Roger.

'John called me out of the blue,' said Roger. 'He asked me if I fancied getting the band back together soon. I was really shocked as I really thought it was in the past, and there had been a lot of water under the bridge.'

But Roger said yes and, when John rang him, so did Andy.

'I wouldn't have done it if Roger hadn't said yes,' said Andy, 'but I think we all came to the realisation that you're never going to do anything as spectacular as Duran Duran again.'

Warren Cuccurullo had no idea what was being planned until, following the end of the band's tour, he headed for home.

'The next thing I heard,' he recalled, 'was when a letter arrived by special delivery at my house sacking me from the band. I read it and I was absolutely shocked because no one had said anything to me.'

Warren immediately phoned Simon, only to be told, 'Sorry, Warren, it's got to be like this', because Simon and the others were getting the original band together again.

'The initial feeling was one of loss,' said Warren. 'I'd dedicated everything to Duran Duran and then it was gone, and I was shocked that they didn't tell me to my face.'

'After that,' said Nick Rhodes, 'Simon and Warren did speak at great length about everything … It wasn't as if Warren had done anything particularly wrong, Simon just felt that it had run its time and he would have started the ball rolling in any case, whether the rest of Duran Duran got together or not.'

The five members of Duran Duran met up in London towards the end of 2000, to discuss their proposed reunion.

'When we sat down and decided how to do this,' said Andy Taylor, 'Nick said, "We've got to do an album." And I said, "Thank God you've said that, because we don't have a future if we don't actually do something new".'

WELCOME TO THE MONKEY HOUSE

Welcome To The Monkey House/We Used To Be Friends/Plan A/The Dope (Wonderful You)/I Am A Scientist/I Am Over It/The Dandy Warhols Love Almost Everyone/Insincere Because I/You Were The Last High/Heavenly/I Am Sound/Hit Rock Bottom/You Came In Burned

Produced by Nick Rhodes, Courtney Taylor-Taylor & Tony Visconti.

UK: Capitol Records/Parlophone 7243 5 90123 1 5 (2003).

31.05.03: **20**-37-59-99

Australia
9.06.03: peakcd at no.**7**, charted for 10 weeks

Belgium
7.06.03: **46**

Germany
2.06.03: **75**

New Zealand
18.01.04: 43-**31**

Switzerland
1.06.03: **83**-98

Norway
31.05.03: **3**-4-8-15-16-16-17-13-12-22-19-30-38-29-34

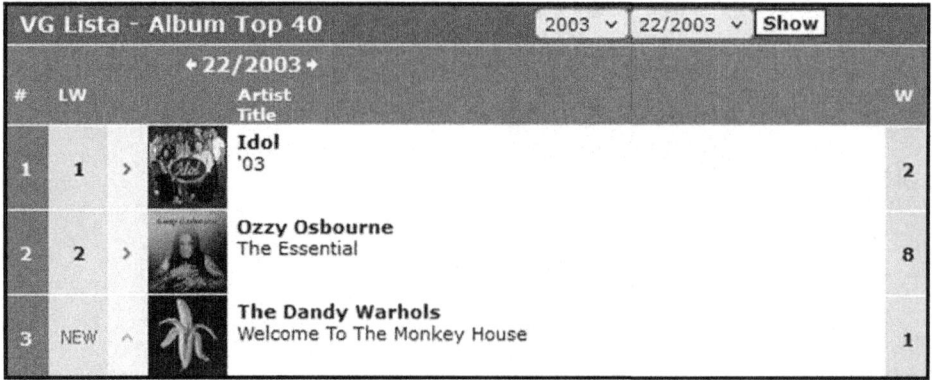

The Dandy Warhols, an American rock band, recorded their fourth studio album *WELCOME TO THE MONKEY HOUSE* between September 2001 and December 2002.

Originally, the album was mixed by Russell Elevado, but Capitol Records weren't happy with the result and decided to release a more polished version mixed by Nick Rhodes instead. Nick was also credited with playing additional synthesizers on nine of the album's 13 tracks, including the three singles:

- *We Used To Be Friends*
- *You Were The Last High*
- *Plan A*

The first two singles were both Top 40 hits, but *Plan A* ~ which featured backing vocals by Simon Le Bon ~ could only manage no.66 in the UK.

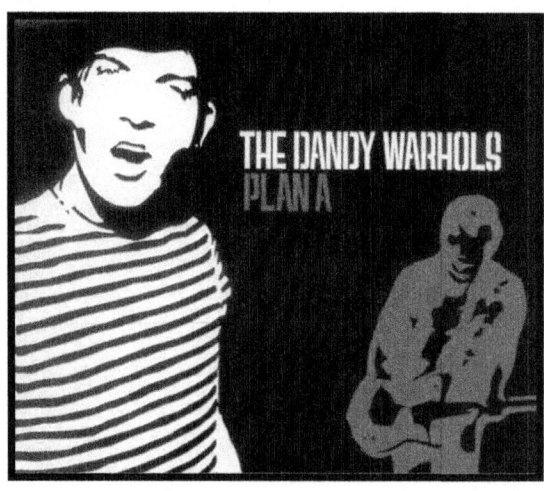

Plan A was released as a limited edition 7" blue vinyl single in the UK and Europe.

21 ~ ASTRONAUT

(Reach Up For The) Sunrise/Want You More/What Happens Tomorrow/Astronaut/
Bedroom Toys/Nice/Taste The Summer/Finest Hour/Chains/One Of Those Days/Point
Of No Return/Still Breathing

Japan Bonus Track: *Virus*

Produced by Duran Duran, Dallas Austin, Don Gilmore, Mark Tinley & Nile Rodgers.

UK: Epic 517920 2 (2004), 517920 5 (Deluxe Edition, 2004).

23.10.04: **3**-17-42-66-93

Pos	LW	Title, Artist		Peak Pos	WoC
1	New	**10 YEARS OF HITS** RONAN KEATING	POLYDOR	1	1
2	1 ↓	**AROUND THE SUN** REM	WARNER BROS	1	2
3	New	**ASTRONAUT** DURAN DURAN	EPIC	3	1

Australia
31.10.04: **22**

Austria
24.10.04: **27**-54

Belgium
16.10.04: 94-44-**40**-61-82-99

Canada
10.04: peaked at no.**9**

Denmark
22.10.04: **8**-25-36

France
10.10.04: **87**

Germany
25.10.04: **23**-65-78

Italy
14.10.04: peaked at no.**2**, charted for 31 weeks

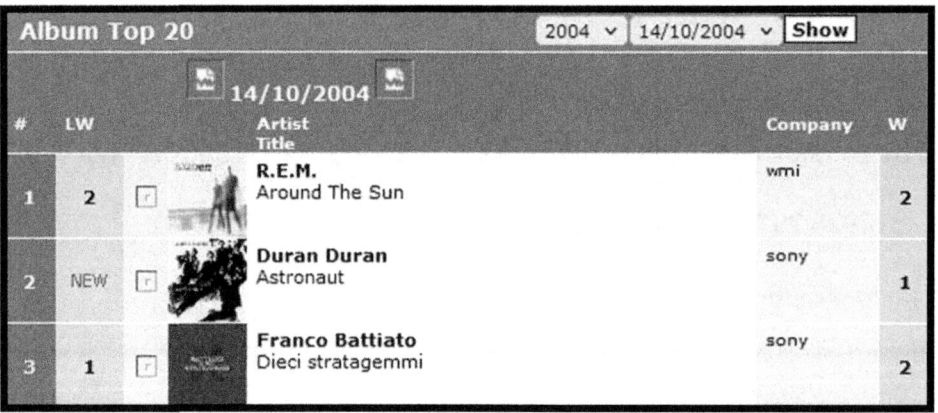

Netherlands
16.10.04: **17**-31-45-59-75-98

New Zealand
25.10.04: **29**

Sweden
22.10.04: **41**

Switzerland
24.10.04: **21**-29-57-75

USA
30.10.04: **17**-38-60-93

Having agreed to reunite the band's classic five-man line-up, Duran Duran wrote thirty or so new songs during a number of sessions from 2001 onwards, which took place in the south of France.

But, at the time, Duran Duran didn't have a record contract and were struggling to find a record company that would give them the control and independence they wanted, together with a commitment to strong promotion and a deal for more than just one album. Too many record companies viewed Duran Duran as an 'oldies' band who had nothing new or exciting to offer.

Duran Duran didn't see things that way, of course, and determined to prove how popular they still were the band embarked on a world tour in 2003, playing sold-out dates in the UK, Australasia, Japan and the United States. The band made a point of including new songs, including *Beautiful Colours, Still Breathing, Sunrise, Virus* and *What Happens Tomorrow*, in their set-list.

Around this time, to the band's dismay, a teaser CD was leaked on the internet, which featured short demo versions of six songs, namely *Virus, Sunrise, TV vs. Radio, Taste The Summer, Salt In The Rainbow* and *Pretty Ones*. Only two of these, *Sunrise* (as *(Reach Up For The) Sunrise)* and *Taste Of Summer*, made the final track listing of Duran Duran's new album.

Following their hugely successful tour, Duran Duran signed a four album deal with Sony's Epic Records in June 2004, and recorded the band's eleventh studio album *ASTRONAUT* at London's Sphere Studios. It was the first album for twenty-one years, since *SEVEN AND THE RAGGED TIGER*, to feature Duran Duran's classic five-man line-up.

As well as the standard CD and double album release, *ASTRONAUT* was also issued as a limited edition CD + DVD, with the DVD titled 'Live At Wembley 2004'. The DVD featured:

(Reach Up For The) Sunrise/Hungry Like The Wolf/What Happens Tomorrow/New Religion/The Wild Boys/(Reach Up For The (Sunrise) (Video)

Two singles and a promotional single were released from *ASTRONAUT*:

- *(Reach Up For The) Sunrise*
- *What Happens Tomorrow*
- *Nice*

(Reach Up For The) Sunrise and *What Happens Tomorrow* were both hits, but *Nice* was only issued as a promotional CD single and it failed to chart anywhere.

ASTRONAUT gave Duran Duran their biggest hit album for more than a decade, rising to no.2 in Italy, no.3 in the UK, no.8 in Denmark, no.9 in Canada, no.17 in the Netherlands and the United States, no.21 in Switzerland, no.22 in Australia, no.23 in Germany, no.27 in Austria, no.29 in New Zealand, no.40 in Belgium and no.41 in Sweden.

'I would have liked it to have sold more copies,' admitted John Taylor, 'but it's put the band back on the map now, and the next one hopefully will do more for us.'

22 ~ RED CARPET MASSACRE

The Valley/Red Carpet Massacre/Nite-Runner/Falling Down/Box Full O' Honey/Skin Divers/Tempted/Tricked Out/Zoom In/She's Too Much/Dirty Great Monster/Last Man Standing

Japan Bonus Track: *Cry Baby Cry*

iTunes Bonus Tracks (various countries): *Cry Baby Cry/Nite-Runner (Live)/Red Carpet Massacre (Live)*

USA Vinyl Bonus Tracks: *Cry Baby Cry/Dirty Great Monster/Last Man Standing*

DVD (Deluxe Edition): The Album/The Artwork/The Video/The Campaign/The Out-Takes/The Stills

Produced by Duran Duran, Jim Beanz, Jimmy Douglass, Justin Timberlake, Nate 'Danja' Hills & Timbaland.

UK: Epic 88697 07362 2 (2007).

1.12.07: **44**-96-90

Germany
30.11.07: **85**

Italy
22.11.07: peaked at no.**10**, charted for 11 weeks

Netherlands
24.11.07: **73**

Switzerland
2.12.07: **39**-96

USA
1.12.07: **37**

Duran Duran began working on the band's twelfth studio album ~ working title 'Reportage' ~ with producer Michael Patterson in September 2005.

'The record will be in some ways a homage to our roots as a band,' said Roger Taylor, 'more direct and a return to our dance and new wave origins.'

But, after just one album together, disagreements within the band led to Andy Taylor quitting Duran Duran for the second time. According to Andy, he favoured a more electric sound, whereas Simon Le Bon wanted to work with people like Timbaland and Justin Timberlake, and he admitted there was a lot of bickering within the band, especially between him, Simon and Nick Rhodes.

On 25th October 2006, Andy's split from the rest of the band was confirmed on Duran Duran's official website.

'As of last weekend,' the statement read, 'the four of us have dissolved our partnership and will be continuing as Duran Duran without Andy, as we have reached a point in our relationship where there is an unworkable gulf between us and we can no longer effectively function together.'

Following Andy's departure, although the band had completed 14 new songs, the four remaining members of Duran Duran agreed to shelve the *REPORTAGE* album.

'When we sat down and listened to what we had done on our own,' said Simon Le Bon, 'we didn't feel we had a lead track, so we got in touch with Timbaland, who was the only producer out there that we knew we all liked.'

As well as Timbaland, Duran Duran worked with Justin Timberlake and Nate 'Danja' Hills on their new album. Guitarist Dom Brown was drafted, to play with the band both in the studio and live in concert, but he was never officially considered to be a member of Duran Duran.

Working with Timbaland took Duran Duran outside their comfort zone.

'The thing was,' said Nick Rhodes, 'we got an opportunity to work with Timbaland, so we thought, "Great, let's go for it!" When Timbaland saw the guitar and the bass and the drums come into the studio, I think he was mortified, because everything's in a box for those guys.'

Duran Duran's twelfth studio album, titled *RED CARPET MASSACRE*, was finally released in November 2007. Only one single, *Falling Down*, was issued from the album ~

it featured backing vocals by Justin Timberlake, and gave Duran Duran what is to date their most recent Top 40 single.

A second track, *Skin Divers*, was released exclusively as a promotional CD single in Hong Kong.

RED CARPET MASSACRE, compared with *ASTRONAUT*, sold poorly ~ it was a Top 10 hit in Italy, but could only manage no.37 in the United States, no.39 in Switzerland and no.44 in the UK. The album was also a minor hit in the Netherlands and Germany, peaking at no.73 and no.85, respectively, but it missed the charts altogether in many countries.

'I do think *RED CARPET MASSACRE* was a bit of a personality issue,' reflected Simon Le Bon. 'We thought we could make an urban album and our fans would like it, but they left us in no doubt about their response.'

23 ~ ALL YOU NEED IS NOW

All You Need Is Now/Blame The Machines/Being Followed/Leave A Light On/Safe (In The Heat Of The Moment)/Girl Panic!/A Diamond In The Mind/The Man Who Stole A Leopard/Other People's Lives/Mediterranea/Too Bad You're So Beautiful/Runway Runaway/Return To Now/Before The Rain

UK Bonus Tracks (Deluxe Edition): *Networker Nation/All You Need Is Now (Youth Kills Mix)*

UK Bonus CD Single (Deluxe Edition): *All You Need Is Now (R2V2 Mix)/(Tom Middleton Cosmos Remix)/(Pablo La Rosa Remix)*

UK Bonus 12" (Deluxe Edition, Limited Edition Clear Vinyl): *Networker Nation/This Lost Weekend/Too Close To The Sun/Early Summer Nerves*

UK Bonus 12" (Deluxe Edition, Limited Edition Clear Vinyl): *All You Need Is Now (Tom Middleton Cosmos Remix)/(Pablo La Rosa Remix)*

UK Bonus 12" (Deluxe Edition, Limited Edition Clear Vinyl): *All You Need Is Now (Youth Kills Mix)/(Youth Kills Alt Doom Mix)/Girls Panic! (David Lynch Mix)/ (Johnson Somerset & John Monkman RMX Remix)*

USA Bonus Track (Deluxe Edition): *Networker Nation*

Best Buy Bonus Tracks (Deluxe Edition): *Too Close To The Sun/Early Summer Nerves/ Networker Nation*

USA Bonus DVD (Deluxe Edition): The Making Of *ALL YOU NEED IS NOW*/All You Need Is … Mark Ronson/The Art Of Clunie Reid/On Se Of The Photoshoot/*All You Need Is Now (Video)*/Behind The Scenes At The Videoshoot/Track By Track

Japan Bonus Disc: *Networker Nation/Too Close To The Sun/Early Summer Nerves/This Lost Weekend/All You Need Is Now (Youth Kills Mix)*

Produced by Duran Duran & Mark Ronson.

UK: Tape Modern Duran 01 (2011), Duran DLX 01 (Deluxe Edition) (2011), The Vinyl Factory VF026 (Limited Edition 2 x LP plus 3 x 12" Clear Vinyl, 2011).

2.04.11: **11**-32-52-80

Austria
1.04.11: **62**

Belgium
9.04.11: **77**-78-82

Canada
04.11: peaked at no.**52**

Germany
1.04.11: **39**-75

Italy
31.03.11: peaked at no.**10**, charted for 11 weeks

Netherlands
9.04.11: **23**-45-50-75-87

Switzerland
3.04.11: **28**-85

USA
9.04.11: **29**

Duran Duran wrote and recorded their thirteenth studio album between February and August 2010 at four London studios ~ Air Edel, Eastcote, Metropolis and Sphere ~ and at 6 Nassau in Toronto, Canada.

A 9-track version of the album, titled *ALL YOU NEED IS NOW*, was released digitally towards the end of December 2010, with a full physical release in a number of different formats following in March 2011.

'It seemed to me that he (producer Mark Ronson) had a magic touch,' said John Taylor, 'and I like him a lot. We did go for a retro-sound on this record, but it was different. He moved his microscope from Sixties soul to Eighties electro-pop, and applied the same kind of detail … He wasn't interested in an Old World type of song on there. He wanted to have that quirky, dark pop thing the first few Duran albums had.'

Three promotional singles were released to promote *ALL YOU WANT IS NOW*, none of which entered any mainstream charts:

- *All You Need Is Now*
- *Girl Panic!*
- *Leave A Light On*

All You Need Is Now, as well as being issued as a free iTunes download, was released as a promotional CD single in the UK, Europe and the United States. *Girl Panic!* was released as a promotional CD single in the UK, and as a limited edition 7" single in the United States, as part of Record Store Day 2011. *Leave A Light On* was issued as a promotional CD single in both the UK and the United States.

Although not a massive success, *ALL YOU NEED IS NOW* did chart at no.10 in Italy, no.11 in the UK, no.23 in the Netherlands, no.28 in Switzerland, no.29 in the United States, no.39 in Germany and no.52 in Canada.

24 ~ LIVE 2011 – A DIAMOND IN THE MIND

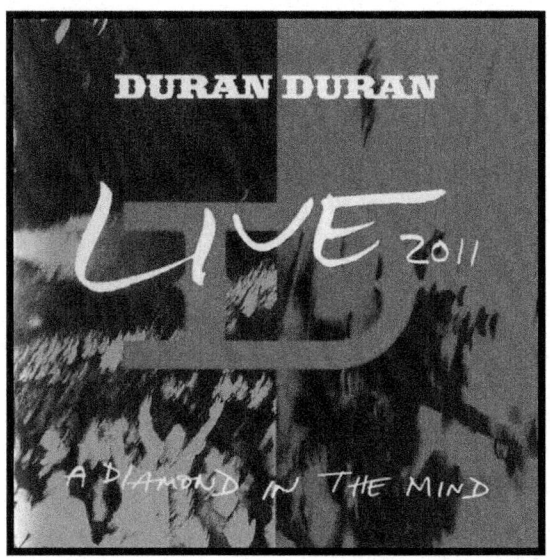

Before The Rain/Planet Earth/A View To A Kill/All You Need Is Now/Come Undone/ Blame The Machines/The Reflex/Girl Panic!/Ordinary World/Notorious/Hungry Like The Wolf/(Reach Up For The) Sunrise/The Wild Boys/Relax/Rio

DVD: *Return To Now (Intro)/Before The Rain/Planet Earth/A View To A Kill/All You Need Is Now/Blame The Machines/Safe (In The Heat Of The Moment)/The Reflex/The Man Who Stole A Leopard/Girl Panic!/White Lines (Don't Do It)/Careless Memories/ Ordinary World/Notorious/Hungry Like The Wolf/(Reach Up For The) Sunrise/The Wild Boys/Relax/Rio/A Diamond In The Mind (Credits)*

DVD Bonus Features: Duran Duran 2011 (Documentary)/*Come Undone/Is There Something I Should Know?*

Directed by Gavin Elder.

UK: Eagle Records EAGCD487 (2012).

LIVE 2011 – A DIAMOND IN THE MIND wasn't a hit in the UK.

Germany
13.07.12: **59**

Italy
12.07.12: peaked at no.**40**, charted for 3 weeks

LIVE 2011 – A DIAMOND IN THE MIND was filmed at the Manchester Arena in Manchester, England, on the 16th December 2011, during Duran Duran's All You Need Is Now Tour.

As well as the four members of Duran Duran, the concert featured:

- Dom Brown on guitar and backing vocals.
- Simon Willescroft on keyboards and saxophone.
- Dawne Adams on percussion.
- Anna Ross on backing vocals.

LIVE 2011 – A DIAMOND IN THE MIND was released on CD and as a home DVD. The album version was a Top 40 success, just, as it rose to no.40 in Italy and no.59 in Germany. However, the live album failed to chart in most countries.

In 2014, *LIVE 2011 – A DIAMOND IN THE MIND* was released as a limited edition double vinyl album, as follows:

LP1: *Before The Rain/Planet Earth/A View To A Kill/All You Need Is Now/Come Undone/Blame The Machines/The Reflex/Girl Panic!*

LP2: *Is There Something I Should Know?/Ordinary World/Notorious/Hungry Like The Wolf/(Reach Up For The) Sunrise/The Wild Boys/Rio*

25 ~ PAPER GODS

Paper Gods/Last Night In The City/You Kill Me With Silence/Pressure Off/Face For Today/Danceophobia/What Are The Chances?/Sunset Garage/Change The Skyline/ Butterfly Girl/Only In Dreams/The Universe Alone

Bonus Tracks (Deluxe Edition): *Planet Roaring/Valentine Stones/Northern Lights*

Target Edition Bonus Tracks: *On Evil Beach/Cinderella Ride*

Produced by Duran Duran, Joshua Blair, Mark Ronson, Mr Hudson & Nile Rodgers.

UK: Warner Bros. Records 9362-49264-2 (2015), 9362-49251-4 (Deluxe Edition) (2015).

24.09.15: **5**-39-57-99
3.12.15: 77

Australia
27.09.15: **19**

Austria
25.09.15: **24**-67

Belgium
19.09.15: **19**-49-75

Canada
3.10.15: **18**

Denmark
25.09.15: **27**

Finland
22.08.15: **28**

France
19.09.15: **60**

Germany
18.09.15: **24**

Italy
17.09.15: peaked at no.**2**, charted for 9 weeks

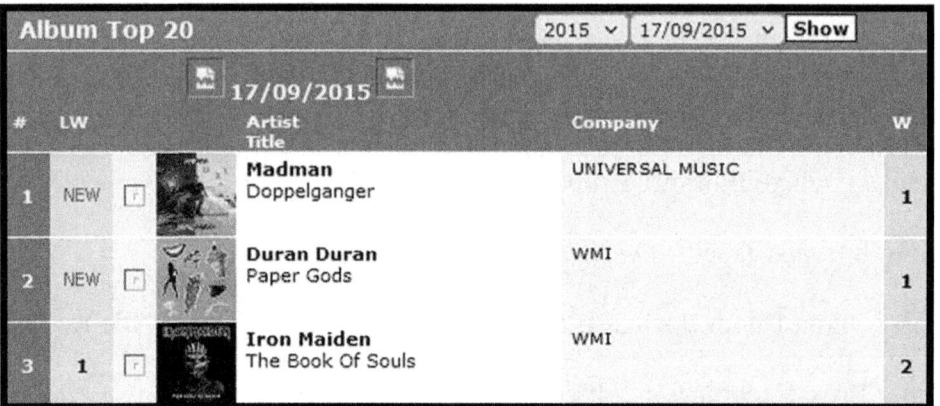

Netherlands
19.09.15: **4**-43-70

New Zealand
21.09.15: **24**

Switzerland
20.09.15: **15**-69

USA
3.10.15: **10**-76
23.01.16: 45

Duran Duran recorded their fourteenth studio album *PAPER GODS* at three different studios, London's Battersea Park and Zelig, and The Village in Los Angeles, California.

'We had little idea of what future direction our fourteenth album would take,' said Roger Taylor, 'other than it should be very different from its predecessor. At times we laboured, other times we were incredibly inspired, but with the arrival of the amazing men and women who came into our world, the puzzle slowly unravelled, and we were taken on a journey that ended some four years later.'

The album's distinctive sleeve design was taken from a painting titled 'Sky Backdrop' by artist Alex Israel, which depicted icons that represented Duran Duran's history. For example, the eye and lips (*RIO*), Eiffel Tower (*A View To A Kill*), snake (*Union Of The Snake*), tiger (*SEVEN AND THE RAGGED TIGER*) and an ice cream cone (*Perfect Day*).

'When we first saw it none of the band liked it,' John Taylor later admitted. 'All our wives and girlfriends did. They talked us into it. Now we all love it!'

Duran Duran promoted the release of *PAPER GODS* with a tour of the UK and the United States, and by releasing three singles:

- *Pressure Off*
- *Last Night In The City*
- *What Are The Chances?*

Pressure Off featured Janelle Monáe and Nile Rodgers, while *Last Night In The City* featured Kiesza.

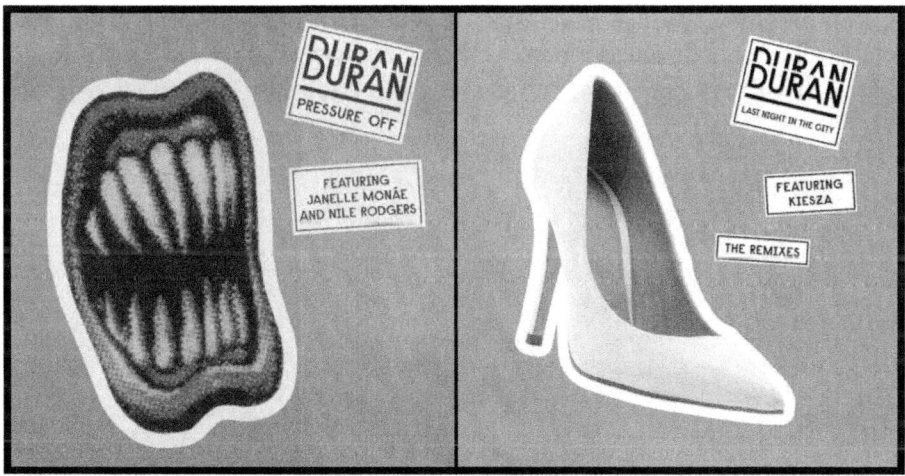

What Are The Chances? was released as a promotional CD single in Japan and the UK only.

As streaming 'sales' now counted towards charts around the world, vintage artists like Duran Duran rarely attracted sufficiently high streaming numbers to enter the singles charts, and as a consequence *Pressure Off*, *Last Night In The City* and *What Are The Chances?* all failed to chart anywhere.

Albums, thanks to physical and download sales, generally fare much better chart-wise than singles, and so it was with *PAPER GODS*. In the UK, the album made its chart debut at no.5, which meant Duran Duran joined a select number of bands to achieve a Top 5 album in four consecutive decades.

Elsewhere, *PAPER GODS* achieved no.2 in Italy, no.4 in the Netherlands, no.10 in the United States, no.15 in Switzerland, no.18 in Canada, no.19 in Australia and Belgium, no.24 in Austria, Germany and New Zealand, no.27 in Denmark, no.28 in Finland and no.60 in France.

'Each album becomes a chapter of our lives,' said Nick Rhodes, 'a long diary entry filled with precious memories, and I think this particular journey was a very special one for everyone in the band. It always begins the same way, with writing the songs, but that process dictates the development of the project and each block of musical DNA changes the trajectory.'

26 ~ FUTURE PAST

Invisible/All Of You/Give It All Up/Anniversary/Future Past/Beautiful Lies/Tonight United//Nothing Less/Hammerhead/More Joy!/Falling

Deluxe Edition: *Invisible/All Of You/Give It All Up/Anniversary/Future Past/Velvet Newton/Beautiful Lies/Tonight United/Wing/Nothing Less/Laughing Boy/Hammerhead/ Invocation/More Joy!/Falling*

Produced by Duran Duran, Erol Alkan, Giorgio Moroder, Hannie Knox, Joshua Blair, Kaz Haga, Mathieu Kranich & Peter Karlsson.

UK: BMG/Tape Modern 538693602 (2021), 538696562 (Deluxe Edition) (2021).

4.11.21: **3**-20-83

Pos	LW	Title, Artist		Peak Pos	WoC
1	New	**THE LOCKDOWN SESSIONS** ELTON JOHN	EMI	1	1
2	New	**BLUE BANISTERS** LANA DEL REY	POLYDOR	2	1
3	New	**FUTURE PAST** DURAN DURAN	BMG	3	1

16.12.21: 61-76-81

Australia
7.11.21: **16**

Austria
5.11.21: **9**-48

Belgium
30.10.21: **16**-86

Canada
6.11.21: **53**

Denmark
29.10.21: **12**

Finland
23.10.21: **21**

France
23.10.21: **83**

Germany
29.10.21: **8**-62-81

Italy
28.10.21: peaked at no.**10**, charted for 2 weeks

Netherlands
30.10.21: **9**

New Zealand
1.11.21: **35**

Switzerland
31.10.21: **10**-78

USA
6.11.21: **28**

Work on the album that became *FUTURE PAST* ~ Duran Duran's fifteenth studio album ~ began when the band entered the studio in 2018.

'I was trying to persuade the guys that all we needed to do was write two or three tracks for an EP,' said Simon Le Bon. 'Four days later, with the nucleus of twenty-five plus strong songs in the can that all deserved development, I realised we'd be in for the long haul ~ but that was before Covid.'

'Many of the songs are about emotional crises,' said John Taylor, 'or long-term intimacy issues, let's call them. When we came back after lockdown, I felt that those lyrics, particularly *Invisible*, spoke to the moment, because the last eighteen months have really been about intimacy politics.'

The distinctive sleeve for *FUTURE PAST* was created by Rory McCartney using two colourised ~ one green and one red ~ black and white images shot by Japanese photographer Daisuke Yokota.

'We open (the album) with the song *Invisible*,' said Simon Le Bon, 'which began as a story about a one-sided relationship but grew into something much bigger, because "a voiceless crowd isn't backing down". John and Roger's rhythm track is mountainous, Nick's melodies twist and soar. Graham (Coxon)'s guitar is a knife. It feels exactly right for right now.'

Invisible was the first of six tracks from *FUTURE PAST* to be promoted as singles:

- *Invisible*
- *More Joy!*
- *Anniversary*
- *Tonight United*
- *Give It All Up*
- *Laughing Boy*

More Joy! featured Chai, and *Give It All Up* featured Tove Lo.

The music video for *Invisible* was created by Huxley, an Artificial Intelligence, and featured a simulated 360 reality audio experience enabling fans to immerse themselves in the music by wearing headphones.

'Sonic architecture has always been incredibly important to Duran Duran,' said Nick Rhodes. 'I think, with *Invisible*, we really have managed to carve the sculpture the way we wanted it. Sonically, it's a very unusual piece of music. I think when you merge all the instruments together, it creates an overall sound that perhaps you haven't heard before.'

However, due to typically low streaming 'sales' for a vintage act, none of the singles from *FUTURE PAST* enjoyed chart success anywhere on any mainstream charts.

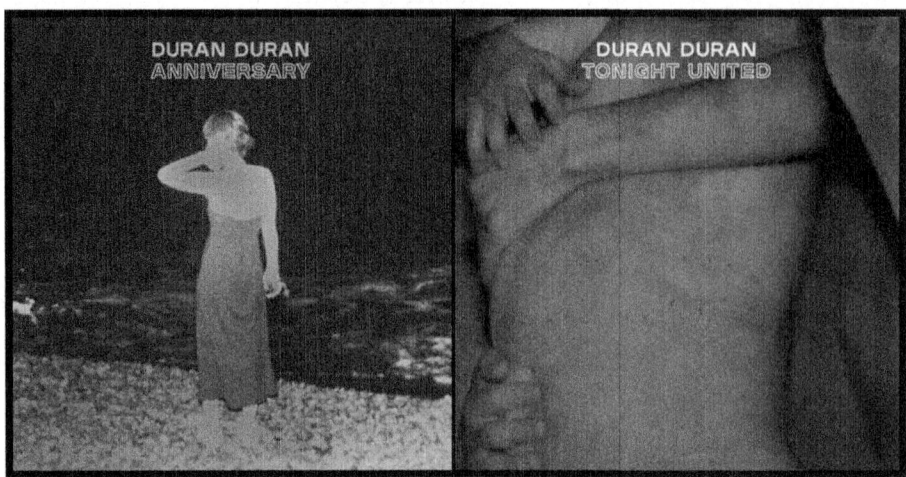

In the UK, in making its chart debut at no.3, *FUTURE PAST* expanded Duran Duran's run of Top 5 albums to an impressive five decades. The album also achieved no.8 in Germany, no.9 in Austria and the Netherlands, no.10 in Italy and Switzerland, no.12 in Denmark, no.16 in Australia and Belgium, no.21 in Finland, no.28 in the United States, no.35 in New Zealand and no.53 in Canada.

In 2022, *FUTURE PAST* was released as a double album, with one green and one red vinyl disc.

DURAN DURAN'S TOP 20 ALBUMS

This Top 20 has been compiled using the same points system as for the Top 30 Singles listing.

Rank/Album/Points

1   *SEVEN AND THE RAGGED TIGER ~*
                                                1,852 points

2   *ARENA ~* 1,688 points

3   *NOTORIOUS ~* 1,291 points

4 *RIO* ~ 1,259 points

5 *DURAN DURAN (THE WEDDING ALBUM)* ~ 1,158 points

6. *PAPER GODS* ~ 1,020 points
7. *FUTURE PAST* ~ 941 points
8. *ASTRONAUT* ~ 918 points
9. *GREATEST* ~ 905 points
10. *DURAN DURAN* ~ 878 points

11. *SO RED THE ROSE* | Arcadia ~ 757 points
12. *THE POWER STATION* |The Power Station ~ 749 points
13. *BIG THING* ~ 740 points
14. *THANK YOU* ~ 645 points
15. *ALL YOU NEED IS NOW* ~ 464 points

16. *LIBERTY* ~ 420 points
17. *RED CARPET MASSACRE* ~ 249 points
18. *DECADE* ~ 234 points
19. *POP TRASH* ~ 118 points
20. *MEDAZZALAND* ~ 104 points

Duran Duran's most successful album in terms of worldwide chart success is *SEVEN AND THE RAGGED TIGER*, which is ahead of the band's live album, *ARENA*, with *NOTORIOUS* ranked in 3rd place. *RIO* and *DURAN DURAN (THE WEDDING ALBUM)* complete the Top 5.

Arcadia's *SO RED THE ROSE* just misses the Top 10, and is ranked at no,11, one place ahead of The Power Station's self-titled album.

ALBUMS TRIVIA

To date, Duran Duran has achieved 19 Top 40 albums and four Top 40 EPs in one or more of the countries featured in this book, with The Power Station, Arcadia and Andy Taylor each adding one Top 40 album to the total.

There follows a country-by-country look at Duran Duran's most successful albums, starting with the band's homeland.

DURAN DURAN IN THE UK

Most Hits

18 hits	Duran Duran
1 hit	The Power Station
1 hit	Arcadia
1 hit	Andy Taylor

Most Weeks

475 weeks	Duran Duran
23 weeks	The Power Station
10 weeks	Arcadia
1 weeks	Andy Taylor

No.1 Albums

1983	*SEVEN AND THE RAGGED TIGER*

SEVEN AND THE RAGGED TIGER topped the chart for one week.

Albums with the most weeks

119 weeks	*DURAN DURAN*
110 weeks	*RIO*
67 weeks	*GREATEST*
47 weeks	*SEVEN AND THE RAGGED TIGER*
31 weeks	*ARENA*
30 weeks	*DURAN DURAN (THE WEDDING ALBUM)*
23 weeks	*THE POWER STATION* ~ The Power Station
18 weeks	*DECADE*

| 16 weeks | *NOTORIOUS* |
| 10 weeks | *SO RED THE ROSE* ~ Arcadia |

The Brit Certified/BPI (British Phonographic Industry) Awards

The BPI began certifying albums in 1973, and between April 1973 and December 1978, awards related to a monetary value and not a unit value. Thanks to inflation, this changed several times over the years, and when this system was abolished, the awards that were set remain in place today:

Silver = 60,000, Gold = 100,000, Platinum = 300,000.

Multi-Platinum awards were introduced in February 1987.

In July 2013 the BPI automated awards, and awards from this date are based on actual sales (including streaming 'sales') since February 1994, not shipments.

3 x Platinum	*GREATEST* (July 2013) = 900,000
Platinum	*RIO* (November 1982) = 300,000
Platinum	*DURAN DURAN* (December 1982) = 300,000
Platinum	*SEVEN AND THE RAGGED TIGER* (November 1983) = 300,000
Platinum	*ARENA* (March 1985) = 300,000
Platinum	*DECADE* (December 1989) = 300,000
Gold	*NOTORIOUS* (December 1986) = 100,000
Gold	*DURAN DURAN (THE WEDDING ALBUM)* (April 1993) = 100,000
Gold	*ASTRONAUT* (October 2004) = 100,000
Gold	*THE SINGLES 81-85* (September 2021) = 100,000
Silver	*BIG THING* (November 1988) = 60,000
Silver	*LIBERTY* (September 1990) = 60,000

The Power Station

| Gold | *THE POWER STATION* (July 1985) = 100,000 |

DURAN DURAN IN AUSTRALIA

Most Hits

13 hits	Duran Duran
1 hit	The Power Station
1 hit	Arcadia

Most Weeks

160 weeks	Duran Duran
20 weeks	The Power Station
10 weeks	Arcadia

No.1 Albums

1982	*RIO*

RIO topped the chart for one week.

Albums with the most weeks

52 weeks	*DURAN DURAN*
30 weeks	*SEVEN AND THE RAGGED TIGER*
27 weeks	*RIO*
20 weeks	*THE POWER STATION* ~ The Power Station
18 weeks	*ARENA*
10 weeks	*SO RED THE ROSE* ~ Arcadia
9 weeks	*NOTORIOUS*

DURAN DURAN IN AUSTRIA

Duran Duran achieved 10 hit albums in Austria, which spent 55 weeks on the chart.

The band's highest charting album is *ARENA*, which peaked at no.7.

Albums with the most weeks

12 weeks	*SEVEN AND THE RAGGED TIGER*
10 weeks	*ARENA*
10 weeks	*NOTORIOUS*
9 weeks	*DURAN DURAN (THE WEDDING ALBUM)*
4 weeks	*GREATEST*

DURAN DURAN IN BELGIUM (Flanders)

Since 1995, when the album chart was launched, Duran Duran achieved six hit albums in Belgium (Flanders), which spent 29 weeks on the chart.

The band's highest charting album is *FUTURE PAST*, which peaked at no.16.

Albums with the most weeks

14 weeks	*GREATEST*
6 weeks	*ASTRONAUT*
3 weeks	*ALL YOU NEED IS NOW*
3 weeks	*PAPER GODS*
2 weeks	*FUTURE PAST*

DURAN DURAN IN CANADA

Most Hits

14 hits	Duran Duran
1 hit	The Power Station
1 hit	Arcadia
1 hit	Andy Taylor

Most Weeks

230 weeks	Duran Duran
31 weeks	The Power Station
18 weeks	Arcadia
9 weeks	Andy Taylor

No.1 Albums

1983	*RIO*

RIO topped the chart for one week

Albums with the most weeks

52 weeks	*RIO*
49 weeks	*SEVEN AND THE RAGGED TIGER*
31 weeks	*THE POWER STATION* ~ The Power Station
29 weeks	*DURAN DURAN (THE WEDDING ALBUM)*
27 weeks	*ARENA*
24 weeks	*DURAN DURAN*
21 weeks	*NOTORIOUS*
18 weeks	*SO RED THE ROSE* ~ Arcadia
17 weeks	*THANK YOU*

DURAN DURAN IN DENMARK

Since 2001, Duran Duran achieved four hit albums in Denmark, which spent 10 weeks on the chart.

The band's highest charting album is *ASTRONAUT*, which peaked at no.8.

Albums with the most weeks

5 weeks	*GREATEST*
3 weeks	*ASTRONAUT*
1 week	*PAPER GODS*
1 week	*FUTURE PAST*

DURAN DURAN IN FINLAND

Most Hits

8 hits	Duran Duran
1 hit	Arcadia

Most Weeks

98 weeks	Duran Duran
10 weeks	Arcadia

Duran Duran's highest charting albums in Finland are *RIO* and *SEVEN AND THE RAGGED TIGER*, which both peaked at no.3.

Albums with the most weeks

36 weeks	*RIO*
19 weeks	*SEVEN AND THE RAGGED TIGER*
14 weeks	*ARENA*
12 weeks	*DURAN DURAN (THE WEDDING ALBUM)*
10 weeks	*SO RED THE ROSE* ~ Arcadia

DURAN DURAN IN FRANCE

Duran Duran achieved seven hit albums in France, which spent 30 weeks on the chart.

The band's highest charting album is *SEVEN AND THE RAGGED TIGER*, which peaked at no.20.

Albums with the most weeks

16 weeks	*SEVEN AND THE RAGGED TIGER*
8 weeks	*DURAN DURAN (THE WEDDING ALBUM)*
2 weeks	*NOTORIOUS*

DURAN DURAN IN GERMANY

Most Hits

13 hits	Duran Duran
1 hit	The Power Station
1 hit	Arcadia

Most Weeks

122 weeks	Duran Duran
16 weeks	The Power Station
2 weeks	Arcadia

No.1 Albums

1984	*ARENA*

ARENA topped the chart for four weeks.

Albums with the most weeks

40 weeks	*SEVEN AND THE RAGGED TIGER*
25 weeks	*ARENA*
21 weeks	*DURAN DURAN (THE WEDDING ALBUM)*
16 weeks	*THE POWER STATION* ~ The Power Station
10 weeks	*NOTORIOUS*

DURAN DURAN IN ITALY

Most Hits

18 hits	Duran Duran

1 hit	Arcadia

Most Weeks

240 weeks	Duran Duran
14 weeks	Arcadia

No.1 Albums

1984	*ARENA*
1985	*SO RED THE ROSE* ~ Arcadia

ARENA topped the chart for two weeks, and *SO RED THE ROSE* for one week.

Albums with the most weeks

35 weeks	*ARENA*
33 weeks	*GREATEST*
31 weeks	*ASTRONAUT*
20 weeks	*NOTORIOUS*
19 weeks	*BIG THING*
19 weeks	*DURAN DURAN (THE WEDDING ALBUM)*
18 weeks	*SEVEN AND THE RAGGED TIGER*
14 weeks	*SO RED THE ROSE* ~ Arcadia
13 weeks	*MIXING*
11 weeks	*RED CARPET MASSACRE*
11 weeks	*ALL YOU NEED IS NOW*

DURAN DURAN IN JAPAN

Duran Duran achieved 15 hit albums (including three EPs) in Japan, which spent 214 weeks on the chart.

The band's highest charting album is *ARENA*, which peaked at no.3.

Albums with the most weeks

47 weeks	*SEVEN AND THE RAGGED TIGER*
26 weeks	*DURAN DURAN*
25 weeks	*RIO*
21 weeks	*TIGER! TIGER!* EP
20 weeks	*NOTORIOUS*

18 weeks	*CARNIVAL* EP
18 weeks	*ARENA*
9 weeks	*STRANGE BEHAVIOUR* EP

DURAN DURAN IN THE NETHERLANDS

Most Hits

15 hits	Duran Duran
1 hit	The Power Station
1 hit	Arcadia

Most Weeks

178 weeks	Duran Duran
8 weeks	Arcadia
5 weeks	The Power Station

No.1 Albums

1984	*SEVEN AND THE RAGGED TIGER*

SEVEN AND THE RAGGED TIGER topped the chart for five weeks.

Albums with the most weeks

37 weeks	*GREATEST*
35 weeks	*SEVEN AND THE RAGGED TIGER*
27 weeks	*ARENA*
20 weeks	*NOTORIOUS*
13 weeks	*DURAN DURAN (THE WEDDING ALBUM)*
12 weeks	*BIG THING*

DURAN DURAN IN NEW ZEALAND

Most Hits

10 hits	Duran Duran
1 hit	The Power Station
1 hit	Arcadia

Most Weeks

228 weeks	Duran Duran
21 weeks	The Power Station
12 weeks	Arcadia

No.1 Albums

1983	*SEVEN AND THE RAGGED TIGER*

SEVEN AND THE RAGGED TIGER topped the chart for five weeks.

Albums with the most weeks

62 weeks	*RIO*
55 weeks	*DURAN DURAN*
45 weeks	*SEVEN AND THE RAGGED TIGER*
37 weeks	*ARENA*
21 weeks	*THE POWER STATION* ~ The Power Station
14 weeks	*GREATEST*
12 weeks	*SO RED THE ROSE* ~ Arcadia
10 weeks	*NOTORIOUS*

DURAN DURAN IN NORWAY

Duran Duran achieved five hit albums in Norway, which spent 37 weeks on the chart.

The band's highest charting album is *NOTORIOUS*, which peaked at no.8.

Albums with the most weeks

11 weeks	*NOTORIOUS*
8 weeks	*ARENA*
7 weeks	*RIO*
7 wccks	*GREATEST*
4 weeks	*SEVEN AND THE RAGGED TIGER*

DURAN DURAN IN SOUTH AFRICA

Duran Duran achieved four hit albums in South Africa, which spent 54 weeks on the chart.

The band's highest charting album is *ARENA*, which peaked at no.4.

Albums with the most weeks

17 weeks	*ARENA*
13 weeks	*RIO*
13 weeks	*DURAN DURAN (THE WEDDING ALBUM)*
11 weeks	*SEVEN AND THE RAGGED TIGER*

DURAN DURAN IN SPAIN

Most Hits

6 hits	Duran Duran
1 hit	Arcadia

Most Weeks

65 weeks	Duran Duran
8 weeks	Arcadia

Duran Duran's highest charting album in Spain is *ARENA*, which peaked at no.2.

Albums with the most weeks

40 weeks	*ARENA*
10 weeks	*SEVEN AND THE RAGGED TIGER*
10 weeks	*NOTORIOUS*
8 weeks	*SO RED THE ROSE* ~ Arcadia

DURAN DURAN IN SWEDEN

Most Hits

9 hits	Duran Duran
1 hit	Arcadia
1 hit	The Power Station
1 hit	Andy Taylor

Most Weeks

105 weeks	Duran Duran
2 weeks	Arcadia

2 weeks	The Power Station
2 weeks	Andy Taylor

Duran Duran's highest charting album in Sweden is *DURAN DURAN*, which peaked at no.3.

Albums with the most weeks

30 weeks	*DURAN DURAN*
18 weeks	*ARENA*
16 weeks	*DURAN DURAN (THE WEDDING ALBUM)*
12 weeks	*RIO*
12 weeks	*NOTORIOUS*
10 weeks	*SEVEN AND THE RAGGED TIGER*

DURAN DURAN IN SWITZERLAND

Most Hits

12 hits	Duran Duran
1 hit	The Power Station

Most Weeks

54 weeks	Duran Duran
5 weeks	The Power Station

Duran Duran's highest charting album in Switzerland is *ARENA*, which peaked at no.4.

Albums with the most weeks

13 weeks	*ARENA*
10 weeks	*DURAN DURAN (THE WEDDING ALBUM)*
9 weeks	*SEVEN AND THE RAGGED TIGER*
5 weeks	*THE POWER STATION* ~ The Power Station
4 weeks	*NOTORIOUS*
4 weeks	*ASTRONAUT*

March 26, 1983   40p

MARI WILSON•TEARDROPS•ALTERED IMAGES•WAH! songwords!

RECORD MIRROR

Thompson Twins dates!

DURAN DURAN

4 page mega–spectacular with colour poster!

DAVID BOWIE
Full tour details!

TRACEY ULLMAN

TRACIE

STAR STYLE

WALL OF VOODOO

Never mind the bollards

BILLY GRIFFIN

TRACEY ULLMAN pic by Eugene Adebari   NICK RHODES pic by Fin Costello

292

DURAN DURAN IN THE UNITED STATES

Most Hits

17 hits	Duran Duran
1 hit	The Power Station
1 hit	Arcadia

Most Weeks

254 weeks	Duran Duran
32 weeks	The Power Station
14 weeks	Arcadia

Duran Duran's highest charting album in the United States is *ARENA*, which peaked at no.4.

Albums with the most weeks

50 weeks	*SEVEN AND THE RAGGED TIGER*
37 weeks	*DURAN DURAN*
34 weeks	*RIO*
32 weeks	*DURAN DURAN (THE WEDDING ALBUM)*
32 weeks	*THE POWER STATION* ~ The Power Station
22 weeks	*NOTORIOUS*
21 weeks	*BIG THING*
20 weeks	*ARENA*
14 weeks	*SO RED THE ROSE* ~ Arcadia
11 weeks	*DECADE*

RIAA (Recording Industry Association of America) Awards

The RIAA began certifying Gold albums in 1958, Platinum albums in 1976, and multi-Platinum albums in 1984. Gold = 500,000, Platinum = 1 million. Awards are based on shipments, not sales, and each disc is counted individually (so, for example, a double album has to ship 500,000 to be eligible for Platinum).

2 x Platinum	*ARENA* (February 1985) = 2 million
2 x Platinum	*RIO* (October 1991) = 2 million
2 x Platinum	*SEVEN AND THE RAGGED TIGER* (November 1991) = 2 million
Platinum	*DURAN DURAN* (January 1985) = 1 million
Platinum	*NOTORIOUS* (January 1987) = 1 million
Platinum	*DURAN DURAN (THE WEDDING ALBUM)* (June 1993) = 1 million

Platinum	*DECADE* (May 1998) = 1 million
Platinum	*GREATEST* (January 2005) = 1 million
Gold	*BIG THING* (December 1988) = 500,000
Gold	*THANK YOU* (June 1995) = 500,000

The Power Station

Platinum   *THE POWER STATION* (August 1985) = 1 million

Arcadia

Platinum   *SO RED THE ROSE* (January 1986) = 1 million

DURAN DURAN IN ZIMBABWE

None of Duran Duran's albums have charted in Zimbabwe.

Printed in Great Britain
by Amazon